W9-CPZ-362

COURT
CONFIDENTIAL

COURT
CONFIDENTIAL

INSIDE THE WORLD OF TENNIS

NEIL HARMAN

The Robson Press

First published in Great Britain in 2013 by
The Robson Press (an imprint of Biteback Publishing Ltd)
Westminster Tower
3 Albert Embankment
London SE1 7SP
Copyright © Neil Harman 2013

All images reproduced by kind permission of Getty Images,
except page 8, bottom, author's own.

Every reasonable effort has been made to trace copyright holders of material
reproduced in this book, but if any have been inadvertently overlooked the
publishers would be glad to hear from them.

ISBN 978-1-84954-507-5

10 9 8 7 6 5 4 3 2 1

A CIP catalogue record for this book is available from the British Library.

Set in Sabon

Printed and bound in Great Britain by
CPI Group (UK) Ltd, Croydon CR0 4YY

To Maureen, Elizabeth and Kathleen.

Acknowledgements

I SUPPOSE I was taking something of a risk with this project. After all, almost everyone told me that tennis books don't sell and, well, this one might not either. I just felt it was now or never, with the Olympic Games to be staged in London, with Andy Murray talented enough to win a grand slam tournament, with the sport in such a healthy state. And so I started to type.

Nothing is possible without faith, hope and love. I wanted to see this venture through, so having faith in myself and many other people was one thing, I hoped it would work out and you, dear reader, have to be the judge of that; the fact is, I love this sport and – in the platonic sense of the word – a lot of those in it.

Because you always think you are going to leave someone out that you should not, I thought it best to keep the acknowledgement section as short as possible. To those who supported me all the way through, I have the greatest time and affection. I strove long and hard to find someone who believed in me and the idea of this book. A lot of folk did not. John Beddington, a good friend, pointed me in the direction of Ros Edwards of Edwards Fuglewicz who wanted to help and she, in turn, found Jeremy Robson of The Robson Press. This book would not have happened without them and I am deeply grateful.

Ros's colleague Julia Forrest read and reread the manuscript; Lewis Carpenter and Hollie Teague took on the task at Robson and their meticulous approach and considered opinions have all been invaluable. In the tennis world itself, I am indebted to players, coaches, agents, administrators, and especially to those superb PR folk too often taken for granted. 'Do you think I could get five minutes of time with [so and so] for the book?' became a familiar request and was very rarely refused. The same is true of those who work very closely with the leading players: Tony Godsick (Roger Federer); Benito Perez-Barbadillo (Rafael Nadal and now Victoria Azarenka); Edoardo Artaldi (Novak Djokovic); Matt Gentry and Louise Irving (Andy Murray); Jill Smoller (Serena Williams); and Max Eisenbud (Maria Sharapova). I badgered them quite a lot and they didn't seem to take offence. Special thanks to Stanislas Wawrinka – a brilliant player and an even nicer person – for keeping me in coffee all year long.

The Times, a newspaper I have been honoured to serve for eleven years (and hopefully many more), backed me all the way. Tim Hallissey, the sports editor, is the most decent of men. Most of my colleagues in the British press were extremely supportive. They know who they are.

Andy Murray won his title. He won the Olympic gold medal. Without him, his performances and his help, I'm not quite sure whether this book would have taken shape. Thanks Andy. And, it goes without saying, my pride in what you have achieved is immense.

Neil Harman
28 March 2013.

Contents

Preface

Who would agree that tennis is perhaps the cruellest of games, as two dedicated combatants bat a ball back and forth, back and forth (audience suffering cumulative neck injury to watch it), in a small rectangle, over interminable hours? Naked as they fail or recover, some see this as the essential bare bones of human encounter. Those who freak out become heroes.

Why? Because the game is a schizophrenogenic event, bringing men and women to the brink of the bearable, and the audience is no different than those who witnessed the lions consuming the gladiators. Whether played on grass, earth, or whatever, it really is an absurd game. As you do, just sound out loud the echo of – 'bong, bong, bong, bong, bong, bong 'out'. And for love. Who the hell ever came up with that as a call in the world's most sadistic game?

Christopher Bollas's comment on my article in *The Times* on Novak Djokovic vs. Jo-Wilfried Tsonga, French Open quarterfinal, 6 June 2012.

IT IS A dwindling species, the tennis correspondent, those employed to articulate the antics of the modern-day gladiators. The post is increasingly at the mercy of declining budgets, dictated to by bean counters and besieged by blogs. In Britain, the spiritual home of lawn tennis, you can count our number on one hand. When I began as a tennis reporter on the *Daily Mail* in 1982 – covering Wimbledon for the first time having started to learn the ropes at the tournaments in Beckenham, Birmingham and Bristol – each national newspaper employed a mainstream tennis writer on its staff. Not any more. Times have changed. Not yet, I am relieved to say, at *The Times*.

Almost everyone who writes about tennis has to try their hand at a little of something else, be it football, golf, rowing, cricket or whatever the office throws at you. And yet the tennis circuit never stops, it rises and falls, courses and flows, as we wax and wane. Every day, somewhere in the world and often logged only in the minds of those intimately involved, a tennis match of professional significance is played and someone's day will end either with a sense of achievement or – more likely – the gnawing worry that this was a sport that you truly have to love to want to keep going at it. Tennis is a bloody and brutal world in which only the most courageous of gladiators will survive.

By a startling irony, as the cutbacks among those who cover it intensify, tennis entered 2012 enjoying its greatest global reach and blessed with talents that resonate with a larger percentage of the planet's population than ever before. There may be a remote part of North Korea or the Amazonian rain forest where Roger Federer is not instantly recognisable, but they are the exception.

The explosion in the number of outlets offering thoughts and opinions – whether tweets, blogs, rolling news or sports pages updated minute-by-minute on the internet – adds to the cacophony surrounding each result, from the distant to the most recent, each jostling for prominence in our heads and profoundly affecting our perception of time and imperatives. Every result brings a cascade of comment. Many times in the past few months, I realised I followed too many people on Twitter and could well appreciate why of many players who chose to use it, some did so sparingly and others quit altogether. I asked Federer why he did not embrace Twitter. 'Why would I want to do that?' he said.

In 2012 – and for the foreseeable future – the staff writer is at the public's mercy like never before, through often visceral comments at the foot of articles posted online as if every word is being microscopically probed for a hidden meaning. Murray's former agent, Patricio Apey, used to say to me 'Neil, with you, I always try to read between the lines'. And there was I simply trying to make sense of the lines themselves.

Work-wise, there is more to be done and far less time in which to do it. I am not one to willingly pare back on quality. That has to stay, however long it takes to 'get it up online'. There are increasing constraints on travel, and night-time tennis at almost every venue on the circuit massively curtails the old-school social delights of the job. Every opportunity to sit and discourse over a bottle of wine during a tournament is to be savoured for they are few and far between. We are slaves to the computer and its latest form, the iPad. To point out these changes is not to evoke sympathy but merely to state a fact – that this job, for all of its myriad marvels, is not as much fun as it used to be. If you are a workaholic like me, there are a lot more hours on site and, consequently, there is a lot less time to relax and recuperate. Of course, you want to be in more place than one, but quite often, that one is more than enough to be going on with.

Invariably though, the locations are warm, the scenery glorious (the mountains around Indian Wells, the royal blue of the Mediterranean at Monte Carlo, the glorious greenery of Wimbledon) and the contests enthralling. I love to write, to talk, to share, to listen, to engage and, yes, to 'gossip' as Switzerland's Stanislas Wawrinka, who has become as close to a friend as it is wise to have among the players, often says. I thrive on deadlines and, if you like all of that, plus you do not mind taxis, airport queues, economy food, non-boutique hotels and having to listen far too often to sensible people being asked all manner of pointlessly daft questions, this life is for you. And as for the pointlessly daft questions, I'm sure I ask my fair share.

I propose this book as a conscious attempt to shine a little light on a pastime where what you see on the court is merely a twinkle in the galaxy of goings-on, intrigues and tales to be told when the lights are turned off and the net taken down. There will invariably be players and officials who do not want to have me around, who don't appreciate what I choose to write, who will fall out with me over what some might consider trivialities but which they take very seriously. A lot of people trust you, some do not. It is the way of the journalistic world.

There is a limit to what you can discover even in such a small world, where most people know everyone else, rely on everyone else, are trying to get an edge on everyone else and where revealing the smallest detail can blow a trust and wreck a friendship. This is to be a study of how the sport works, who makes it work, who is trying to make it work better, who has an appreciation for how that might happen, who stands in its way, what pressures people are under. After all, at the end of a year, there are only two No. 1 players in the world and behind them are extended crushed dreams, broken promises, rude awakenings, missed opportunities, angry exchanges and terrible mistakes.

Memory (if slowly fading) tells me it had been a lot more fun and professional in the bygone days. Sometimes I yearn for those years when the scores at the US Open were chalked on a scoreboard at the back of the now decapitated press box level of the Louis Armstrong Stadium, when we actually had to go out and watch the tennis 'live' to know what was going on, to attend every press briefing we could because there were no transcripts and you had to be in there to 'feel' the interview and inform the reader of the manner in which the words had been spoken. Now, press interviews are regularly shown live on websites across the world, though the journalists doing the work on site for the rest of the media resting at home have cottoned on too late to how much their intellectual property is being abused. We are losing, indeed have probably lost, that battle.

A Melburnian Introduction

ACROSS THE DUSTY red-soil plains, rivers and deserts, we return for a fresh start. It has been like this for years, and a quarter of a century since my first visit to this mighty land in 1988. The load of the previous season is barely set down and we reset our compass to the bottom of the world, full of hope and promise.

Taken from the Australian version of 'All Things Bright and Beautiful', the sense as I land in Melbourne is radiantly captured in the words, 'The wildflowers in their beauty, the mountain ranges tall, the billabongs and rivers, and friendly birds that call'. We are here for sport but we cannot overlook the nature which surrounds it and to what backdrop it is played. This is a lovely, vast place, where friendliness and frightening events mix, where bushfires rage in one state, rivers rise in another, and tennis is but a sideshow, albeit a beautiful one.

Like the Australian weather, the tennis year is brutal, not only in its length, but its complexity, its scope and yet, my arrival – whether or not the route has taken in Abu Dhabi, Doha, Chennai, Brisbane, Perth, Hobart or Sydney – refills the mind with wonder. The competition is back, though it has never really gone away. There is so much to be thankful for in the year passed, the story of which will unfold as you turn the pages of this journey through the sport's corridors the like of which I walk to take my usual seat in the media room at Melbourne Park – an ever-improving monument to progress and sunny optimism – and into the fresh air of the challenge. For the moment, we look forward. Invigoration fills the lungs.

Almost the first person I see is Novak Djokovic, the two-time Australian Open defending champion, and if anyone radiates invigoration, it is the 25-year-old from Serbia. We talk about the new beginnings in 2013. 'What is the definition of better?' he responds when I ask him to consider if such a thing is possible, for he is pushing the boundaries ever wider with his game of defiance, balance, beauty and savage artistry. 'Is it having more variety, coming to the net, playing more efficiently for yourself, just playing from the baseline and physically wearing your opponent down? It depends.' Djokovic said.

Every surface is demanding and requires a different adjustment from the player, so that's why it is so difficult to compare tennis from twenty or thirty years ago to now because technology is so different. We don't know what technology is going to bring tomorrow, maybe we just sit on the bench and let the rackets play themselves.

The vast majority of the players are taking care of what they do, how many hours they sleep, what they eat and drink. There is more efficiency. I consider the semi-finals and finals last year (over ten hours of tennis inside two days that defied athletic logic) as two of the three most exciting matches I played in my life and winning a grand-slam title in such fashion was fantastic. It was so gruelling and physically so demanding that at times it felt like an out-of-body experience.

I've been preparing well but what makes the change is the mental desire and that flame for success, that hunger to win. I think in life it can always get better, I don't know why and how or where but I think that it can.

Later that same evening, Djokovic emerges from the annual pre-Open gathering of the male players and bursts over to report: 'The best-run meeting I've ever attended,' which suggests a burgeoning concept in the tennis world, that of unity among players, great and small.

Next to gravitate over is Brad Drewett, the executive chairman and president of the ATP World Tour, the governing body of the men's game. His eyes are wide and light but his walk is stooped, laboured. Brad has not been at his best for a while now. We will have coffee in a couple of days, he says, to talk about the sport we both love. I get back to the hotel and there is a note waiting to join a conference call with Ross Hutchins, the 27-year-old British Davis Cup player, one of the gentlest of souls, the like of whom you would hope your daughter might bring home one day, who has been diagnosed with Hodgkin's lymphoma. Your spirit is crushed. Invigoration gives way to deep sadness.

Within forty-eight hours of that sledgehammer blow, it is revealed that Brad Drewett is suffering from motor neurone disease and a daze descends. What on earth is going on? Two of the world's nice people, the bedrocks on whom a sport depends for certainty and scrupulousness in a world often shorn of those characteristics, are not well at all. The confident air of a few days ago is replaced by a degree of fatalism that makes you wonder what can go wrong next.

Tennis is shattered by the news of Drewett's illness, not least because he has a wife and four young children; but he is also the quintessential tennis person, who has just achieved what became a burning ambition, for none before in the sport has checked each box from player, to player council, to tournament director, to CEO. Of that, tennis cannot lose sight, nor will it I am sure. He will be supported and succoured by the hierarchy and rightly so. In the short to mid-term, he is to remain as the men's leader and the certainty that he can still lead is all-pervasive.

But just as the unity the men's game has been striving for – the driving ambition of Drewett's leadership – is within their grasp, there is certain to be a period of instability, of reflection, and of a jostling for position. Justin Gimelstob represents the dynamic, go-getting, edgy front tennis requires; he is a man who might challenge a sport in which most people who clamber to the top hope that nothing changes and their privileges remain untouched. The survival rate among 'leaders' in tennis is a testament to their ability to preserve the status quo.

Gimelstob, a former player of decent standing, has a gift for self-promotion that irks some but, channelled properly, can have an effect both lasting and beneficial. He is one of three player representatives on the ATP Board. This makes governance tricky in that there are also three tournament representatives, an alignment of the two strands of the sport which makes for delicate and often irreconcilable negotiation. 'I've worked my butt off and there's nothing I take more pride in than representing the players and doing that while maintaining the balance of doing what's right for the tour and the tournaments,' Gimelstob says. 'I live and breathe this every single day at a tournament. There is no level player, no management company, no executive staff and no tournament that doesn't have full access to me every single day of the year.'

Gimelstob accepts that the ATP structure is not perfect.

My determination is to represent the players fairly in the partnership to work as hard as possible to make sure that their ratio in the partnership is being maximised. One of the things thrown out indiscriminately is 'players union' and some players would be better off for that. If you look at the history of basketball, football, baseball, ice-hockey with purely player unions, these sports have had major work stoppages in the past decade; my standpoint is that we run our tour on the players' side like a union but they own half of their league.

It is a 365-day-a-year job trying to manage and stay on top of all the moving parts of the sport. You cannot compare the player board job to the tournament board job, it is an incomparable challenge and one I love. I can't tell you how much I appreciate trying to represent these players. It's not all piña coladas and birthday cake, it's tough, especially as a former player who is seen in one way. I don't always stand behind the way I acted, what I said and how I handled things as a player but that coming with the maturing process of realising that tennis is a very brutal, tough individual sport and a lot of the qualities you pick up aren't commensurate with being successful or playing nicely in the sandbox post-tennis life.

I could be put off by Gimelstob's ambition but I am not. Tennis needs leaders with ambition. He refuses to stop trying to move the margins in favour of the players. He gets frustrated. He is drained. Even at the start of a year with so much to look forward to, the amount that needs to be done can unnerve the sturdiest of souls. The grand slams have their desires, the tours their own; there is the stultifying bureaucracy, the Davis Cup to sort out. 'I refuse to say, "it is what it is". I believe in it too much,' he says.

One constantly hears that tennis is in such a great place, but for how long? It cannot stay this way forever: even Roger Federer, the lead man, the multi-garlanded heartbeat of the game, this exceedingly special person, won't be around forever; Rafael Nadal is suffering from the effects of a game that borders on the maniacally physical; and Djokovic and Andy Murray, the British hero, are attempting to shoulder the burden of taking it on and up. It is imperative – especially as we set out on another year – that the sport looks further afield, secures its markets, expending time and effort preparing for the rainy day that is bound to come, perhaps sooner than we think. What worries Gimelstob and worries me is that tennis has a tendency towards internal quarrelling which disrupts its capacity to build on what it has and that opportunities – rare and exciting – can be lost. It is with Drewett and Hutchins at the forefront of my mind that I intend to tackle the year. Let us all do tennis as much good as we can. Where they would love to be bounding right now, out to the courts warmed by the sun, it is my honour to bound. This is a grand slam tournament, one of the four cornerstones of the year and, truthfully, it hardly gets much better than this.

On a barge down Melbourne's Yarra River come Djokovic

and Victoria Azarenka, the two defending champions, the two No. 1 players in the world, with the trophies for presentation at the draw for the 2013 championships. It is a novel means of introduction and it works. Djokovic has won the title for the past two years and only Roy Emerson and Jack Crawford from the halcyon days of Australian domination have three consecutive titles to their name. It has not been achieved in the Open Era of tennis, which began in 1968.

Azarenka has shown since her first – and so far only – grand slam victory a year ago that she possesses the capabilities and the drive to do more. She is not universally popular, which is a shame because deep down she is a person of immense warmth, possessed of an absolute drive to succeed which, were it not for the unappealing noise she makes as she strikes the ball, would be something to admire, rather than scorn. I suspect that, as they chug their way along the calm waters of the Yarra, things will get a lot choppier in the next two weeks, but these two voyagers will be the people to beat.

There is no undergrowth for Djokovic and Azarenka to hack their way through and yet, more and more, professional tennis in the twenty-first century is akin to a jungle. Strange shrieking and grunting noises abound, there is as much shadow as there is sun, and the sport has its fair share of reptiles and lizards. It is about finding a way to negotiate with all of the threads – the top professionals, the coaches, the agents, the tournament staff, the officials – to disseminate and to distil, to filter the rumour, disturb the status quo, set the agenda, lead with your chin and determine fact from fiction. And to survive.

There are monster companies at work by all of which a word or a gesture out of place can be interpreted in so many ways. The monsters are ubiquitous: IMG, Lagardère Unlimited, CAA, Octagon, new kids on the block like XIX Entertainment (Murray's representatives). There are also the individuals who see the talent in a young player, sell themselves to that player and their parents, watch them grow and protect them when they become real stars.

I admire the likes of Morgan Menahem (Jo-Wilfried Tsonga); Lawrence Frankopan, who has built a company, Starwing, that represents Stanislas Wawrinka as well as a collection of top juniors; and Ugo Colombini (Juan Martin del Potro). All these people do sterling work for their clients against the multi-million dollar machines who want to own and manage as much of the sport as they can lay their hands on.

The *Times* office back home is largely fixated with Murray, and why wouldn't they be? The British No. 1 is the face and the heartbeat of the game in a country that has trouble deciding whether it likes him or not. There is no doubt in my mind, there never has been and I would quite like a pound for all the times I am asked 'what is he really like?' and 'how do you get along?' The answer in the first case is that he is a shy, sensitive, inquisitive, straightforward, intriguing young man blessed with a glorious talent and an athletic aptitude I have not seen in any British player; to the second it is 'pretty well, I think'. He understands and accepts what the press does, that he has his business and we have ours and that is about it.

'The thing that makes me nervous is the winning, being part of history,' he has said.

> That's what I play for. I don't know if that's what everybody plays for. But I'm sure if you ask Rafa [Nadal], Roger [Federer], Novak [Djokovic], what makes them nervous, [it] is the history of being part of such a huge match. The grand slams mean so much now. I think they've become such a big part of the sporting calendar, not just in tennis. They've become a huge deal over the last few years. All of the guys are playing all of the events. Even when Ivan [Lendl] played, guys missed a lot of slams. That doesn't happen any more. That's what motivates me, the slams. That's what I train hard for and that's what gets me pumped.'

Celebrity is not at the centre of Murray's life. He has never chased a headline, not exactly been driven to market himself and, as a consequence of that and some of his behaviour on the court, he has not been an easy marketing tool.

> I'm not really into that stuff. I know a lot of people that are. I don't really get it. Now it's actually much less. I think if you live kind of a normal life and aren't out doing stupid things like falling out of night clubs with no pants on, after a while the paparazzi lose interest. I'm pretty much going home, walking my dogs, practising. Still, around Wimbledon time, it's different than the rest of the year. I have TV crews calling my house phone early in the morning. Mornings of big matches, you're getting followed. It doesn't help, and in the UK I don't think we really do that good a job with it. If you want your sports teams and athletes to be successful, you don't really want to be throwing them off their stride in the most important moments. And when you lose, they'll be like, 'Oh, you're useless, you don't ever win anything.' So at least [they should] try to help while we're in the event.

I think that we do, but perhaps Andy isn't talking about me specifically but us as a group. The week before the first week of a slam is an experience in itself. For a British writer, the demand is to cover – and support – those from home in the qualifying event. In the men's event, there is Jamie Baker, a contemporary of Murray, a Glaswegian whose spirit and determination are exemplars; and James Ward, a Londoner who has a talent and will not stop trying to make the most of it. In the women's event, Johanna Konta, a recent recruit to the British ranks courtesy of a long process of courting from the Lawn Tennis Association, is trying to negotiate the jungle. By virtue of their surge up the rankings, Heather Watson and Laura Robson are in the main draw, as is the veteran of the group, Anne Keothavong.

I see my role as to report and offer (considered) support. I have a strong belief that sitting courtside – and the players knowing you are there – acts as a stimulant. They may raise their game a differential notch or two. A gesture (of the appropriate kind) is acceptable. We are trained to write objectively – but that does not mean I don't want the British players to succeed.

The rankings may not say so officially but the leaders of the respective packs are Federer, the cheetah, and Serena Williams, the lioness. For the languid Federer, his levels of commitment to the sport in court-time in 2013 will be reduced. He has paid his dues. At thirty-one years of age, having played for over twelve years and with 600 Tour matches under his belt, the Swiss qualifies for exemptions from the tour. He does not have to play the mandated ATP Tour 1,000 events, so he is leaving a couple from his schedule. 'I'm giving myself space, I have to make sure I create a schedule so it makes sense for my practice,' he says. 'I have some catching up to do from that standpoint.'

Federer is adored and respected. When he walks onto a court, the court is his. He is the lord of the manor and, as such, his every movement and stance is uniquely monitored and examined. We know what he does for the sport; what he does outside of the game – though much of it private – offers him a role in the sport that only the absent Nadal comes close to replicating. The women's game is defined by Serena Williams. Hers has been the most extraordinary story, her family the most remarkable people. Like Federer, she is in her thirties now, and like Federer, she holds the court in her thrall. She is box-office. They start the tournament in pleasing style, Federer does not drop a set in four rounds; Williams drops only eight games by the same stage.

The major incidents in the first week involve a third-round, five-set loss for Juan Martin del Potro of Argentina, the No. 6 seed, to the Frenchman Jérémy Chardy. In conversation with del Potro before the event started, he tells me he is 'a changed person' though he does not elaborate. I get the sense that something is troubling him but that is where we leave it. On the women's side, there is the usual and apparently inevitable loss for Samantha Stosur, the Australian hope, in the second round (better than usual) to China's Jie Zheng, 7–5 in the third set.

In the fourth round, there is one match that stands above all others. Djokovic plays with relative calm in the early stages and now plays Wawrinka, a man who could be an absolute star in his homeland were it not that he shares that particular piece of Europe with Federer. Since speaking to him at Wimbledon in 2009 (the day before he played Murray in the fourth round), a conversation that was marked by him falling through his canvas chair, Wawrinka and I have spent a lot of time together discussing the sport. I like these chats and so, it seems, does he. I sometimes watch him and wonder, with that talent, and those shots, why is he not an established top ten player. It has to be that he doesn't believe in himself enough. I don't know what possesses me but I go up to him before the match against Djokovic and say I want to see the real Wawrinka play tonight. It may flout journalistic rules to express my opinions to a player in this manner at all. I don't really care. I know that Novak will give it his all, he never fails to do that. I just want to see Stan do the same. He says he will. I send a Twitter message saying I believe it will be a firecracker of a match. It turns out to be the best I've seen since the 2008 Wimbledon final.

Wawrinka is leading 6–1, 4–1. It is astonishing stuff that has the world No. 1 rocking, as if on the ropes, dodging some punches, but the Swiss is landing with three-quarters of them. Were he to build a two-set lead, surely, in this form, he would prevail, but he drops serve at 5–2 and a sense of 'uh-oh' is in the air. Djokovic wins five straight games to take the second set and then the third 6–4. It is time for Wawrinka to fade, but not only does he not fade, he plays with such an air of certainty it is barely credible and he wins the fourth set on a tie-break.

There are many points in a match more crucial than others and one such arrives at 4–4 in the fifth on a fourth break point for Wawrinka when a forehand return is called long. He has a Hawk-Eye challenge up his sleeve but the umpire's upraised index finger (indicating he agrees with the call) is enough to dissuade Wawrinka from asking for the replay. He will live to regret coming over shy Stan. The replays we see indicate the ball skimmed the line.

On such infinitesimal margins can great matches be determined. Trailing 11–10, both players seizing up with cramp, Wawrinka is match points down. On the first he delivers a 124mph serve through the 'T', on the second he plays the most sublime backhand of his life down the line and on the third, a rally that will go down as one of the best of all, it is Djokovic who – as usual – has the last word, as a perfectly rolled cross-court backhand leaves Wawrinka stranded, winded, devastated, at the net.

Djokovic wins 1–6, 7–5, 6–4, 6–7, 12–10 in five hours and two minutes. The rest of the tennis world has been watching, and tweeting, in admiration and disbelief. Within an hour of the match, the players have tweeted to each other, a new and fascinating phenomenon. Marks of respect are everywhere. It is, to my mind, the defining moment of the championship.

There are matches of distinction and matches (and performances) we would best forget. The rise of 19-year-old Sloane Stephens as a player of regard is much enhanced by her victory over Williams in the quarter-finals. I recall being introduced to her in Indian Wells in 2012, and how engaging and confident she seemed. I see why now. She is not put off when Williams takes a timeout after a heavy fall and instead keeps it all together to win 3–6, 7–5, 6–4.

In the semi-finals, she will play Azarenka, a match that will go down in the annals more for what happened off the court than on it. Cries go up all around when Azarenka, who has blown five match points in the eighth game of the second set, and then lost serve, calls for the trainer. She takes the equivalent of two timeouts, for injuries to her rib and her knee; there is a nine-minute hiatus before Stephens is allowed to serve. She is a point away from 5–5 but loses serve and the match. There is a misunderstanding in the on-court interview when Azarenka says that she almost did the choke of the year. She thinks she has been asked where her game has gone, whereas the question was why did she 'go' from the court. The Americans are up in arms, seizing on what they regard as gamesmanship against their player and the Twittersphere is blue with complaints. The Melbourne press feeds on this, describing the final between Azarenka and Li Na as 'Melbourne v. Azarenka'. Azarenka's coach, Sam Sumyk, describes the media as 'sharks'.

There is much mending of fences behind the scenes but what is clear is that medical timeouts are open to abuse and if you give a player an opportunity to use a rule to their favour, they are almost certainly going to take it. We cannot know what goes on out of public view, we have to take a player's word for it and, call me naive, I take Azarenka's. She calls Stephens the next day to express her regret that it had to end the way it did; Stephens accepts the call and the emotions that inspire it with good grace. Azarenka wins the final against Li with some aggressive tennis, though she has to do it with the crowd almost entirely in the Chinese corner. Her will to win remains remarkable. The champion plonks a can of Red Bull – one of her sponsors – on the table in front of her during her TV interviews, which is strictly against the rules. No one does anything about it.

For Djokovic, life is like a box of chocolates. After his momentous struggle against Wawrinka, he defeats the No. 5 seed Tomáš Berdych for the loss of twelve games, the No. 4 seed David Ferrer for five (a stunning success) and then has an extra day to rest ahead as those in the second semi-final, Federer and Murray, extend each other to four hours before the British player prevails in five sets, having played poorly in two tie-breaks, but serving twenty-one aces and hitting his spots as well as he has ever done. And so, for the second grand slam in succession, Djokovic meets Murray to decide the outcome.

Djokovic ought to win the first set, but loses it when Murray plays a tremendous tie-break. Murray ought to be 2–0 up in the second, the Serb is teetering yet somehow holds on despite three break points and we enter a second tie-break during which there is an extraordinary moment when a feather floats into Murray's eye-line as he prepares for a second serve at 2–2. He stops to retrieve it, he moves back to serve and misses. Djokovic is never behind in the match again and wins 6–7, 7–6, 6–3, 6–2, a final that is not a classic but which encapsulates Djokovic's further dominance of the sport: his movement, his power, his ability to transfer defence into attack, his impossible drive.

Murray, chastened but not depressed, flies home that very night. Though suffering from the effects of twenty-three hours in the air, he drives to the All England Club for dinner with his contemporaries: Baker, Colin Fleming, Jonny Marray and the stricken Hutchins. They laugh and they cry. A couple of days later, I sit down with Hutchins at the club, a lad I have known since he was thirteen, for one of the more remarkable conversations of my career. He is fighting the good fight, taking it to the enemy, in his case, cancer. For months now he has been troubled with pains in his back and hip. He appreciates he may have endured them for longer than he should since he did not pick up on the signs. He says:

> Being a sportsman helped me to overcome the initial diagnosis and mindset but the weakest points in my body are hip and back and being used to playing with pain there meant that it made me not look further into it and maybe I could have caught it earlier. I had been playing with pain in my body so it helps in one way and maybe not in others. The support has been incredible and a little unreal. When you see all these messages and cards, emails and letters from people you've not spoken to for a long time at the start I was thinking 'who is this for?' because it didn't feel like it was for me. And then you start to realise it is you and you are quite over- whelmed by it. You are lifted, you feel special that people want to reach out to you. You text me and I think 'oh I wonder what Neil's up to' and I go and read your paper. I know there are hundreds of people around the world who have experienced it because they write and tell me 'I went through stage four' or 'my husband did this ten years ago when the medicine wasn't that good and now he is sitting here next to me' and that kind of makes you realise (not that people would write to you saying they didn't get through it),

but those who write about living a happy life force you to believe you will do this. This can give me 2–3 per cent of a lift.

When I walk into the Royal Marsden Hospital, I see so many people affected by cancer and I know it is curable and this is the process by which, if the body accepts the drugs, you will get over it. I don't think anything other than that. Maybe a couple of seconds every day you allow bad thoughts to come into your head, you have to have some realisation and respect that it could happen but you mustn't allow negativity to come in. This is an evil trying to push me off my path but I intend to stay on the path.

He tells me he has become engaged to his sweetheart of ten years, Lindsay Wood, and I shake him by the hand and wish him well. He is in my head as I write, dreaming of a better tomorrow.

Chapter 1

Arranging a Game

THE POLITICAL SHAPE of professional tennis has not altered much over the years – the roadblocks, enmities and challenges remain and in some cases have become more entrenched as the years have gone by. Too few people in the sport want to open their eyes to the possibilities for change, innovation and risk. Those who do will risk a slapping down along with those who offer them the succour of publicity. The status quo favours those who have forged their positions of power and do not want to lose their front row seats and who, inevitably, fight extremely hard to keep things as they are.

Before the start of the year no one could remember the last time the seven different bodies representing the sport's leadership – the four grand slam tournaments, the ATP World Tour, the WTA and the ITF – had met in the same room and by the end of the year nothing had changed. This is not joined-up leadership in my opinion.

Every now and again, there is a new face in the seat of power. After a protracted, often hapless process, Brad Drewett became the executive chairman and president of the ATP World Tour from 1 January, 2012. The 54-year old Australian, who reached the top forty in his playing days, had been elevated from his role as the CEO of the ATP's 'International Group' helping to spur the growth of the game in the Far East, especially China, with whose leaders, both in tennis and beyond, he was on excellent terms. For a large part of the year, Drewett was troubled by a problem with his vocal chords which hardly made an unenviable task any easier, for there was much that needed to be talked about, to debate, to engage with. By November, at the O2 arena, he looked dead beat. By January 2013, we would know the full savage extent of why.

Before his illness took a defining hold, would Drewett be able to deliver change? Did he want to? Was it worth the opprobrium? At the start of the year, I spoke to Etienne de Villiers, who had been in charge of the tour between 2005 and 2008; a man brought in by the ATP from the world of Disney to instigate change, to make new things happen and yet, when he did, he was roundly castigated and more or less driven from office.

De Villiers and I became good friends and I found the condemnation of him after he had left office far too personal and extreme. He did what he thought was right, he tried to make a difference and that is the best much of us can hope for. We had a wide-ranging discussion about the structure of the association and whether he thought the ATP, where the decision-making was shared between tournaments and players, required a redefinition of values and priorities.

He said:

I took a lot of flak for being the architect of change but I knew from day one how tough it would be. I had this wonderful meeting in Dubai three months into my tenure with [Marat] Safin, [Lleyton] Hewitt, [Roger] Federer, [Andre] Agassi and Rafa [Nadal] who was just a kid. Rafa said 'don't listen to anything I have to say because I don't know anything about tennis, you are the businessman.' Then he gave me hell about wanting to change the clay court season. When I see him now I ask: 'Whatever happened to that innocent guy?' 'I grew up', he says.

Andre said: 'Are you going to listen to me if I tell you what to do? I'm the No. 1.' I said it had sounded like a trick question. He gave me this incredibly steely intelligent stare. I said, 'No, I'm not going to listen to you, I'm going to do what I think is right', and he said, 'Then you have a chance of succeeding, but understand this – you will be hated by everyone for doing what you are going to do, even if you believe it's the right thing and only ten years later will you be given credit for it and if you can live with that, you'll do a great job because the lows are going to be lower than you ever imagined.'

De Villiers said he went into the job with his eyes wide open. He was a bit of a table-banger, he ruffled feathers, he upset folk, he wanted to move faster than tennis had moved for a long time. 'So none of what happened to me ever came as a shock,' he said.

The trouble with the ATP is that it is a fundamentally flawed concept. As Churchill said, 'Democracy is the poorest of all of the solutions but it's the best solution we've got'. I don't know that any structure is better. You could argue that the players could have their own union but then you would have inherent conflict and employer/employee always arguing about how to divide the spoils and I think that would be very difficult.

For as long as you have sixty-three disparate tournaments that have to be drawn and dragged to do things that are not only in their self-interest but in the sport's and ultimately everyone's interest they will resist because it wasn't their idea or it's not what their owner thinks or their federation thinks, or they think because they hit a tennis ball twenty years ago, they know how the sport should be run.

Following De Villiers's departure in 2008, the ATP launched its 'Brave New World' of two strong top tiers in key markets, with nine Masters '1,000' events in Europe, the United States and Asia which culminated in the Barclays ATP World Tour Finals in London in November as well as ten '500' tournaments (from twenty-two applicant cities) that also included Latin America. By 2011, six of the leading events would be combined with the Women's Tennis Association (WTA).

There was much talk of consistent delivery of stars with a guaranteed player commitment of eight of the 1,000 events and four 500s, including one post the US Open (after September). There would be $800 million in facility investment, a greater than 50 per cent rise in prize money and, in total, more than $1 billion of added capital and increases in tournament 'on-site financial commitments' would be made via the Masters 1,000 and 500 events and spectacular new stadia have and would be built around the world.

At the onset of 2012, the ATP World Tour promotes itself as 'entering its fifth decade as the leading governing body in professional tennis' – a bold pronouncement and not entirely in keeping with reality (hardly a new sensation in tennis). Beneath the board operates a council of twelve players from various levels and a thirteen-member tournament council of whom ten are in place at the start of the year. Federer is the incumbent president with Nadal and Novak Djokovic as premier aides. That players of this stature are willing to engage in the process is welcome but do they have the best intentions of the sport as a whole at heart? The year ahead will tell us the answer but several of those lower down the rankings are wary.

The players are looking enviously towards the money paid by the grand slam tournaments – one of the running stories of the year – but the ATP sets its own compensation levels and there is much to be done to improve the lot of those in the lower echelons. In over twenty years, the prize money at the Futures and Challenger levels has barely risen and inflation has bitten ravenously into everyone's earning potential. There is little monetary incentive for the lower ranked players to want to improve and the ATP needs to keep all of its family members happy.

The WTA's 'Leadership team' is fifteen-strong and headed by Stacey Allaster, a Canadian named by *Forbes* as one of the most powerful women in sport. She had replaced Larry Scott – once a politician for the ATP before generating astonishing sponsorship deals and securing equal prize money across the grand slam board

– as the chairman and CEO in mid-2009 and signed a five year extension of her contract which was a significant achievement. The WTA is made up of seven directors and also has an eight-woman player council and twelve-person tournament council.

In 2008, the WTA introduced a Roadmap designed to shorten and streamline the season, increase prize money and the bonus pool payments (for those who lived up to their playing expectations) and provide more breaks for the top players by reducing their commitment, with the goal of generating healthier players who showed up more regularly for the tournaments they had committed to. This year would mark the fortieth anniversary of the birth of the women's tour, perhaps the most significant moment ever in the advent of women in sport.

The ITF, the International Tennis Federation, is the governing body of world tennis which 'oversees administration and regulation; organising international competition, structuring the game, developing the game and promoting the game'. The Board of Directors is elected every two years by national associations while the president serves a four-year term. The current incumbent, Italian Francesco Ricci Bitti, is in his third period of office, spanning twelve years. He has an executive vice-president and a dozen vice-presidents, whose number includes at least one from each of the four grand slam tournament nations. The day-to-day duties are carried out by a 'secretariat' of six that includes the president and executive vice-president.

Last and most powerful of all are the four grand slam tournaments, comprising in the order in which they are played, the Australian Open, the French Open, Wimbledon and the US Open. Together their chairmen form a grand slam committee, of which American Bill Babcock, formerly legal counsel at the defunct Men's International Professional Tennis Council and subsequently the grand slam administrator employed by the ITF, is the paid director. Few people have more experience of the political machinations of the tennis world than Babcock.

The structure of the calendar remains a lifelong conversation piece. As the cornerstones of the sport, the grand slam tournaments decide their dates and everything else works around them. The Australian Open is staged in the last two weeks of January, which coincides with school holidays and when the weather in Melbourne is invariably perfect.

If the sport were to start all over again with a blank sheet of paper, the 'Aussie' would almost certainly be staged later in the year, with mid-March the optimum after a strong hard court build-up. The tournament is remote in more ways than one, far away in travel terms and further away from any other event of substantial significance in distance and time. Once the sport departs from Melbourne, there is a four-month hiatus filled with tournaments of varying hues and values (from clay courts, to hard courts and back to clay again) until the next major, the French Open in Paris's late spring.

The chequered nature of the tennis season, where one element does not always flow straightforwardly into another, makes it difficult to follow and thus the story often becomes disjointed.

After Paris, there is a strangulated grass court season of two clear weeks until the grand-daddy of the slams, Wimbledon. Six weeks later, we are in New York City for the US Open. This year the Olympic Games will be staged at the All England Club with a three-week gap both after Wimbledon and before the US Open. It means that working through the 2012 schedule will require a player's greater care and attention than usual.

Dotted through the year, the weeks for the Davis Cup and Fed Cup competitions are slotted in, two events which, were it not for their historic value, the ITF would have very little with which to bargain at the top table. They know it and so does everyone else. The ITF is as protectionist of its events as any wildlife organisation of an endangered species. The Davis Cup, which began in 1900 as a friendly fixture between the United States and the British Isles, has grown into a huge competition so confusing that those of us who have written about it for thirty years still have trouble explaining its more intricate variants. The ITF, on behalf of the Davis Cup, haggled for and won ranking points for player participation but points are awarded only at world group level and not lower down, which makes for a two-tier system. This is plainly ludicrous. Without these two events, the ITF almost forfeits its reason to exist. No one wants to lose the Davis or Fed Cups, but almost everyone (bar the ITF) wants to change them.

Beneath these major events is a tranche of smaller tournaments of varying prestige, and lower still the Challengers and Futures for men, Tiers III and IV for the women. This is where the matches are at their most raw, where a player's first ranking points are accrued, where the pain of the weekly defeats (for there are many more of those than there are victories) have to be utilised to a player's benefit, where teenagers become grown-ups and the grown-ups staying in the game bully the teenagers. There has not been an increase in prize money for years at this level, which is where the potential for match-fixing is at its most acute.

Then we have the juniors, the fresh-faced, driven boys and girls, more often than not with fixated parents pushing them all the way, who are looking to make their mark, to grab their slice of the fame, often calling their own lines knowing that sometimes, to be scrupulously honest may cost them in the long run. The junior matches are increasingly intense and ferocious and pored over by a phalanx of agents. I will learn during the year of a leading executive of a national association accused by several parents at a small tournament of openly encouraging his son to question line calls that should not have been questioned. This is the world we are in.

Of course tennis is a sport that has its fears for corruption. Such is its cut-throat nature, so ferocious has the competition become, such is the physical power required to succeed in it that it is increasingly exposed to the threat of corner-cutting and cheating. There have been doping charges in the past and there will be more in the future for sure. The testing procedures are alleged to be flawed and the amount of money required to police it properly is not made available. No one can be 100 per cent certain that no one has ever doped, indeed there are those on the internet who are insistent that the sport cannot be played at its current levels unless someone somewhere is supplying something that is both illegal and undetectable. The sport has to guard, too, against the ever-present threat of match-fixing. There are hundreds of matches played every month at numerous levels and the demands on policing and enforcing the sport's codes of conduct require eternal vigilance. Does tennis have the means and the where-withal to pronounce without doubt that it is clean? It does not.

The superstar players are truly stunning in so many respects, as people, as athletes and as representatives of their sport. Golden age is an over-used phrase but it is difficult to come up with anything better. Djokovic, Nadal, Federer and Murray are the John, Paul, George and Ringo of the men's game, a set of four individuals who together make such sweet music. Yet, like the Fab Four, they have their foibles. On the surface they get along fine, but underneath they want to beat the others' brains out. There are those who want to join the band, but they have not been allowed to play along. The four men at the top have lent the sport a mystical, magical sense of well-being such that tennis wishes it could stay like this forever and fears what might happen if one or more of them fades away. Then we might all be in trouble.

Through no fault of their own, the women's game is in the shadows. It does not have a Martina–Chrissie hegemony, rather there are lots of fine players milling around waiting for someone to make an expressive mark. A lot of sponsors clearly want to be a part of women's tennis but they have been unable to find the single company that wishes to have its name adorning the tour, as Kraft, Sanex and Sony Ericsson had in the past. Tennis is in a stunningly successful period, for all its disparate and fragmented structure. Fernando Soler, the Spanish head of the tennis division of International Management Group, IMG Worldwide, the world's pre-eminent sports management agency, puts it best.

> Men's tennis has never been as high as it is today and it is a credit to these four guys, but there is sometimes a lack of recognition for what some promoters have done for the sport. You have seen the evolution in facilities, of building tennis events, improving the quality of TV product and distribution of the television rights, the evolution of the TV world from terrestrial, to digital to satellite and how well tennis feeds into the channels, from Monday to Sunday, seven hours per day. Look at what has happened at the grand slams, notably Wimbledon and the Australian Open [both of which IMG represents], the facilities are incredible and the level of investment behind this and the quality of the management and their commitment so that the players can perform at the level they do, is better than it has ever been.

Along the way we know there will be good times and bad, happy times and sad, great matches, questionable ones, debate and disturbance, glorious wins and gut-wrenching despair but through it all, there will be tennis – schizophrenogenic or not – and this is the sport we cherish. At its professional peak tennis is a travelling road-show, featuring the same people meeting in the same places, queuing for the same courtesy cars, scrambling for the same locker space and practice courts, bumping into each other in the same cafes, nurturing the same lofty ambitions, and all trying to seek that defining edge, that moment in the stars which will mean them crushing those they see each week of their lives. It is both delicious and terribly dysfunctional.

In April 2012, I lost my old mentor, Laurie Pignon, a great man and former *Daily Mail* correspondent, who fought the good fight all his life and passed away at ninety-three. As I set out on this journey, I recalled his recollections and the fondness he maintained until the last for the glory days of old. He wrote:

The players of my era, like Fleet Street, are gone for ever, but the biggest difference in reporting tennis in this day and age is not all the electronic paraphernalia about the place, but the contact – or rather the lack of it – between the press and the players. Gone are the golden days and swinging nights when together we used to celebrate hard won victories, or soften the bitterness of defeat with a shoulder to cry on. In some cases players became our lifetime friends.

In the quiet hours when the music is soft and the scent of an old whisky lingers on the lips, my mind often travels back to those times when matches had been played and the stories filed, and the little parties of us and them, when we used to amble into the night and forget that it all had to be done again in the morning.

Chapter 2

Winter

IT WAS THREE days before Christmas Day 2011 when the telephone rang. What did the office want at this usually peaceful time for the tennis correspondent? The voice was instantly recognisable. 'He's going to go with Lendl,' my friend said. The remark came out of the blue, though I wasn't entirely nonplussed since it had been in March that I had written a story linking Andy Murray and Ivan Lendl which was never completely dismissed as fanciful. I was picturing how the story might play out in the paper when the caveat arrived. 'You can't use it yet, not until it's settled.'

I knew the information was genuine but the caller would be implicated if I ignored the wish that it stayed between us until told otherwise. I was committed to upholding one of the basic tenets of this profession – you do not let a contact down. Trust was vital and always would be. I would have to keep the information to myself however agonising that choice might be.

On the Friday evening of 29 December came a more definitive whiff that Lendl was primed to take the job but my contact asked that I hold tight for a couple more days. I had that stomach-churning sense that the story was slipping away. I hoped nothing would be disclosed over the weekend and would have an article ready for Monday's edition of *The Times*.

The deal had been completed without fuss. Murray was taken with Lendl's character, what he had said about how he felt Murray would go about beating Roger Federer, Rafael Nadal and Novak Djokovic, the loose ends were tied up quickly, there was no messing. 'The playing side is the be all and end all as far as we are concerned and the rest of it follows, Andy wanted to sign Ivan and so the deal was done,' Matt Gentry, Murray's PR point man at XIX Entertainment said.

In Brisbane, Australia, where he had decamped for the new season, Murray knew what I didn't – he knew I knew about Lendl. His team discussed it over dinner the night before New Year's Eve, as the ink was drying on the contract signed with the former world No. 1. 'We were talking about it and couldn't believe you didn't write it,' said Darren Cahill, a member of the coaching team formed by the clothing firm Adidas, who had been working with Murray on an ad hoc basis for nine months. 'You must be going soft.'

It was difficult to settle into my seat for the flight to Brisbane for the opening tournament of the year, notwithstanding its (lack of) width. I festered and fidgeted. We crossed Poland at midnight on New Year's Day, which was being celebrated with huge bonfires easily picked out from 35,000 feet. The stewardess asked if I wanted a glass of champagne to toast the occasion and I declined. I kept looking at the front page of the *Times* sports section and knew that my story should have been there. It was not an auspicious start to this venture, a book I'd had in mind for some time, to uncover, explore, dig deep and penetrate if possible what had been described as the least penetrable of world sports. I'd missed a sitter.

There was a desperate need for some shut eye after landing in the furnace of Brisbane but I did not want to sleep so it was a case of shower, change and hasten into a van that trundled up and out of the city to the Queensland Tennis Centre and fifteen minutes later, Pat Rafter Arena appeared in the distance. This was my first (bleary-eyed) sight of it. It had the feel and layout of a mini-Melbourne Park. That it was here at all, staging tennis, was something of a miracle.

Two days after the event was completed in 2011, the venue was beneath four metres of water as floods which had been spawned by a shift in the La Niña weather pattern struck the state of Queensland with such a devastating force that three quarters of its 1,852,642 square kilometres of land had to be declared a disaster area.

Not just the main tennis centre itself but thirty-four clubs in the region were submerged to the extent that Tennis Australia, Tennis Queensland and the State's Government joined forces in a $1.8 million Tennis Flood Fightback Infrastructure Programme, the results of which could be seen as we reached the brow of the hill with the Pat Rafter Arena below.

Reviewing the improvements, tournament director Cameron Pearson – the former head of operations at Tennis Australia – was justifiably proud. 'The floods provided us with an opportunity to create more space for the players, bigger changing rooms and more space for them to chill out,' he said.

> The gymnasium has been expanded. We have land set aside for a second stage of development and judging by the numbers coming through the gate this year we may well have to do that. This is a tournament TA and Queensland want to invest in because it's so popular and we may have the funding to build another stadium court with 50 per cent of the capacity of the main stadium.
>
> The vision for this facility came from Ashley Cooper [a Wimbledon and Australian Open champion in the late fifties] years and years ago. He loves this place, I see him at least once every couple of weeks out here pulling out weeds from the car park – he is a keen gardener.

The Brisbane International had become a combined event, an ATP World Tour 250 Series (the winner received 250 ranking points) and a newly-sanctioned Premier 600 tournament on the WTA Tour, which meant it was markedly more important for the women than the men. Hence Pearson could attract a stellar field that included grand slam champions Kim Clijsters, Serena Williams, Ana Ivanovic and Samantha Stosur, who was playing in her home state. Maria Sharapova was a late withdrawal with a recurrence of a shoulder injury. Murray had not played the event before, having preferred to start his year on the opposite side of Australia in the Hyundai Hopman Cup mixed doubles event in Perth for the previous two years. He was the top seed in the men's draw; Gilles Simon, the world No. 12 from France, was seeded No. 2.

The fun was about to start again. After her first round victory, Serena Williams walked edgily into her first press conference of the year. I had first met Serena as a happy-go-lucky teenager when she was eager to engage and buzzing with energy. As the years had gone by, she had grown tired of them and, often, so had we. There were several reasons for Serena to be glad just for being there. After all, here was someone who had survived surgery on a pulmonary embolism in March 2011, having been whipped into Cedars-Sinai hospital in Los Angeles the moment she stepped off a plane from New York. 'The doctors said that I had several clots bilaterally in both lungs,' Serena had recounted at Eastbourne that June – her first tournament back since the surgery.

> They said if they had caught it two days later, it could have been a lot more serious, possibly career-ending. A lot of people die from it because you don't recognise it. I couldn't breathe. I honestly just thought I was out of shape and needed to hit the cross-trainer.

The blood clots had formed during Serena's recuperation from a second operation on her right foot, lacerated by glass in a restaurant in Munich – the German city where her hitting partner Aleksandar 'Sascha' Bajin lived – the previous July, an event that was shrouded in mystery. Even now, when pressed, she could not remember the name of the restaurant and, despite every German media organisation poring over the story, none could establish the name and exact location of the restaurant where the incident had taken place.

The reporters present at this Brisbane rendezvous were keen that the conversation did not extend beyond tennis. The trouble with many such conferences – I'd done a few hundred over the years – was the conflicting agendas and muddled thinking that dominated them, and so it was no surprise that Serena was soon reduced to a rambling discourse in which she did not manage to complete one train of thought before being led to another. It was difficult to sustain a line of enquiry or build the thread of a decent conversation.

She was asked about missing almost all of the 2011 season after the US Open final. 'Officially I … I don't know. I'm going to be honest. I mean, Asia's so far and I was so tired,' she sighed. How powerful remained her inner drive to succeed, I wondered? 'For me it's all about motivation, as opposed to my skill, or anything else, so as long as the motivation's there it's definitely going to be cool,' she said. 'I'm not playing a full schedule this year. I just want to be able to do other things and expand on that. Everywhere I go is going to be really special for me and for the fans and that's what I want it to be.'

She said she had been preparing herself for a life after tennis but could not be explicit about when that might be.

I've never played a lot, but I'll probably play a little less. I think even if I hated it, I mean I don't love tennis today but I'm here and I can't live without it, so it's a difference between loving something and not. Right now I can't live without tennis, so I'm still here and I don't want to go anywhere any time soon.

It's not that I've fallen out of love – I've actually never liked sports, and I never understood how I became an athlete. I don't like working out, I don't like anything that has to do with working physically. Now, if it involves sitting down or shopping, I'm excellent at that. So that's kind of always been my Achilles heel – the workout portion. I'm like, 'Aaaah … how do we do that?', so that's my main problem.

Like so many of Serena Williams's conferences, the press filed out at the end wondering quite what she had been trying to get at.

The following day, she was scheduled for an interview with *The Times*. These 'one-on-ones' were difficult to secure and until you walked into the room there was an anxiety that the person who agreed to the interview might not be as good as his or her word. For the most part the system of partial cooperation worked between the press and the tours, but generally one way. The writer turned up, notebook and pen at the ready and hoped the player would make it as well.

The Williams family had not always been the easiest to pin down. The WTA staff did their best to accommodate the multiplicity of requests they received for these special sit downs with a player and they, too, knew that Serena and Venus could often be tricky customers.

But that morning I received a nod and a wink. It was on. Even the chance to talk to Serena for fifteen minutes with a WTA chaperone (I was old enough not to need those now) meant making sure preparation was thorough. No time for ums and errs. But first, they had to get through the day's match and your objectivity was often tempered by the feeling that you wanted the interviewee to be in a good mood. You hoped that they would win.

Serena was playing Bojana Jovanovski of Serbia and all was well, for she led 6–2, 5–3. As I made final preparations for the interview with one eye on the television screen in the press room, Serena moved to her right, had to alter course quickly and stumbled, rolling her ankle. There were gasps as the fall was replayed over and over again. My heart sank. Even though she managed to win the next game and the match, Serena said she would play no further part in the tournament. My interview was off as I somehow always knew it would be.

Stosur lost in the second round, miserably, to Iveta Benešová of the Czech Republic, who was newly on the arm of Austrian Jürgen Melzer, which was some consolation for his first round defeat in the singles to Phillip Petzschner, his (other) doubles partner. Clijsters was here for the first tournament of her final, final year on the tour with Carl Maes, the coach who had departed from her team in 2006 to spend a few years at the Lawn Tennis Association in Britain, as the head of women's tennis.

Maes did not leave Britain on good terms with many people and clearly he did not like the fact that I was around. I sensed his unease when we crossed paths, which (as often happened in these cases) felt like it happened every five minutes. He was here with his wife, spending down time pushing his two young children along the riverside in their buggy. I received one forced handshake. He had not appreciated the tone of a number of articles I had written about him during his LTA tenure and I was not enamoured by certain elements of his behaviour while he was working in the British game. I would not be doing my job properly if I got on with everyone. I didn't get on with Maes.

Kim was a different kettle of fish altogether, approachable, sincere, loveable, still trying to overcome the loss of Leo, her father, three years earlier, while juggling the demands of Jada, her daughter who was now four years old, as well as the knowledge that she had decided that this would be her final full year on the circuit.

In her third match, the semi-final, she played Daniela Hantuchova – who received a walkover on Serena's withdrawal – and started brightly, winning the first set on a tie-break. As the second set unwound, she felt her left hip tightening to the point where she could not turn her upper body into her shots, which is so essential. She said that the 'smartest choice' was to stop for fear she would only make matters worse. She said she would go to hospital the following day for an MRI scan.

'This is such a strong sport where physically it is so much more demanding on the body,' she said in response to my question about what effect that many hard court events has on the body.

When I started playing, there were very few players travelling with a physiotherapist and no one was hardly ever in the gym except those with a skipping rope or maybe doing some shoulder exercises, but now everyone is in there because it is necessary. I can only speak for myself but the tennis I play is so demanding on the body and combine that with a hard court, well...

The new team of Hantuchova and her coach Claudio Pistolesi would last all the way to the final where Daniela met her match in Estonian Kaia Kanepi, an exceedingly powerful ball striker. Hantuchova won only three games in the final but as a preparation for the Australian Open her coach was as content as he could be.

There was not a Slovakian journalist at the event and besides me no British writer either. This was almost unheard of for an event in which Murray was competing so close to a grand slam tournament. You took such decisions – and hoped the office backed you up – with a finger or two crossed behind your back because an early loss would be a crippling blow to everyone's morale – player, entourage and writer. It was nice to be welcomed by some friendly faces: Sam Smith, the former British No. 1, was forging a career as an excellent commentator and was on secondment to Australia's Channel 7, there was a knowledgeable trio of Belgian writers shadowing Clijsters and a decent smattering of locals, from their always affable journalists to former pros turned television folk, Todd Woodbridge, John Fitzgerald, Geoff Masters and Rennae Stubbs.

Murray knew I had reported on Lendl in his playing days, that we had got along and thus the tone of my relationship with him would be markedly different from previous coaches he had dissuaded from talking to the press. It would work in his favour and, in any case, with Lendl it would be futile. He was too strong a personality. Murray would do well to let Lendl say whatever he wanted whenever he wanted and suck it up. The coach called me and said he would be in Brisbane on Friday if his man survived that long, which he fully expected him to do.

One wondered if Lendl was going to speak to Murray about the tetchy demeanour on court that cost him badly at critical moments, especially in major tournaments. 'All that will be said to Andy on that subject will be said by me to him and to nobody else,' he replied. I knew where I stood.

The initial indication was that Lendl intended to work with Murray at the four grand slam tournaments and 'a handful' of other events in the year in what I believed would be one of the more open-ended relationships forged in international tennis. But would a hands-on/hands-off situation work? 'We will adjust as we go along but you know me, when I am in something I am in it totally,' Lendl said.

The international response was immediate and, to a great extent, flatteringly positive. Peter Bodo, an American writer and author with a distinctive pedigree, saw how it would work. 'Lendl is a supremely logical guy with an abiding faith in the empirical who will help Murray find his most efficient game'.

> And that is a very big deal for Murray. One of his weaknesses, which is also a source of some of his appeal, is a tendency to lose the plot in any given match. Nobody in the top four gets as careless as Murray, and none of his rivals are as prone to getting sloppy.
>
> It's taken me a long time to figure out with any clarity how I feel about Murray, but now I know. He's an enthusiast – the eager, determined amateur holding his own, or trying to, among the polished pros. In some ways, he always seemed an outsider, the bony, pasty-faced Scot among all those tanned European, American and South American dudes with their crisply laundered shirts and cool haircuts.

To make certain Lendl diverted to Brisbane after his long haul trip from Florida, Murray had to win three times in consecutive days. His first opponent in 2012 was Mikhail Kukushkin, a Russian by birth, who now popped up under the Kazakh flag, an arrangement acceptable in the eyes of the International Tennis Federation. Since 2008, several invitations had gone out from the cash-rich Kazakh Tennis Association to Russia, its northern neighbour, for help with players.

Shamil Tarpischev had long been Mr Russian Tennis, captain of the Davis and Fed Cup teams and a member of the Organising Committee of the International Olympic Committee. He gave the deal his blessing, which made it all right. 'This arrangement has helped a lot of players receive extra funding from the Kazakh Federation for their development. There were problems in Russia and we were unable to give them the financing they needed as we have so many good players,' he said. In the wake of this 'understanding' Kukushkin, Andrey Golubev, Yuri Schukin and Evgeny Korolev had traded nationalities and were strong enough as a bloc to form a Davis Cup world group team. How many long-established nations (including my own) would give their eye-teeth for that?

Neither political consideration nor the fact that Kukushkin was coached by his wife Anastasia Ulikhina (a rare breed) was uppermost in Murray's mind half an hour after he took to the Pat Rafter Arena on a sticky Wednesday evening. It was the shock of a prospective humbling. The top seed had lost the first set 7–5 and was 1–1, 15–40 in the second. I was beginning to think I had embarked on the wasted journey to end them all.

It is incumbent on the best players to step up in these circumstances and Murray did just that, a forehand cross-court winner saving one break point, an unreturnable serve the next. From there, he broke Kukushkin in the next game and a sense of calm settled over the top seed and this anxious scribbler. He won in three sets.

The next two rounds taxed him further. Gilles Muller, an eleven-year circuit veteran from Luxembourg, who peaked at No. 42 in November 2011, also won the first set and was a break up in the second before Murray recovered strongly. Muller unravelled when his opponent played a tie-break befitting a top-four player and the Scot won the final set to love.

Next up was Marcos Baghdatis and, thus, in the opposite corner sat Miles Maclagan, Murray's former coach. This time, perhaps spurred on by the opposition's mentor, Murray took a match by the scruff of the neck, was 4–0 up in a blur and won 6–2, 6–2 in sixty-five minutes. Lendl was half way across the Pacific Ocean as Murray's net cord winner landed within the court boundaries on the Cypriot's side. He was into the last four against Bernard Tomic, the enigma from the Australian Gold Coast.

It was good to have Ivan Lendl back. He looked to have put on a couple of extra pounds around the middle but I decided it would be best not to bring that up straight away. Better make sure we still worked together well. The first couple of times he took the piss out of me (within a minute) I knew we were all right. 'Still writing the usual shit,' he said.

When people talk of Lendl's sense of humour they largely mean his ability to make fun of others while retaining a psychological upper hand. I had heard it called 'jovial sadism'. I liked the fact that he seemed nervous. He was as much the new kid here as he was the first time he came to America, all those many life-forming years ago. He wanted and indeed needed to do this job well.

The electricity generated by his arrival in the grounds was emphasised by his pupil's performance on the court. Murray was mesmeric against Tomic, winning 6–3, 6–2, rounding off the first set with a trio of aces, serving two more behind a break in the first game of the second and requiring just seventy minutes to get a really professional job done. 'I'm just interested in winning,' Murray said, and this was how to win well.

In the final he would play Alexandr Dolgopolov, of Ukraine, coached by Jack Reader, born in Fleetwood, Lancashire over half a century earlier, one of the original 'Ten-Pound Poms' uprooted from the old country in the 1960s and who took the boat to Australia for a better life. Reader looked like something out of an episode of Skippy, with his shoulder-length dark hair, perennial cigarette perched between his fingers, and his eagerness to swap stories and gossip. He said that a story doing the rounds about him earning money as an exotic dancer earlier in his life, under the name 'Jack The Stripper', was entirely the figment of someone's imagination. You rather wished it wasn't.

What was true was that two years earlier, as he and Dolgopolov were sitting in Nice airport trying to board a flight to Paris, they decided as a ruse that they would pose as a gay couple to make use of a lovebirds' cheap flights offer. Dolgopolov went along with it as far as the check-in counter and then lost his nerve.

As it transpired, the final was a bit of a damp squib. Perhaps Dolgopolov was trying not to overdo it, as he was broken twice in a first set Murray completed with a twenty-eighth hold of serve in succession. Quickly into his stride in the second, Murray stalled only when he dropped serve in the sixth game but secured a 6–1, 6–3 victory and a title paraded as one for the new team. He thanked 'Mr Lendl' for being here for him. Lendl, in turn, praised Murray's 'fantastic composure' before sliding away saying he was in desperate need of some sleep.

The night before he left for Melbourne, Andy and I had a long and, I felt, revealing chat. Obviously, the appointment of Lendl was the hottest topic. He had been searching for a compatible 'full-time' coach and none had fitted his bill. Cahill had been a superb stop-gap but that was all he would ever be, given his Adidas commitments.

After he had met Lendl a couple of times the prospective coach had become more and more flexible in terms of the time he would be able to devote to Murray. 'I'm sure Ivan will tell you that he had doubts, because when you've been on the tour as long as he was, he knows the sacrifices,' Murray said. 'He has a wife and five daughters, he loves his golf but he's willing to give up a lot of that for me.'

I have chopped and changed, a lot of the situations weren't [of his making]; when I went with Brad [Gilbert] it was done through the LTA and it was a big mistake on my part. It didn't work for me. I've always tried to find the best person and help and the way I play the game is a lot differently to how a lot of people see the game. It might look like something from the outside but the reality is when I'm on the court I'm feeling something completely different to what the person who is coaching me sees. That's what it's about having a great coach, someone who can see the game through your eyes and what you can do on the court.

He accepted that his negative behaviour and impulses had slowed down his progress – the critics might have had a point in some respects.

It's something that would help and that I'm working on and that I'll get better at. It's a good thing that it is that and not something that's glaringly obvious in my game that needs to improve. At no stage last year did I see Djokovic go through a match without saying anything. I saw him go nuts on the court and win matches and almost like he wasn't trying for a set and then coming back. It is how you respond. You can break a racket but if you go and serve an ace on the next point – the whole of this week, every time I was down, I was coming up with first serves. So long as you have a clear head when the next point starts, who cares? That's what matters.

I feel more accepted in the US or here than I do at home, more comfortable in the surroundings. You don't feel you are getting judged if you get annoyed on the court – 'He's spoiled or he's this or he's that.' Maybe this year I won't get emotional, I don't know, we will have to wait and see.

We parted with the firmest handshake I could remember from him.

In the final three rounds of his first event of the year, the British No. 1 had given away thirteen games; he had won his eight sets at the tournament and as he looked back over his shoulder before heading to the airport, he said: 'I am going to show up and give 100 per cent on every point from now on.'

Roll on Melbourne.

Chapter 3

Australian Open

MANOEUVRING THROUGH THE players' restaurant two days before the Australian Open was not an easy task. Around people and over bags – or was it the other way around? – I was making a beeline towards Britain's James Ward who had won his second round match in qualifying. The mood in his group was buoyant, though the same could not be said for every table. There were plenty of tears and traces of smudged mascara. Coaches sought explanations, some spoke in loud, accusatory tones and when these chidings were delivered to a young female – and not in a whisper too discreet to be overheard – you could not help but shudder a little. But this was the life they had chosen. This was not a pleasant time to experience a loss, on this huge but isolated island.

The temptation was to offer a consoling look to anyone who appeared in need of one – even to not immediately familiar faces, a kind of fatherly instinct. Just at that moment, a hand landed with a thump on my left shoulder and a mobile phone appeared across my right. 'Hey, Mr Twitter friend.' There was a flash from a camera and Novak Djokovic and I greeted each other with beaming smiles and firm grips. I beheld a man comfortable with world dominance.

I had not seen Djokovic in the flesh since November at London's O2 Arena where, for the one and only time in 2011, he was crushed. Everything else in his year had been stupendous, all those titles, all those headlines, all that wild celebration. At the start of the New Year he was the man everyone was looking up at – the world No. 1 and reigning champion of Australia, the United States and Wimbledon.

The hierarchy in the men's game was shifting. Djokovic discomfited Roger Federer and Rafael Nadal – there was a self-confidence about him that went more than skin deep. It was noticeable that when Djokovic mentioned Nadal he called him 'Rafa' and when Nadal was asked about Djokovic, he most definitely never said 'Nole' (as rhymes with Ole and by which friends and family knew him).

The 'old' guard had become used to splitting the majors, they appeared side-by-side in commercials, apparently relishing the company, and flew together in one's private jet to appear at the other's charitable foundations. McEnroe and Connors they were not. Connors would tell me he found this idea of chummy familiarity particularly off-putting. And so Federer and Nadal did not take kindly to Djokovic kicking their butts throughout 2011 (aside from the French Open semi-final when Federer ended the Serb's 43-match unbeaten run, which prompted the Swiss, a good deal too precipitately, to raise his index finger to suggest he had merely loaned the No. 1 ranking).

Federer had not lost a match between the semi-finals of the 2011 US Open, when he had two match points but was beaten by Djokovic, and the end of the year, when he landed his sixth victory in the end of season Barclays ATP World Tour Finals in London. 'I think that shows, again, how tough I am, the right decisions I can take,' he said.

These are the kinds of reactions I expect. I always have to explain myself. But I don't have a sheet where I say, I have to achieve everything. I really don't. The effort that goes into all this is equally big. Every tournament I play in some ways is a priority for me, otherwise I wouldn't be playing. I don't play thirty-five tournaments. I play, you know, a certain amount where I know I can perform well.

But Djokovic had clearly got Federer's goat and that's the way it should be. The Serb was a natural, that much was clear, and his ease on the big stage was getting to the opposition. I recalled his stage presence at the age of nineteen, representing Serbia and Montenegro in a Davis Cup tie in Glasgow, at which the British LTA tried unsuccessfully to persuade his family to sign for Britain as they sought to use the break-up of the two nations to offer sanctuary in the British game. His mother and father were wooed but the idea crashed and burned when Djokovic decided, wisely, that it could cause him and his family too much grief if he gave up on his homeland, as generous as the offer was. It had, frankly, been embarrassing that the LTA would even contemplate such a move.

Novak was the dominant personality at his team's press conferences, even though the captain was present and all his teammates were senior in age. He was straightforward, thoughtful and approachable and spoke perfect English. I am thirty years older than him but, in truth, I felt we had the same sense of humour; we both appeared in the players' show at Monte Carlo and he was amazed that a journalist – especially one from *The Times* – was not averse to stepping up and taking part in something a bit risqué. We had that in common.

Djokovic pushed a lot of people's buttons, with the infernal ball-bouncing, an unpardonable past reluctance to complete matches and times when his on-court demeanour appeared disrespectful to his opponents. I had questioned all of this. I was straight with him and, having never discovered anything to the contrary, believed he was completely straight with me.

He opened the year in an exhibition in Abu Dhabi, playing quite brilliantly. The event had the brass neck to market itself as a world championship though it was merely an oil-rich nation's attempt to join the tennis 'club' by offering thousands of dollars to persuade the best in the world to give up a weekend. The guarantees of around $1 millon in the case of the top three competitors made it a very acceptable as well as lucrative three days' labour. There was virtue in these events for the participants but, respectfully, it was nonsense to make them out to be anything other than what they were – a means of accumulating large sums of money without the pressure of defending your ranking position.

From the unreal world of petro-dollars and artificial competition it was time to embark on the first grand slam tournament of the year. There could be no more distinctive leap from pseudo-grand to one of the four ultimate 'grands' of tennis.

The purse for 2012 would be $A27 million, men and women receiving an equal share – as they had since the reintroduction of parity in Australia in 2001 – and the champions would take home $A2.3 million each. The rump of those players whose anticipation was not to last beyond the first week did not fail to notice the bumper packages and at whom they were weighted.

Everyone was doing their sums. The winning mixed doubles pair would earn more for an event that would barely make a line of coverage in the newspapers, than the average Australian took home in a year. The singles winners would fly home featherbedded by the equivalent of forty years' pay for a local worker. There was very serious money in grand slam tennis.

The man at the heart of the Open's renaissance was tournament director Craig Tiley who, at the same time, was head of performance for Tennis Australia, an exquisite job-share that required cunning and astute business acumen in equal measure and Tiley, a South African (a fair few folk in Australia turned their noses up), was one of the most adroit political minds in the sport.

'My role is unique and I believe it should be copied,' said Tiley, who oversaw participation, performance, tournaments, facilities and coaching, a total of 130 employees and a budget in excess of $A80 million. It had taken time for Tiley to be accepted – he still wasn't entirely – but he had played the tour and coached in the United States collegiate system which was a solid grounding. But it was the case in Australia as in the other grand slam nations that being a former top level player granted an assumed privilege. How could 'an outsider' teach us, a great tennis nation, how we might make things better?

'The fact is that I have coached and I understand the sport,' he said.

To me, this is not about the gravy. I had no vested interest in relationships when I came into the job. It was a question of 'you look like you can do the job – and you don't'. I had a mandate for change, so in the first year I was able to set the strategy, put the structure in place, make the decisions on people. I was able to grow exponentially every part of the business. In player development, we are getting wins on the board and more kids in the top 100 and that's always a long journey, that doesn't happen overnight.

If you make a decision to have a short term fix because it looks good, you will never have a long term solution. Any decision we took, we made certain it would have a long term impact. I did take flak early on – 'why don't you hire this high profile player, this ex-player?' – but my view was that well, maybe that ex-player didn't have experience working with fourteen-year-olds, so I'll have the coach who has the experience and I'll happily bring that ex-player into an area where they have expertise on what it was like for them on the tour. In an environment where there are a lot of people like that, it becomes more challenging but now we are at a point where I don't know of anyone who didn't do something in Australia who is not having some impact on a full time or part time basis.

Rod Laver earned a total of $1,565,413 in his playing career – an undefeated winner in the Barclays ATP World Tour Finals at the O2 in London in November would make more than that in a week. Laver was one of the true tennis gods, a small, wiry man, soft of speech, shy of manner, who played so wonderfully and earned the respect of everyone in the sport.

The Centre Court at Melbourne Park was named after him and, though initial indications were that the great man, now seventy-three, would not travel from his home in California, whispers increased that he might indeed show for the second week. The

humblest of champions, Laver – the only man in tennis history to
win all four majors in a calendar year as both an amateur (1962)
and a professional (1969 when he took home $5,000) – spent a
lot of time caring for Mary, his wife of forty-six years and only
left her side when it was absolutely necessary.

Laver's victories in the Australian legs of those 'slams' had
come in Sydney in 1962 and Brisbane in 1969 as the tournament shuttled between the nation's major cities before settling in
Melbourne in 1972. For the next fifteen years, it was staged on
grass at Kooyong until it outgrew the suburban club and moved
to its new site on the banks of the Yarra River, a brisk walk from
the throbbing city centre.

At Kooyong – whose grass courts remained lovingly tended –
in the week preceding the Open, an eight-man 'exhibition' was
masterminded by Colin Stubs, the former Open tournament
director. Herein lay one of the many contrary quirks of the sport:
why did the ATP Tour not complain about an exhibition event in
Melbourne in the same week as an official tour event in Sydney?

Stubs gathered a hugely marketable line-up for the AAMI
Classic, duly announced with all the fanfare he could muster. Andy
Roddick, Mardy Fish, Tomáš Berdych, Gael Monfils, Jo-Wilfried
Tsonga, Milos Raonic, Jürgen Melzer and top ranked Australian
Bernard Tomic formed a highly compelling field. Channel 7
covered the event as if it stood for something more than the
opportunity to give eight players a few friendly knock-ups.

Sydney, in the meantime, promoted the profiles of Juan Martin
del Potro of Argentina as top seed and the No. 2 American John
Isner, happier than ever to be a combined event as the women
attended in considerable force, with nine of the top ten headed by
Caroline Wozniacki, the No. 1.

Craig Watson was tournament director in Sydney (now the Apia
International), which, as the former New South Wales Open dated

back to 1885, is the fifth-oldest event in the world. It had moved from its old home of White City in 2001 to Homebush, the site of the 2000 Sydney Olympic Games. Watson extolled Sydney's virtues – and they were many – but like every other tournament director, he needed a field.

> Tournaments have been struggling with player commitment for as long as I've been involved and I started with Tennis New South Wales in 1984. Everyone wants the top players, they are the ticket sellers, they fuel the need for tournaments like ours to find enough in guarantees [payments to players to ensure their participation] but there are only so many [top players] to go around.

But, emphasising the affection in which tennis continued to be held in Australia, Watson's attendance figures were up, broadcast hours increased and 'we sold every bit of moving inventory'. He was within four hours of a completely dry week and was a reasonably happy man. His champions were Azarenka of Belarus, who had to be considered as a real chance for the Open, and the veteran Finn, Jarkko Nieminen, who was unlikely to be a contender at No. 77 in the world.

Kooyong's crown went to Tomic, which pleased the locals and delighted Stubs. Murray played one match against Argentina's David Nalbandian on a tricky broiler of a day. The result didn't matter. Ivan Lendl decided it was time to talk to the full ranks of the British media, the majority of whom he had not met. He shook hands and attempted to memorise names. He spoke for half an hour, initially cautious, before relaxing and opening up more. What he said was utterly absorbing.

> I admire Andy's guts for hiring me because he had to know it would create a lot of interest and that it's not going to go unnoticed and be a quiet thing. It ups the ante a little bit and that just shows me that he wants it. It would have been very easy just to hire someone, just another coach and not get a high profile person.

So would Lendl have come out of purdah for anyone other than the present world No. 4? 'Unlikely' was his response.

> I knew I would be asked that so I tried to count. I've had between seven and ten enquiries over the last eighteen months, some more serious than others, but I didn't consider any of them seriously.
>
> I see a guy [Murray] who wants to win, a guy who wants to work hard. Obviously I see parallels between his career and mine. The way I look at it is that we work hard and we prepare the best we can and that is success itself. You have to focus on the process – you cannot be glued to results.

It was an interesting theory.

Lendl already had plans for his charge to loosen up a bit and speak to someone he knew, he trusted and who had helped Lendl to get over the line when it mattered. He would recommend Alexis Castorri, from Fort Lauderdale in Florida, who had bet Lendl $1,000 in 1985 that she could design a mental and physical programme which – if he followed it to the letter – he would win the US Open that year and become the No. 1 player in the world. If not, he would pay her $1,000. Suffice to say she was the richer at the end of it. Seven months after their first conversation, Lendl won the Open.

Castorri had designed a programme for him based on 'logo-therapy' which argued the theory that man's only freedom was the attitude they chose, that they must face up to the prospect of losing before they walked onto court, to confront the fear and then put it behind them. Murray had won in Brisbane, which was all well and good, but could he go on to put fear behind him in the first major of the season? How much might Castorri help in the weeks and months ahead? Lendl was determined to find out.

While the coach was planning for the short and long term, the qualifying tournament for the Open – very much the present – was reaching a crescendo at Melbourne Park. Those of us of a particularly manic disposition dashed (well, hailed taxis) back and forth between Kooyong and Melbourne Park, catching a set here, a set there. I loved the 'qualies'. They were the heart and soul of the sport, where players outside of the ranking cut-off for the main draw fought and scratched to get into it. Quite often the qualifying tournament would throw up more interesting storylines and matches than the early rounds of the tournament proper. There was so much to gain, so much more to lose.

The robust depth of the game was epitomised by the strength of the qualifying draw – Germany's Rainer Schuettler and Arnaud Clement of France, two former Australian Open finalists, were in the men's event. Melanie Oudin of the United States, a quarter-finalist at her home Open in 2008 and Sesil Karatantcheva of Kazakhstan were entries in the women's competition. Karatantcheva (then representing Bulgaria) had sat in front of an incredulous audience of which I was a member at Indian Wells at the age of fifteen in 2005 and said she was going to be a superstar. Oh the bounteous bravado of youth.

Of the four, only Schuettler made it beyond a round. Nothing quite prepared a player for a first round loss in qualifying. The recompense was $A2,860 in prize money and not one ranking point – little compensation for a ton of hurt. For those who had fallen in qualifying, there was little point hanging around, it was time to pack and prepare for the next tournament, the next chance to earn a dollar or a ranking point and to make any kind of headway – which brought us to the first hint of the political tensions that would engulf the sport through the year.

On the Friday evening before the championships, I was the lone journalist (remarkable I thought given the advance notice of the meeting) outside a room at the Sofitel Hotel, inside which were gathered the members of the ATP Tour to hear Brad Drewett, the new executive chairman and president, make his first and most important speech. He needed to make an instant impression. Tiley, as the Open tournament director, and Steve Wood, the CEO of Tennis Australia, were given ten minutes to deliver their welcome addresses and then they, like all non-players, were asked to leave.

Players' coaches used to be allowed to attend these meetings but that was stopped when they continually tipped people (like me) the wink about what had been said behind closed doors. Player attendance was mandatory; the risk of a hefty fine hung over the non-compliant. It necessarily followed that all the members of the ATP Board in the city would attend such a potentially defining gathering. I was told not to. I tried to gain admission on the premise that only by hearing the players' views at first hand could I express them fully and fairly. But security was tight and I got only as far as a sofa outside the conference room before being told – in friendly tones by a security man – to stay put and have a coffee.

Murray gave me credit for turning up – 'not surprised you're here,' he said, laconic smile in place. Many players were happy to acknowledge my existence; Nadal made a point of breaking away from a group of fellow Spaniards for a handshake and nod. I was told to expect the meeting to last a lot longer than the hour or so these things usually take.

There was rumour of a major resignation. Nadal – a vice-president of the ATP Players' Council, a group of twelve players representing the views of the competitors – was poised to step down because he had had enough of political wrangling. His disaffection had grown at the previous year's Barclays ATP World Tour Finals at London's O2 arena, when he had put it to his fellow competitors that the ATP ought to consider the introduction of a two-year ranking system.

The strength of the idea, for those superstars at the top, was that it would offer a greater sense of ranking protection because, if a player missed a couple of months through injury, their ranking average would be taken over two years, rather than one and they would almost certainly restart about where they had left off. When it came to endorsements, bonuses and other favours for the elite, it helped enormously still to be ranked at or near their ranking peak.

Nadal gained the signatures of six of his fellow competitors in London; the only player to demur was Federer and when I asked him about it during the championship, the Swiss was quick to nail the idea as a non-starter.

'I'm not a big fan of it just because I think it would make things rather boring,' Federer explained.

As the president of the Player Council, I think it's not a good thing for the lower-ranked players, to be quite honest, it's going to be a struggle for them to make a big breakthrough. It's going to take them multiple breakthroughs. So the dream of having one great tournament, then making a move, in my opinion, is never going to happen. I like golf, but I couldn't tell you who's in the top ten of golf right now. I couldn't even mention four players. This is where I think tennis lives from the weekly rankings we have, the changes. You guys (the press) love it, I think.

If we have a two-year ranking, things would be so slow and nothing would really move. I can't support it as a president of the Player Council and I have to look at all the players in the eye. I know it could be a good thing for me or for Rafa or for other good players because we would stay at the top for a very long time. For us to move down in the rankings would take something extraordinary. But for the lower-ranked players, I don't think it's a good thing and that's why I can't support it.

The case against had been conclusively stated.

Two hours after they had entered into the Sofitel meeting, the bulk of the professional tennis playing community was on the march. One or two made 'call me' gestures, others winked, but no one stopped and spoke. Fear of reprisals, perhaps. The rump of the ATP board and its associated partners remained in the room, locked in discussions. They had several problems.

The Bryan Brothers, the doubles twins from the United States, talked of a fiery meeting, with the demand for scheduling changes to the fore. 'In a perfect world,' they said,

We'd have the US Open [in August/September], have the tour finals for the top guys then shut things down. As far as the rankings go, look at golf, theirs are over a two-year period which means Tiger Woods can take a year off, come back and still be No. 1. But everyone [in tennis] has their agendas, when you talk about cutting the schedule the clay courters don't want to lose their events and the hard court guys are the same. We have friends who have had hip replacements at forty and we don't want to see guys limping around when they are twenty-five.

Nadal was only twenty-five yet had been limping for a long time. His petition raised at the London finals in November may have been forgotten by others but he did not forget. The grievances were getting too much and spilled over the day after the player meeting when he greeted the press as the defending Australian champion. His words in English were not particularly contentious. 'I am not going to be the one who is going to talk about these things, especially because I am always the one and I am tired,' he said.

> You are talking about a movement. I don't know which 'movement'. This is a sport that's an individual sport. So when you are talking about individual sport, what must happen if a super majority thinks one thing, the rest of the players have to support that. So if a super majority thinks one thing, I will support them – that's all – in anything. Not in a strike, not in calendar, in anything, because I understand democracy is like this.

A little later, in Spanish, more meat was added to the bones of his discontent – a generous and controversial portion. 'It is very easy for him [Federer] to say: "I am not going to say anything, everything is positive" and come off as a gentleman and burn the rest. To finish your career with pain in all areas of your body is not positive,' Nadal said. 'He finishes his career as fresh as a daisy because he is physically privileged, but Murray or Djokovic or I are not fresh as a daisy.' Nadal had assumed the moniker

'Red Rafa'. Federer was pressed on the remarks and played the diplomat. 'Nothing has changed in our relationship,' he insisted.

Nadal remained distracted. This time a year ago we had been debating his attempt at a genuine, four-in-a-row 'slam' and utter domination of the sport on all three surfaces. He had won the French Open for a fifth time, Wimbledon for a second and the US Open for the first. The world was at his feet but David Ferrer defeated him in straight sets in the quarter-finals in Melbourne and Djokovic trampled on his chances of winning on hard courts in America by beating him in the finals of Indian Wells and Miami and, to everyone's astonishment, on clay in the finals of Rome and Madrid. Nadal won Monte-Carlo for the seventh time but Djokovic had not entered there, preferring to rest.

The Spaniard contested ten finals in 2011, losing six to Djokovic. He was hollow-eyed in London for the tour finals, came back to life in Seville on clay to lead Spain to Davis Cup glory but declared himself unavailable for his country in the competition throughout 2012 and was riding his anti-hard court hobby horse as Melbourne approached.

'The [hard] courts are very aggressive on the body,' he said.

> I feel I can say these things now because I have won here in Australia and the US Open on hard courts. The only negative thing about tennis, if I have to say one, is that the competition is too much. The calendar makes the sport too hard. Without health [performance] is impossible. This surface is, in my opinion, very bad for the lower back, for the knees, for all of this. It makes me scared for my body for when I have to retire.

To cap it all off, on the night before the tournament started and while lazing in a chair in his hotel room at the Crown Casino, he felt his right knee lock. We pictured a scene much like the semi-comic slide from his chair underneath the press conference table at the 2011 US Open when seized by cramp. I talked to a couple of former players, on the basis that I would keep their names secret, who said that their knees had locked in the past and it had hastened the culmination of their careers. Nadal was genuinely shocked and troubled. He said he was in tears. Could he possibly start the tournament, let alone complete it?

The wider Australian audience, while perturbed that one of the world's leading players was suffering from more physical pain, was more pre-occupied with local prospects. The top seeded Australians this year were Tomic and Samantha Stosur, Gold Coast residents both, but markedly different as characters.

Stosur was the beach girl with the wrap-around shades and shapely, toned biceps, who could quite easily pass for a triathlete. She was the US Open champion, backed by a team of unobtrusive compatriots, manager Paul 'Killer' Kilderry, her coach David Taylor and partner Jane Morrow, a former Australian softball international.

Stosur had recently changed clothing sponsors. The story was that her sponsor Lacoste did not find her dynamic enough – quite a decision since she was the sport's newest female grand slam winner. Now, she had a multi-million-dollar account with Asics, the first time the company had branched so decisively into tennis.

Asics must have been getting twitchy. Stosur had lost fretfully in Brisbane and again in the first round of Sydney. Most of the headlines concentrated on her prospects but the sense was that inside the No. 7 seed's stomach there was a chill in concert with the unseasonable Melbourne thermometer readings.

Any time you're a top player, let alone a grand slam winner, every match is more closely followed, win or lose and especially lose, I guess. I know everything is going to be heightened. But it is what it is. I think it's been building in the last couple of years and I know this is going to be bigger again.

As it turned out, she had to cope with such pressures only for a couple of days. In her first round match, against Romanian Sorana Cirstea, the worst, for Australia, came to the worst. Stosur lost in straight sets. She played as if in a trance. 'Now the weight is over for Sam,' opined the *Melbourne Age*. Greg Baum, the paper's sports columnist, wrote: 'Everything was heavy, the atmosphere, the balls, Sam Stosur's legs and shoulders, question marks about her form and above all, the cursed weight of Australia's insatiable sporting expectation.'

Stosur had said after her New York victory that she could not wait to hear Craig Willis, the finest MC in tennis, introduce her on Rod Laver Arena as the US Open champion but when he did, her knees buckled. 'Immediately three cameras were trained on her, including one dangling from a spidery web. Australia was in her face,' Baum wrote. She called it her Open disaster. 'I think all the work I have put in is going to work for me down the track, so it's not a waste of time,' she said. Those who worked tirelessly on the posters, the emblems, who painted the signs on the side of the Melbourne trams, may have thought otherwise.

Tomic had grown to 6ft 5in. and grabbed headlines because of the belief – which some of his behaviour did little to debunk – that he was 'a bit of a lad'. His father John was a menacing presence to many in the Australian game, a Croatian by birth whose guttural delivery was such that you had to strain to pick up every word; a lot of what he said could be misconstrued because it was not understood perfectly. I recalled one thing he told me very clearly when I wrote two years earlier that I thought his son could be a top ten player: 'You are nine places out.'

Bernard was something special, he played in a throwback style, sucking up the pace of his opponent, generating sudden bursts of speed and possessing the court savvy of a player ten years his senior. He was without doubt a potential goldmine but agents at IMG representing him had come and gone, exasperated with John more than anyone. Now he was in the hands of Max Eisenbud, who also took care of Maria Sharapova and Li Na, so there was nothing to catch him unawares. Yet, Tomic had a Qantas logo on his racket bag (John wore a Qantas cap), which contravened Virgin Australia's sponsorship of the tournament.

Was this commercial naivety or 'you can't touch me' bravado? The authorities seemed powerless or perhaps they were afraid of incurring Big John's wrath. Either way, they let it go.

The best match of the first round was between Tomic and Fernando Verdasco, the body-beautiful left-hander from Madrid, a semi-finalist in the tournament in 2009. The statistics indicated that Verdasco made eighty-three unforced errors but, in its four-hour-and-eighteen-minute duration he was so often tormented by Tomic's effortless indulgences off the ground it was made to look as if that was an imperfect count.

The home flag was also being hoisted once more by Lleyton Hewitt, who played his home championship for a sixteenth straight time and never offered anything less than all that he had. But, he was thirty and had endured months of trouble, especially with his hips and now his toes. He was at No. 181 in the world and this was rough for him, but you knew they would have to scrape him off the court. A couple of victories would suit a lot of people, but not him.

Hewitt was the Vegemite of Australian tennis, you either loved him or you hated him. He sparked a certain level of indifference in those who recalled the good old days of Australian tennis, a period in which camaraderie prevailed after a hard day's slog on the court. Hewitt was much more of an acquired taste, a hell of a champion but with an edgy, abrasive side to his nature that did not suit everyone's taste.

Every match of Hewitt's appeared a swansong, as if we were about to witness the last scuffing of the baseline by the old soldier. In the round of sixteen, the home nation's interest finally faded away though Tomic and Hewitt fought the good fight to the end. Hewitt was the first player to take a set from Djokovic on a boisterous night inside Rod Laver Arena when the impossible was dreamed before reality took an uncompromising hold. Tomic lost in straight sets to Federer but his credentials had been endorsed.

The lion's share of the pre-championship publicity was taken by these Aussies and Andy Murray, to whom the Australian media had taken a genuine shine. The Lendl–Murray axis was a fascinating new element and the player was happy to engage in it. Darren Cahill, the Australian who played a significant part in bringing the pair together, was now in the commentary box for ESPN, though he would happily venture to the side of the practice court to offer any expertise required.

It was difficult to see a winner in Melbourne beyond one of the top four, Djokovic, Nadal, Federer and Murray. The arrival of Lendl aside, their backroom teams had become as familiar as an old blanket, trusted cabals of tennis-specific assistants and off-court staff, PRs, agents, their clothing reps, wives and girlfriends.

In the Djokovic stable was coach Marián Vajda, physiotherapist Miljan Amanovic, and physical trainer Gebhard Phil-Gritsch; Toni Nadal had coached his nephew since the age of four and Rafael 'Titin' Maymo travelled to every tournament with Nadal, watching over his physical preparedness like a hawk.

Federer employed twin coaches: Severin Lüthi, Switzerland's Davis Cup captain, and American Paul Annacone, who worked with Pete Sampras and Tim Henman and had been handed down from friend to friend to friend. Physiotherapist Stephane Vivier, once an ATP staff man, had joined the team in 2010. Vivier, especially, rather enjoyed the renown of working exclusively with Federer, having lived the humdrum existence of jobbing physio. Dealing with Federer's limbs was altogether more exotic.

Murray's corner consisted of Lendl, Andy's best friend Dani Vallverdu, physical trainer Jez Green and physiotherapist, Andy Ireland. Neither Federer nor Djokovic's parents were at the event this year but Nadal's father and mother Sebastian and Ana-Maria (though they had separated in 2009) were together and present at the tournament, as was his uncle Miguel Angel, once a formidable centre-half for Barcelona and Spain (I had reported on England vs. Spain at the 1996 European Championships in which he played in the middle of the back four).

Judy and Will Murray, Andy's divorced parents, both attended, though in Judy's case it was largely in her capacity as the recently-appointed GB Fed Cup captain. How she would react to Lendl taking charge, and how much time she would spend around her younger son, was the subject of much speculation. Whatever happened, she would go home after the first week to prepare for her captaincy debut, a Europe Africa zonal championship in Eilat, Israel. That was unless any of the British team survived beyond the middle weekend, which was considered unlikely. Indeed, by mid-afternoon on the first Tuesday, they were all biting generous portions of Aussie dust.

The first contentious match came in the second round, casting another unsatisfactory spotlight on the perennial conflict and concern over officials at major events. The ITF had a group of nine officials engaged by them for the slams, the Davis and Fed Cups. There was an ATP group of umpires and another for the WTA; they were augmented by a troupe of freelancers who travelled the world working for the tournaments that would pay their way.

My view is that the best events should be umpired by the best officials regardless of the initials after their names. Imagine the outcry if a World Cup took place without half a dozen of the best referees. This happened at too many grand slams. Nowhere in tennis were the levels of jealousy and sheer paranoia as evident as they were in the secretive world of officiating. I was thought to be closer to too many of the ATP umpires than to those of the ITF but that was because I saw them more often and they were entirely more approachable (though always nervous that supervisors might see them talking). Such a notion was incredibly counter-productive but tennis does counter-productivity extremely well.

When a tournament referee worked through his list of matches one assumed they were aware of which match would require the most sensitive handling. David Nalbandian of Argentina needed that for he could quite easily blow – it was best to watch him closely and assign wisely. Kader Nouni, a French umpire who received important assignments in the women's game, was a rare visitor to high profile men's matches and yet here he was, on Margaret Court Arena in charge of a potential fireball.

This was as spicy as they came. Nalbandian was 8–8 in the fifth set against John Isner as the shadows lengthened. Isner faced a break point in the seventeenth game, and fired down a first serve which was called wide. The crowd erupted, obscuring the fact that Nouni had overruled the call. Nalbandian sought clarification before deciding to check the mark. The Argentine looked over to Isner, who seemed to suggest he might want to challenge. Nalbandian said 'challenge' but Nouni deemed the request untimely (as he was allowed to do) and refused to allow it.

Nalbandian was beside himself that a challenge at such a critical point had been timed out when he had not heard the umpire. He demanded to speak to the supervisor, Andreas Egli of Switzerland, who did little but throw up his hands and say the chair umpire had made the call and he could not interfere. To make matters worse, TV replays showed that the original call was correct and the ball was out, which Nalbandian would have known had he been allowed a challenge. The overrule cost him a second serve on break point that, had he converted, would have given him a chance to serve out the match. Instead, Isner was credited with an ace (one of forty-three in the match) and it was deuce. Isner held for 9–8 thanks to a forehand passing shot and an ace before breaking Nalbandian's serve to win the match.

The ensuing press conference was not one to miss. There were next to no Argentine press at the tournament – the downturn in their economy taking a severe toll on their capacity to travel – and Nalbandian was a notoriously frosty customer. And yet I got to know him well after his appearance in the 2002 Wimbledon final, we happily chatted and I had the sense that a familiar friendly face might settle him and allow a conversation to develop. Barry Flatman of the *Sunday Times* joined me in the interview room, where players sat at a lower level to the rows of seats for the press, the only event where they were not set higher than us. It all felt very uncomfortable, as if we were somehow superior. Initially,

Nalbandian was monosyllabic but as we became a little more persistent with each question, he relaxed. 'It's ridiculous playing this kind of tournament with these kinds of umpires,' he said, rising to the theme and becoming more straight-backed in his chair.

> What is this? What did the ATP do for this? I didn't understand in that situation, eight-all, break point. I mean, can you be that stupid to do that in that moment? What the umpires need, press? Be on the picture [TV] tomorrow? Incredible. Anyway, I didn't lose for that, but that was a very bad situation.

Nouni was wrong, not by the letter of the law but by refusing to use common sense – that fundament of umpiring. Nalbandian was well within his rights to ask for a challenge and should have received it. How could you not let technology decide upon a call on an ace at 8–8 in the fifth set? It was absurd and smacked of arrogance. Nalbandian lost 4–6, 6–3, 2–6, 7–6 (5), 10–8. We all lost really. The determination of what was or was not 'time-honoured fashion' had to be less subjective. There had to be a distinct time limit, otherwise the sport looked stupid.

Nalbandian was then summoned to doping control. He had washed his hands in the locker room and was asked to repeat the procedure in the testing room. Upset at having to repeat the task he turned the taps so quickly that water splashed over his hands and across the floor. At least that was his story. It would later be suggested that he had tipped a bottle of water over a tester's head, an incident for which there were apparently witnesses. He told me that such a charge was utterly baseless but was fined nonetheless and did not put up a fight.

Only eight of the thirty-two matches in the second round of the women's singles reached three sets, one involving Petra Kvitová, the Wimbledon champion, who expended more energy than she would have liked to see off Carla Suárez Navarro, a Spaniard who adapted a clay court game impressively to a hard surface, albeit a very slow one. Three of the sixteen matches in the third round lasted the distance; and just two in the fourth. Of those, the match between Kim Clijsters – once Hewitt's fiancée – and Li Na was utterly memorable.

Clijsters's ankle was still not right. She admitted to having considered withdrawing at 3–3 in the first set when she was treated. 'I knew if I just let the medication sink in, if I could get through the first twenty minutes or half an hour maybe the pain would go away a little bit and with the adrenalin, I could fly through it,' she said. 'I'm happy that I didn't give up.'

Leading 6–2 in the second set tie-break, with the first set in her pocket, the Chinese could smell victory. This is such a difficult moment for a tennis player. Point by point, the mantra goes. On the fourth match point, the Belgian attempted a do-or-die drop shot; Na reached it but with all the court to aim at, directed the ball right back into Clijsters's strike zone and the devastation of the loss of that point drained all the life from her. She fought gamely but lost 6–4 in the third and dabbed away a tear in her conference – 'maybe 6–2 up in the tie-break it was a little bit shocking,' she said, 'but doesn't matter close or far away – in the end I lost the match.'

Clijsters would now play Denmark's Caroline Wozniacki, who had teamed up with a Spanish coach, Ricardo Sanchez, to help share the load with Piotr, her father. The aim, obviously, was that elusive grand slam. Not this time. If the pre-match sense was that Clijsters's injury would be decisive, the Belgian dug as deep as she always had and rallied to win in straight sets. The Danish reporters packed their bags.

Murray had made it to the last four, past Ryan Harrison of the USA, two Frenchmen Edouard Roger-Vasselin and Michael Llodra, Mikhail Kukushkin (his second match against the Kazakh in two weeks) and Kei Nishikori, the Japanese who had played the match of his life to defeat Jo-Wilfried Tsonga, the No. 6 seed from France, in the quarter-finals and was staggering around like a man who had enjoyed one too many glasses of sake.

Tsonga could not believe how poorly he played, his rackets

were trashed and his mind was a mess as well. He felt he was in the best condition he could possibly be to face Nishikori and yet nothing quite happened for him. He was at a complete loss. Tennis has a way of doing that to you. We were left, as we felt we would be, with the Fab Four in the last four once more.

On the morning of his semi-final with Djokovic and against local rules I sneaked onto Rod Laver Arena to watch Murray practise with British junior Kyle Edmund. I feigned importance, chatting with the backroom team, sharing a joke with Lendl, prepping the man from Channel 7 before he conducted his courtside preview, but the 'heavy' in yellow with a security badge spotted me and I was told to leave, like the schoolboy who flicked an ink dart at teacher. There had to be security, no one argued against that, but mostly they got on my nerves and none more so than in Melbourne. This was the only grand slam where you had to be accompanied to watch a practice session. What did they think we were going to do?

I was there long enough to sense a mood of keen anticipation. Practice was low-key and high-spirited, a prelude to one of the more remarkable matches in Murray's life. He led the champion two sets to one having played a third-set tie-break full of clutch winners; serving first in the fourth set was a wonderful opportunity to push on and win. So many of the service games in the match began with the server losing the first two points, it was no surprise Murray was 30–0 down but at 30–15 he had the court at his mercy and took an exaggerated swing at another of the teasing retrievals with which Djokovic kept himself in so many points. Murray missed.

Losing his serve there was a considerable blow; worse that two more breaks followed in quick succession and a previously discouraged Djokovic had new life. It did not aid Murray's cause indulging in a really loose service game to relinquish the set 6–1, thus having to come from behind in the final set. Each rally, each point, each game was a drain. Murray was going for his shots more than ever – an immediate sign of his relationship with

Lendl – but against Djokovic that was not enough. The man was a compound of granite and elastic. When he exhaled loudly as he strained to stay in a point, it sounded real; when the women did it, it sounded less so.

Murray was forced to hold serve and nerve. In the fourth game, he withstood three break points, but as the pressure mounted, Djokovic nabbed his serve in the sixth (Murray led 30–0) with a punishing forehand winner. At 5–3 the defending champion served for the match. Here Murray, downing an entire bottle of energy drink, found another surge, forcing Djokovic to miss, then taking on a couple of forehands British watchers had longed to see, flat, with intent, scarring the surface.

At 5–5, Djokovic wobbled and trailed 15–40. A forehand service return failed to carry the net on the first break point; on the second a rally was extended to twenty-nine shots before Djokovic cut it off with a forehand down the line, at which he let out a roar from the depths of his being. On the third chance, on what looked like a bread-and-butter backhand down the middle, Murray netted. The loss of his next and final service game was no great surprise. Djokovic had been utterly clinical.

As the winner thanked Rod Laver for remaining in his seat until the early hours – 'I wish I could play more serve and volley like you sir', he said – Murray was scooped up by the blood testers for an immediate doping control. How to heap indignity on hurt.

The *Times* headline the following morning FOURTH AMONG EQUALS was quite brilliant and had nothing to do with me. At every turn it had been Murray's deepest desire to change the dynamic. He produced what was his finest major semi-final; and it was almost impossible to believe it was still not enough. It had been the matter of a point here and point there, but he did not win either. Did it mean he was within a whisker of a breakthrough, or that the breakthrough was as far away as ever?

Nadal, who defeated Federer in the 'other' semi-final over four sets (for once a match between the pair would pale when set against Djokovic against Murray which Nadal explained because he had 'more time over best of five sets to find solutions'), now had to contend with the Serbian who, surely to goodness, had to be out on his feet. Thanks to her offer of a courtside seat three rows behind the Djokovic bench, I settled in beside Vika Azarenka to watch the early stages. It felt an uncomfortable place to be and not just because my pink polo was soon imbued with sweat from the early evening humidity. I needed to make sure no one could suspect I was in favour of one side over the other. Objectivity was imperative. I decided I would move at the end of the first set. I was still sat there over an hour later.

The women's final, heralding an astonishing breakthrough for Azarenka, lasted only sixty-eight minutes. Once she conquered the nerves that affect most players in their first grand slam final (perhaps not Boris Becker or Steffi Graf) and the loss of the first three games, Azarenka played awesome tennis to stun Maria Sharapova 6–3, 6–0 and land not only her first major crown but become world No. 1 at the same time.

I liked Vika but not everyone did. We had become close since the WTA Tour was at a loss to understand her reticence to the point of obstinate non-communication in press conferences and asked if I might try to help her express herself better. This did not fall under a journalist's regular remit. I suppose I could have refused and I can imagine some in my peer group thinking a) I was totally wrong and b) why should they ask me and not them? I thought it through but felt if I could help Vika come out of her shell, it would do everyone in the tennis world a favour and, not least, the young girl herself. What I said to her and she said to me will always remain private. I would do the same for anyone if asked again.

Azarenka's newfound honesty and openness were something the sport should cherish and yes, after her victory over Sharapova, one of tremendous bravery and maturity given the immensity of the occasion, I was invited to a private party at the Crown Casino for a celebratory cocktail. The next day, on rather high heels, she walked along the Yarra with her trophy, posed for pictures and then sat with a group of international journalists and handled herself superbly. I have to say, I was rather proud.

Azarenka was unable to stay after the first set of the men's final, in a stadium so enervating it was difficult to believe Djokovic and Nadal could breathe, let alone run. It was time for her flight home and she could not know the wonders she was going to miss. The final assumed an extraordinary sheen.

In the opening exchanges, when Djokovic came to the end where his team were seated, he appeared listless and irritable. There was much eye and shoulder rolling. Nadal won the first set in eighty gripping minutes. But Djokovic picked up his game, as he tends to do, his shoes scraping across the synthetic surface, leaving long streak marks. Thanks to outrageously long reaches, as we entered a fourth hour, he was two sets to one up and led 4–3, with Nadal 0–40 on his serve. This was the time to close it. But the Spaniard refused to be cowed and fought with all in his power, to the extent that it was now two sets all and, with his forehand landing more prodigiously, he was 4–2 ahead in the fifth and was standing at 30–15 on his serve. The next rally was supremely intense and Nadal carved out an opening: it was on the backhand, he had two thirds of the court at which to aim but he nudged the two-hander wide. His entire body sagged at the same moment Djokovic received an infusion of adrenalin.

He knew what it was like to defeat Nadal in finals and now he believed this would be no different. Girding himself for one last effort, Djokovic rallied to break back and with a forehand of sublime mastery, he sealed a 5–7, 6–4, 6–2, 6–7, 7–5 victory. We looked at the clock. It was 1.30 a.m. We had sat through five hours and fifty-three minutes of tennis and Djokovic had emerged the master.

We were in the realms of fantasy. The speech by the man from Kia Motors – contractually obliged – was so long-winded that the chairs the players used on the changeover had to be brought over to the side of the dais so that Djokovic and Nadal could sit through it, otherwise they would collapse. It was faintly cruel and utterly ridiculous. An announcement was made that the last media transportation would leave the stadium at 4.15 a.m. Never in the field of tennis writing had so many been required to write so much about such a remarkable match so early in the morning. In his speech, Djokovic talked of his appreciation of the multiculturalism of tennis supporters in Australia. It was amazing that he could contemplate such a thing at such a time. I was reminded that, in the Australian Open final of 2005, between Federer and Marat Safin, 395 points were played in 268 minutes. In this final, 369 points were played in 353 minutes.

Tiley, the tournament director, could not have been more ecstatic with the success of the Championship.

This year we saw an exponential improvement – helped by good weather. We had some great matchups, the top four seeds in the men's reaching the semi-finals, a new women's winner and new No. 1. There are many things we did, like scheduling matches earlier [e.g. Tomic vs. Verdasco] to accelerate the interest in the event. It worked out, with a bit of a risk. This was far and away our finest Open. On every metric you want to measure it by, the attendance, website hits, broadcast numbers, media, quality of tennis, we exceeded our expectations. In the last six years we have almost doubled our prize money and doubled our attendances. Now we have to do better next time.

My attention was drawn to two letters in the *New York Times* which helped explain that what was happening in tennis reached out and touched so many different people in so many different ways.

To the Sports Editor: Victoria Azarenka and Maria Sharapova, the Australian Open women's finalists, are great tennis champions. But the shrieks they belt out during their matches are irritating. As a classically trained soprano with a good ear, as well as a big tennis fan, I was curious to find out what musical pitches they actually use. When the shrieking started during coverage of the Australian Open, I would immediately run to the piano, singing the pitch repeatedly until I found the exact piano key that matched. For the record, Azarenka shrieks on high G and Sharapova shrieks on high A flat. They are probably unaware that they are sopranos. And I am amazed that their speaking voices reveal no signs of misuse. (Classical singers would be hoarse for days.)

Marilyn Vondra, New York

To the Sports Editor: Re: 'In five hours, fifty-three Minutes and Five Riveting Sets, Djokovic Retains Title,' Jan. 30: After a heart-rending match, Rafael Nadal and Novak Djokovic treated each other with humility, respect and admiration. I'm so pleased that my three young children heard the players' post-match remarks. The presidential candidates should be forced to watch the match and learn from these two remarkable men.

Shirley S. Meyer, Maplewood, N.J.

Chapter 4

All Change Please

AN EERIE SENSATION descended on Melbourne Park with a couple of days of the tournament left to run. A site once bursting with humans, hustle and bustle, conversation and conspiracy was now a near-empty cavern, the corridor that ran past the players' locker rooms bereft of all but the security folk perched on their chairs outside the doors, as if there were still passes to check.

Well, not quite everyone had gone. The officials were still in place, so were the media, tournament staff, juniors, wheelchair competitors and those players who had reached the finals of singles and doubles in the main draw; otherwise all life had scarpered to outposts like Viña Del Mar, Zagreb, Honolulu, Antalya, Burnie, Kazan (where James Ward had all his rackets and kit pilfered), Eilat or wherever else this wacky world took them. In Chile, the temperature was a pleasant mid-sixties Fahrenheit; in Kazan, a bone-chilling ten.

Most of us still could not get the Australian Open final out of our head. Jason Gay, writing in the *Wall Street Journal* (yes, it covers tennis, and exceedingly well) wrote:

One of these days men's tennis is going to get boring again. There will be a fallow period. Greats will retire, get hurt, fatten up, open bad restaurants and buy vineyards. There will be a new, unremarkable No. 1. Maybe a US player – a real, live US player! – will crack the top five. Grand slam finals will shrink to three uneventful sets.

Tennis will return to that stale-aired foyer it got trapped in a while ago – dull, characterless and skip-able.

That time isn't now. Men's professional tennis may be the most satisfying sport on the planet at the moment.

Rafael Nadal decided to take the month off – hoping for some peace and quiet – Andy Murray spent time in London and Edinburgh before heading to his 'third' home in Florida for a critical training block with Ivan Lendl – and his first session with psychologist Alexis Castorri – while Roger Federer said, this time, he would play for Switzerland in the Davis Cup, enhancing the sense that 'when they want to play they will play'. Novak Djokovic, citing excusable exhaustion, chose to skip Serbia's world group tie against Sweden and instead spent a few days at home in Monte Carlo.

Murray's first speaking engagement after the Open was at a sports forum at the National Museum in Edinburgh, a chance to mix with Scots, young and old, who delighted in having more light shed on his personality. 'I am completely different, in psychological terms, to, say, five or six months ago,' he told his audience.

> I feel more mature and calmer. I think you could see that in the semi-final [against Djokovic]. In the past when I lost the opening set of a big match, like last year's final, things would spiral out of control. I was too emotional, too bound up in what was going wrong, and I have learned from that. I am able to process things and make adjustments. It is about being less wound-up on court, and more rational. Like an assassin. I think Ivan has helped with that.

'It is impossible to ignore the level of expectation, particularly when a grand slam comes into view,' Murray confessed.

> At the Australian Open I was so nervous in the first round that I could not move my legs. They were like stone. But once you get a couple of matches under your belt, you relax into the competition.

The problem in the semis or final is not nerves; it is staying in the moment. The temptation is to start thinking about victory, about what would happen if you could just win the next few points or games. But that is deadly, because you stop thinking about tactics and the other things that really matter. The trick is to stop your mind running away.

How the British would have liked him to play Davis Cup a few days later, but he declined this particular tie.

As irony would have it, the nations shorn of their leading stars were victorious, with the Serbians thumping Sweden, Spain far too strong for Kazakhstan and Great Britain, whose tie in the Europe/Africa Zone Group I was staged in Glasgow – a venue largely chosen to accommodate Murray – triumphed against a strong Slovak Republic while the Scot was relaxing near South Beach.

Cast in the unlikely role of British saviour was 21-year-old Daniel Evans, who stepped up in great style to win his two singles against Lukas Lacko and Martin Klizan, players with significantly higher rankings. These surely had to be the victories upon which the Birmingham player would build, for he had the talent and, when the mood took him, the discipline required to use it properly. I am a devotee of Evans but, over time, patience with him had worn thin. He had been restored to the fold after a period in the wilderness, a sighting of him in Wimbledon village the evening before a boys' doubles match in the Championships having incurred the wrath of the Lawn Tennis Association and led to him being stripped of funding assistance. For once, if they had their man nailed, the response was proportionate and proper.

Now Evans, peppering the court with brilliance and bravado equally, was doing the right things and was eventually bounced shoulder high around the Braehead Arena. We really hoped this would be the change. The headlines declared the bad boy had come of age yet there was anxiety on the dais where Leon Smith, the captain, was seated, as well as among those of us listening to Evans's

Brummie accent. There was no doubt Evans enjoyed the praise and so I awaited his response in the tournaments that followed, in those corrugated, cold venues where he would flourish into a player or retreat into anonymity once more.

As Britain celebrated an improbable success, Federer's Switzerland was devoured in a World Group first round tie by the United States who won 5–0 in Fribourg on a testing clay court. In the opening singles rubber, Stanislas Wawrinka, Switzerland's No. 2, lost to Mardy Fish and then, in a seismic shock, Federer was beaten by John Isner in five sets, which was, in the circumstances, a performance on a par with his Wimbledon heroics in 2010. In the doubles Wawrinka and Federer played meekly against the scratch American team of Fish and Mike Bryan and the Swiss were defeated inside two days.

Then it all became a bit messy. Depending on how he was interpreted, Federer was either critical of Wawrinka's performances as the two sat side-by-side at a press conference, or he was being honest and his words were misconstrued. In the French part of his conference, where the different language could lead to different interpretations, Federer was reported as saying 'Stan, unfortunately, didn't do his best match, but he was close. It's a shame he wasn't able to put the pressure on the Americans from the start. After that, me against Isner, in a match like that, anything can happen. We knew that from the start.'

When he reached Rotterdam for his following tournament, the ABN AMRO sponsored event, and was made aware of the furore his words had caused, Federer sought to clarify them: 'It was a tough weekend for us. I did have a day to recover on Sunday and weather the press because it was taken completely the wrong way, me blaming Stan. I would never do that and it was just an unfortunate weekend.'

Wawrinka knew he could never win a public relations joust with Federer and so kept his opinions relatively private saying: 'There is no problem between Roger and me, nor with anyone on the team. I am the first to accept the criticism about the level of play, that I didn't play well enough and that Roger didn't play that well.' But Stan, a sensitive guy, departed for the South American clay-court stretch with an injured shoulder and a heavy heart. Federer was settling into the warm embrace of Dutch tennis, cushioned by a guarantee topping €750,000.

The Rotterdam tournament was re-christened Roger-Dam. Everything possible was done to make life as comfortable as possible for the return of someone who had last appeared there in 2005 and he reciprocated. His first practice session was played to a full house inside the Ahoy Stadium. When his quarter-final was cancelled because of an injury to Russia's Mikhail Youzhny, Federer suggested he should play a golden tie-break against Igor Sijsling, the Dutchman, to placate disappointed ticket holders. When that was completed quickly, he said they should play another one. The crowd lapped up such professionalism. It was Roger being Roger. Richard Krajicek, the tournament director, whose bid for the ATP presidency had not earned Federer's endorsement and had thus been scuppered, beamed broadly as he presented the trophy. It had been a very lucrative week's work.

Guarantees paid to players to appear in certain tournaments are the unspoken truth of the game. For many tournament directors they had become the only means of 'guaranteeing' the presence of one of the leading players. It was a gamble, using a share of anticipated profits to secure the services of someone who would fill a stadium. How, for instance, could a small tournament like the Open 13 Marseille – played the week after Rotterdam – have a viable future without digging deep for certain star players? Jean-François Caujolle, the silver-haired and silver-tongued tournament director, had spent years developing the kind of relationships with players that became the essence of his event's survival.

'Today it becomes very hard to have a player in the top thirty unsecured,' he said.

It creates, logically, a [tournament] table with two speeds. So if the Open 13 stayed in the top three of all 250 ATP Tour events in terms of sporting value, it was not because I am the tournament director or that we play beside the sea, but because our schedule is favourable and we are generous with the players and their guarantees.

I am he who pays the best.

Djokovic, still shattered from his labours in Melbourne, had arrived in London for the Laureus Sportsman of the Year Ceremony – a little like the Oscars but without the gushing oratory. Federer and Nadal had both won the coveted award in the past, so Djokovic's presence was further confirmation that no sport in the world had as much resonance as men's professional tennis.

It was nine days after his historic victory in Melbourne and, magically, he was still able to walk straight. I marvelled at the man and we chatted away from the throng in the hotel lobby. 'I'm recovering quite rapidly,' he said.

'I have this live spirit. I try to absorb every challenge that is presented and take the best out of it, and learn and improve every day. The biggest change I feel in my overall game is the emotional stability. I don't know what the limits are right now.'

Across the city – with no audience to play to – there was momentous change at the All England Club. Ian Ritchie, the chief executive since 2006, had been lured by the Rugby Football Union, ambitious to have him in place in time for the 2015 World Cup after the disastrous fall-out from the 2011 event in New Zealand where the England team's excesses were laid bare, the sport was held in contempt and the smack of firm leadership was clearly lacking.

Ritchie was an enormously popular figure in the game, engaging, approachable, chummy, and much respected. Wimbledon had benefited greatly from his five years at the helm. 'The club has been commercially successful without hurting the brand but I believe we have to be a bit more innovative in the way we deal with our partners,' Ritchie said.

I brought the conversation around to the grand slam tournaments, their success and the spread of their largesse. 'It's a statement of fact that the four slams are in more than pretty good shape, whatever parameters you want to look at – attendances, commercial activities – and that is a direct response to the success of the game and the players,' Ritchie explained. But there was increasing dissent among the playing fraternity at what they considered to be paltry pay.

Crumbs, over the last six years there have been more issues involving players than a simple 'let's have more prize money', like what's the situation with the calendar, what's the situation with a two year ranking list as opposed to one. And it is not just what the prize money is but how do you allocate the prize money, the total pot – all of these things are quite difficult.

Ritchie reached for a piece of paper on his desk.

As a matter of fact at Wimbledon in 2006 [his first year], the winner received £655,000; and in 2011 it was £1.1 million. That's a 68 per cent increase in five years; I think that speaks for itself. The total prize money was £10.3m and is now £14.6m. That's 42 per cent up. You take any argument you like but in the last six years those are very decent increases. The abiding point that applies to all the slams is that all the profit goes back into the game. It's very important to generate that interest. I believe we are very player friendly.

An abiding memory of 2011 was of Novak Djokovic going home to Belgrade after winning Wimbledon to be greeted by 100,000 people. I was watching on YouTube and I could not believe that his members badge was still on his blazer. There was no horde of PR people there saying 'make sure you wear the right tie,' and there he was wearing his badge and as we know of that crowd of 100,000 – 99,998 probably didn't know what it was, but he knew what it was. All of the guys who have won here feel that affinity with the club. When Andy [Murray] became a member here [late in 2011], I know he was delighted.

But if everything in the garden was so rosy, why did Ritchie need to leave? 'I will always have affection for here but you look for new challenges. It's as simple as that,' he said.

Perhaps the management committee was impinging on Ritchie's space, forcing him to consider different options. Philip Brook, who had become chairman of the All England Club in January 2011, was an invigorated new leader, a 54-year-old retired actuary who wanted to be at the sharp end of decision making. The ATP had invited Ritchie to be a part of their interview process as the new chief executive and hoped their interest in Ritchie might remain secret but I got wind of the news and it had to be speeded up.

Nadal invited Ritchie to Majorca for a conversation about the role. He wanted him to take over, believing his brand of experience, respect and straightforwardness was just what the position demanded. There was a rumour that Tim Phillips, whom Brook had replaced as Wimbledon chairman, was asked if he might be considered for the ATP post. I sent him a note asking if it was true and in the midst of a short and extremely courteous reply, he did not deny it.

Of the prospect of leading the ATP, Ritchie said:

> It was a fairly loose and informal [recruitment] process and I'm not going to deny there was an approach, and frankly, I was very flattered to be thought of, never mind asked about, but it wasn't a thing that came about or that I was [that keen on]. I'm just the bloke in a suit. On the broader issues, everyone has to work at partnerships and relationships. I'm not trying to be a Pollyanna about it but why wouldn't you try to treat everybody decently, properly and recognise what they do. It's not difficult.

So Nadal had been thwarted as to his preferred ATP choice. There were plenty of other major players in the game, both on and off court, who knew that Ritchie would have been perfect for the men's tour for all the reasons that persuaded Nadal to invite him to his home: respect, affability, professionalism and cool, clear-headed decision making.

Tennis moved on. The men were in San Jose, the women in Paris; they would team up in Memphis, another tournament where a combined event was regarded as chic though it clogged up the order and frustrated several (mostly male) players. Andy Roddick was not so much upset with that as his form. He fell in the first round, which extended a sequence of a year without a title, and was ranked No. 27, his lowest mark since 2001. From hip to shoulder, from hamstring to ankle, Roddick was hurting.

'You are always at the mercy of the [tour] schedule,' he said.

> Unfortunately if you get hurt, the tour doesn't stop. There's a significant gap from where I am and where I need to be. It would be abnormal if I wasn't frustrated, the question is how to figure your way through it. There's a fine line [between deciding whether to rehab or play on] and something I don't know if there's a perfect answer to.

One certain thing was that these small events, like Roddick, were taking a beating. Compared to the grand slams and the Masters 1,000s, not only did they devote more of their revenues to prize money, but they needed to pay guarantees to induce the better players to come to their town. Unless they possessed a sugar daddy, this was not usually considered a sound investment. The problem was that these tournaments needed the top players more than the top players needed the tournaments.

Roddick just wanted to feel like a player again – 'walking into a tournament, playing a match and having it be second nature and not having it be a thing that happens once every month.' His return to Delray Beach for the first time since 2003 – scheduling and a full commitment to Davis Cup had kept him away – allowed him a reality check regarding how much he had achieved. A teen-on-the-scene in 2000, the seventeen-year-old played his first ATP Tour-level match there. 'I had these dreams that you never think you'll be able to reach out and touch and I've got to do a lot of them,' Roddick said. 'At that point I was wondering would I ever be good enough to make a living at it.'

The men's tour split into four sections in February, with South America, North America and the Middle East hosting mainstream events. Though it was only designated an ATP Tour 500 event and thus considered only half as important as one of the nine Masters, few tournaments were more eagerly anticipated then the Dubai Duty Free where it was six-star glamour all the way.

The main draw contained two fascinating names: Marko Djokovic and Omar Awadhy. The first was Novak's kid brother, the second a local from the UAE. Marko's entry caused a stir, because his wild card was awarded at the last minute having initially been promised to Malek Jaziri of Tunisia. Kid Djokovic was ranked No. 869; Jaziri No. 104. 'We wonder why there are no top Arab players in tennis, and then we witness situations like this,' a local writer objected.

There were calls for Marko to reject the wild card but he had applied for it and was not likely to suddenly trash his own application. Ironically, Jaziri won his first match in qualifying, and if he could defeat Andrey Golubev of Kazakhstan in what was akin to a sandstorm in the second, he would face Novak Djokovic in the first round proper. But he lost; as did the younger Djokovic.

In Doha, Agnieszka Radwańska defeated Germany's Julia Goerges for her eighth career singles title and climbed to a career-best ranking, No. 5. For the second time, Sofia Arvidsson of Sweden won Memphis, rising to No. 55 on the WTA Tour, with three of her four singles finals appearances having been in Tennessee where she had the most match wins of any player in the tournament's history. Some players and events are a natural fit. At this stage of the year, in the top 100 on the WTA Tour, there were eleven Russians, eight from the United States (including teenagers Christina McHale and Sloane Stephens), seven from the Czech Republic and seven Romanians.

The men's title in Memphis – the penultimate time the event would be staged there as it was subsequently bought for around

$7 million by IMG and would be transported to Rio de Janeiro for 2014 – was won by Austrian left-hander Jürgen Melzer, who had slipped to No. 38 in the world but stood strong, despite a broken toe, to defeat Milos Raonic of Canada in the final. 'If anybody would have said last Friday after seeing the doctor, that I would be holding the trophy the following Sunday, I would have said he was a fool,' Melzer said. 'But sometimes life plays games like that.'

Federer's victory in Dubai – he defeated a rather lacklustre Murray in the final – could not have been better timed for those, including Ivan Lendl's manager Jerry Solomon, who were about to stage the BNP Paribas Showdown 'Tennis Night in America' at Madison Square Garden, a made-for-TV sport spectacular which involved the Swiss along with Roddick, Sharapova and Wozniacki.

'Star Power in New York' it was called and star power it exuded. 'Tennis belongs here,' said Scott O'Neil, the executive director of MSG, and there was little doubt in their proclamations and body language that this was the prelude to a serious effort to muster the city's considerable forces and bid once more to stage the end-of-season championships that were both played in the Big Apple until the late 1980s. New York taxis were festooned with advertisements for the event. It was an 18,000 sell-out.

Lendl was in attendance as a guest with his wife Samantha, whom I had not seen for years and who had not changed a bit. Solomon and I retired for a coffee and a chat. He had been Lendl's first manager for seven years at ProServ, until they had a bitter falling out in 1987, with lawsuits and counter-suits to follow. Lendl had required attention twenty-four hours a day and when Solomon married, he could not be Lendl's constant eyes and ears as much as the player demanded.

Solomon was now married for the third time, to Nancy Kerrigan, the ice skater who had gained notoriety in 1994 when she was attacked in a nightclub at the US Figure skating championships, an assault that was planned by her rival Tonya Harding's ex-husband and an accomplice. Although the injury forced her to withdraw from the championships, she won a spot on the team for the Winter Games in Lillehammer, Norway where she won a silver medal. Solomon, her manager at the time, married her a year later. He had subsequently become CEO of StarGames Inc., a sports marketing and entertainment company, intent on creating sports and entertainment content for live audiences, TV and DVD, and decided tennis was a natural partner. He brought Federer and Pete Sampras to the Garden in 2008 and the event was a huge success. In the meantime, he had also kissed and made up with Lendl.

We spoke about the partnership with Murray, which if it was not the talk of this town today, might be at some time in the future. 'The name Ivan Lendl has a certain connotation to me and people in tennis which means "you are going to challenge yourself at the ultimate level".' Evidently he saw Murray as the 'ultimate level'.

> For him to become Federer's coach, where do you go with that? For him to become Nadal's coach, where do you go with that? He's not going to coach those guys. For him to take a guy at this stage ranked 100 and work that all the way through the time commitments – to do that is enormous. Ivan had to have a situation that worked for him as much as it worked for the player. That's not typically the case.
>
> The way I look at it, he has been brought in to refine a thoroughbred rather than breed a racehorse. That's a very big difference and the decision issues on travel, commitment and all those things were very important and so those discussions with Andy were 'are you going to need me twenty-six weeks a year because if you are, I'm not your guy'. Part of the reason Andy's situation is so attractive is what he already had in place Ivan found to be very complementary to him. If Ivan is not going to be at an event, he and Andy talk on the phone, Andy has Dani [Vallverdu] who understands what Ivan's issues are and what they are trying to accomplish.

Vallverdu had first met Murray as a fifteen-year-old when he was a graduate at the Casal-Sanchez academy to where the Briton had been sent when his family could find nowhere at home to satisfy his desire for round-the-clock tennis of the highest calibre. Vallverdu, from Venuzuela, first looked upon Murray as a threat to his position at the academy only to come to befriend his fellow teenager, a move that would have a lasting impact on both men.

Solomon said that Lendl getting on with Vallverdu and the rest of the team was essential to make the association work.

> So you have a guy [Vallverdu] with him every day, who Andy likes so it works from that standpoint and therefore there was a certain set of circumstances surrounding Andy that allowed it to work for Ivan.
>
> You know that within him [Lendl] is the potential for a phenomenal coach. He's not the guy who will go out there and change the grip on the forehand and move your elbow on the serve. I don't think that's what Murray is looking for. It is about subtle changes in fitness, mental approach, strategy, preparation for the matches, dealing with the rain delays, night matches, all of these little things that nobody really realises goes into what happens between the coach and the player. There are a handful of other guys with the same experience but we are talking about a handful.

Considering Solomon had worked so closely with Lendl during the days when he was not accepted by large swathes of the public – Lendl used to expect Solomon to curtail press conferences if questions strayed into territory where he was uncomfortable – I wanted to know how he saw the relationship between Murray and the British public and media.

'I do think that one of the nuances in all this is how to lower that temperature a little bit on Andy,' he said.

> I always knew there was a lot of scrutiny but now we are involved in it, the amount of attention paid to his every move is crazy. There are a lot of people who could not deal with it. He's twenty-four

and he has a great team but it's still a lot [to handle] and it's something that Ivan is very aware of.

Wozniacki's boyfriend, Rory McIlroy, the brilliant Northern Irish golfer, was sitting a little sheepishly in the fourth row, trying not to notice that each time he looked up to the giant screens that hung over the court, it was his puckish face that was staring right back at him. Caroline could not resist and persuaded him onto the court to play a point against Sharapova.

The crowd lapped it up and for tennis it was a golden nugget, for it was this cameo rather than the brilliance of Federer or Roddick that was replayed on all the morning television shows and on ESPN's sports news programme, where at this time of the year, tennis would do well to get a sniff what with the descent of March Madness, Little League and lots of Nascar, where the Daytona 500 is the feature event of the week.

I knew this would be a relaxed time to talk to McIlroy and Wozniacki about their burgeoning relationship. John Tobias, president of Lagardère Unlimited, the new kids on the tennis management block, was at the Garden representing Wozniacki and he said he would try to make it work, but in the frenzy of the night, with the pair shuffled through the underpasses of Madison Square Garden by burly security men, there was no way of getting close. I would try again later in the year.

New York had more to anticipate in tennis terms because on 4 April *Federer Versus Murray* would make its US theatre debut. Terrence McNally, the playwright, said it was a play in which 'comedy and tragedy collide', which incorporated bereavement and war on three levels: man versus wife, nation against nation, and Scotland's golden boy versus the Swiss master at Wimbledon. Shortlisted in 2010 for a London Fringe Theatre writing award, *The Independent* marked it 'taut and punchy'. Unfortunately, due to the non-stop life of a tennis correspondent, I would not be in town for the show but wondered if I might see the tie staged on court later in the year.

Chapter 5

Indian Wells and Key Biscayne

'CAUTION – STRONG WINDS AHEAD'. It was the last, weary leg on the long and winding Interstate 10 which threads its way from Los Angeles, through the mountains which encase San Bernadino before entering the Coachella Valley with hundreds of wind turbines as a guard of honour. Those whose planes attempted the approach to Palm Springs spoke of the buffeting of their flying lives. The winds were outrageously powerful. I was thankful to have hired a car in LA, a cranky blue Ford, but even that required a firm hand on the wheel.

Roger Federer's private jet, with wife and twins on board, endured a landing to prove the great man does sweat. A plane carrying ATP bigwigs Flip Galloway and Mark Young and a number of umpires and linespeople veered at such a wicked angle that those by the windows gasped as they felt sure it would land on a wing rather than its wheels. 'I'm sure if it was one of those props, it would have flipped right over,' one umpire told me.

It was a portent of a series that would see its fair share of bumpy passages. Within three days of the start of the BNP Paribas Open in Indian Wells, second only in importance to the grand slams, one player after another was complaining of severe stomach pains. Some of my colleagues in the press box were affected, indeed one was so ill that she required hospital treatment. The first commercial I heard on the grounds was for the Eisenhower Medical Centre, which was not a response to the viral outbreak but nonetheless rather apt. Players were either off sick, playing sick or, in Andy Murray's case, about to be sick at their performance.

The source of the infections was a surface-borne 'norovirus' that could be contracted from touching any surface where it was present and on which it was able to survive for days unless everything was scrupulously scrubbed clean. The first batch of players to feel poorly and discount themselves included Nikolay Davydenko, Gael Monfils, Mike Bryan and Francesca Schiavone. Federer also complained about sickly symptoms but said he hadn't been well since before he arrived, a sensation exacerbated by his stomach-churning landing.

There was little the tournament could do about this other than keep everything scrupulously clean, much like the roads, pavements and grass verges of Indian Wells. The tournament itself had been the dream of former professionals-cum-business partners Charlie Pasarell and Raymond Moore, who had seen its rise from transient beginnings to a bit of a wonder in the desert, an event that is coveted by the local communities who flock to this 'city', which is little more than a continuation of Rancho Mirage before you arrive in La Quinta. In a nice touch, the streets were named for the rich and famous who had made this their home: Bob Hope, Frank Sinatra, Gerald Ford and Fred Waring, 'The Man Who Taught America To Sing'.

Any discordant notes were more or less confined to the sound of vomiting. For this was a place that, even if not everyone there looked it, made you feel young. It was one of the most hospitable, people-friendly tournaments of the year, aided and abetted by the near constant sunshine, equable temperatures, ease of movement and the growing support of Californians and those from further afield. Simple things mattered. Red Vines in the media centre. The erection of temporary stands around the practice courts was a master-stroke. 'There were more people watching Nadal practise the other day than watched me play tennis in seventeen years,' Moore said. 'Girls were screaming, guys were screaming. It was unbelievable.'

The screams of those demanding more in terms of compensation – the fancy word for prize money – were also being heard. Wimbledon chairman Philip Brook and Tim Henman, a member of the management committee and twice a former finalist in Indian Wells, were here to talk about money and the future of grass court tennis, and what better place to do that than one of the 100 prized golf courses scattered across the district. A lot of business was done on the cart-paths between green and tee. If Brook and Henman wanted to keep their presence a secret, the cat was let out of the bag by Justin Gimelstob who shared the course with them and couldn't stop himself from tweeting about it.

Not only were the British pair on the premises representing the All England Club but it was increasingly impossible to turn a corner and not bump into grand slam bigwigs – Craig Tiley and Steve Wood from Tennis Australia; Gilbert Ysern and Guy Forget of the FFT and Gordon Smith, the executive director of the USTA. They were not here exclusively to work on their tans or reduce their handicaps.

The top four male players had asked to see the grand slam leaders to state their case for a more significant player share of prize money but this was no selfish cause, instead there was an overarching sense of *noblesse oblige*, four honourable men atop the game speaking up for the rights of the lower-ranked players. It was going to be hard to refuse such a persuasive force.

As for Indian Wells, it had skewed the players' pitch for a more equable spread with its decision to top-load the prize money and reward the champions to the tune of $1 million each, a far cry from ten years earlier when very few would have bet a dime that the event would still be around in 2012.

Not long before the cataclysmic 9/11 attacks on the United States sent the world economy into a convulsion, there was the collapse of the biggest deal ever in men's tennis. The Super Nine tournaments (the forerunner to today's Masters 1000s) had agreed to pool their domestic, international television and sponsorship rights in an unprecedented $1.2 billion package and sell them to ISL Worldwide, a Zurich-based Swiss marketing company, thus negating the need for individual deals. No more would these events need to strike out on their own in an attempt to balance their books – the finance would be delivered up on a plate for them. You can find many reasons why it seemed like a good idea at the time but the sums involved and the thought of what might happen if it all went wrong made a lot of people extremely nervous.

Within a year the whole enterprise had crashed and burned, for ISL had bitten off far more than it could chew, financially speaking, and it pulled out, a decision that provoked sound, fury and contempt (but no resignations) and left the tournaments wedded together by the proposed pooling of resources cruelly exposed and wondering if they would ever get back on their feet. The men's game was in a state of shock it needed to recover from quickly.

Pasarell and Moore, like many others, had therefore been left to secure the future of their tournament without a sponsor and on paltry reserves. The death in 2003 of Mark McCormack, the founder and ruler of IMG which was a 50–50 partner in the tournament, required a significant re-evaluation of the event's status. Did Indian Wells stay, or would it go?

McCormack had been succeeded at IMG by Ted Forstmann, regarded by Moore as a leverage buyout specialist and asset stripper. Indian Wells wasn't making enough in profits to satisfy Forstmann, who informed Pasarell and Moore of his intention to find a way out. There were offers in writing from Shanghai and Doha, but PM (Pasarell and Moore) Management had a veto and used it. IMG began to apply legal pressure so Moore provided Forstmann with a figure at which he and Pasarell would consider doing business – 'a ridiculous number which they would never get, or so I figured,' he said.

But both Shanghai and Doha stunned Moore by matching what he had asked for, so PM Management was stymied. To save the tournament for southern California, their only recourse was to raise enough money to purchase IMG's 50 per cent share and, after lengthy negotiations and much desperate last minute haggling, they came up with the requisite cash. IMG's share was bought out and a syndicate of thirty-two investors, some of whom were just seeking a profit, others who simply shared a love of tennis, was assembled. All were promised an annual 9 per cent return on their investment.

In the midst of this process and through an old tour chum Sandy Mayer, Moore got to meet Larry Ellison, chief executive officer of Oracle and the third-richest man in the United States. Moore sensed a once-in-a-lifetime opportunity. 'Mr Ellison agreed to see me up at his house, there were several people in the waiting room,' he recalled. 'I had an hour to speak to him and we spent fifty-five minutes talking tennis and the other five about buying the tournament. I told him what I thought we needed in order to stay here.'

Moore worked keenly on the relationship: 'Twice I got to the altar and twice I was jilted,' he said.

> Then Doha upped the ante and they had put so much money on the table that our thirty-two investors wanted to take it. Charlie and I didn't have the power to stop it. We reported to the board, they said this was a huge amount which doubled everyone's investment. I went to Larry again and told him the tournament was going to Doha and he said 'No way, I won't allow it, how much do you want?' In the six months it took to close the deal, he didn't backtrack once.

Ellison was now the tournament's owner and as part of his takeover he insisted Moore and Pasarell remained to run the show for at least four more years. The thirty-two investors received a 100 per cent profit on their initial outlay. 'It's going gangbusters,' Moore said of the current strength of the tournament.

> In 2010, we made some money and ninety days after the tournament, Steve Simon [the tournament director] and I had paid all

the bills, we had a wad of cash and I called the guy I speak to on
Mr Ellison's behalf and asked into which bank he wanted me to
deposit it. He said: 'Larry doesn't want it. My instructions are that
any profits have to be reinvested in the site, he just wants to build
the tournament.'

Moore almost fell off his chair.

Reaching Ellison was not easy. For the third year in succession
I made a plea to speak to him, one of the most significant game-
changers in the sport. He had shelled out for Hawk-Eye to be
installed on every court on site and even the grand slams baulked
at stretching to that. Plans were afoot to increase the tournament
acreage, to purchase more land from the city and construct over
1,000 more car parking spaces. In his hands, Indian Wells was
absolutely booming.

This time around, there was a sense he might speak to me.
'He'll do it on Saturday.' Saturday came and went. 'He'll do it on
Sunday.' Sunday came and went. Then, on the second Wednesday
I was told to drop everything and go to the boardroom to join
two other writers sitting nervously outside. My twenty minutes
of fame was sandwiched between the *New York Times* and the
Desert Sun.

Ellison's secretary was making notes and the press chief Matt
van Tuinen sat in, obviously offering moral support. Ellison, in
a Fila top, slacks, sneakers, and a baseball cap, could pass for
many 67-year-olds in the Valley, except that he had $36 billion in
his account and owned the Porcupine Estate in Rancho Mirage
where Rafael Nadal and his team were staying as his house-
guests. Ellison revealed that the Nadal party had eschewed a more
luxurious offer and had chosen to share rooms – the all-for-one,
one-for-all attitude that summed up the Spaniard so precisely.

Nadal had a hit for an hour-and-a-half with his landlord
and pronounced him 'very good'. In turn, Ellison watched
each and every Nadal match, singles and doubles, with an
almost paternal concern.

I like the quality of the people who play tennis, both Roger and Rafa are very bright, high-quality people and that is very important in terms of me spending my time (and money) working on this. I like to be inspired by people. Business is more of a marathon and there is something beautiful about 'you won, you lost, give me the trophy, go home'. I think that is why we all love sport – it's the challenge, the competition and the clarity when it is over.

Ellison had bold plans and you do not make $36 billion without being bold. 'I love the fact we have the best doubles event in the world,' he said. 'You don't get to see shots like Rafa's forehand on the normal doubles tour. I want to bring Connors, Lendl, McEnroe here and team them up with Roger, Rafa, and Novak for a small tournament with these great stars of today and yesterday playing for real.'

The doubles tournament this year was indeed spectacular and special. Nadal played in it as did Djokovic and Murray with brother Jamie. The courts were packed and the interest frenzied. There was no seat vacant for me to watch the Murrays against fellow Britons Colin Fleming and Ross Hutchins so I stood on the steps. This was crazy in its way but so much better than those events where the doubles competition drew 'doubles only' players. More often than not, they played to half-empty stands.

It was the end of my allocated time with this wealthy man who could move into a business, click his fingers, demand perfection, examine the fine print and make a real difference. I hoped that he might be able to get more decisively involved for we need effective game-changers in tennis. As I left the room to be replaced by the man from *Desert Sun*, my single thought was whether anyone who worked for the LTA would last ten minutes in his employ.

Milos Raonic was eager to prove to Ellison, and to the world at large, that he had what it took to be a champion and that he was more than a big serve and a big forehand. The ATP, seeking to build the media profile of a new breed of player, was pushing for people to spend time with him – a sound strategy. After all 'Who will next challenge the top four?' remained the fiercest debate in the men's game after, 'Can Murray win a major?' which had become such a preoccupation for me.

Raonic emigrated from Montenegro to Canada with his parents when he was three years old and retained a fluency in his national tongue. Djokovic insisted I ask Raonic which were the harder workers, the Serbs or the Montenegrans. 'We work the hardest but they are the smart ones,' Djokovic said. 'When they split from Serbia, they kept the part with the beach.'

The Canadian – known as The Missile or The Big Leaf – was utterly engaging. He was fighting back after a couple of tough injuries, one to his hip during Wimbledon in 2011 which could have threatened his career had it not been handled with absolute care and, more recently, a niggle he felt in the Canadian Davis Cup tie against France. Interest in him was growing although, as he came from a non-grand slam nation, his progress was always likely to be spared the intense intrusion into the progression of Murray, Tomic, Tsonga et al.

'There's not a lot of awareness of me out here but hopefully if I can get some more marquee matches it would be a great thing,' Raonic said.

It's always the top four, they sell the tickets but the mentality is changing. I'm not that big into being in the spotlight, unless it's for the right reasons. I wouldn't want to be in the spotlight for someone I'm dating, I want to keep this to myself. If my tennis is in the spotlight and there's a lot of international appreciation for my tennis that's what I want. When I think about somebody thinking about me I would want them to say 'Oh did you hear about Milos Raonic?' – he did this in tennis not that he was out that night.

It doesn't take away from my focus because the most important thing is winning. That's what I care about more than anything else, I'm going to do what I need to do and also I think it helps that I stay with a tight group, an international group; being in Spain [he was coached by former professional from Spain, Galo Blanco] helps me get away from it. My parents travel a few times and are very easy to have around. They ask for my practice time, my match time, what time is dinner and that's it. I don't see them for the rest of the day. They know that I'm used to being around my coach and physio and they try to help out as much as they can. It makes it easy and it helps me not get caught up in a lot of things like outside expectations. I simply expect more from myself than anybody else.

There's a lot to the year, there's going to be some great weeks and some not so fun weeks but the way you have to look at it is that tennis is a sport with a lot of losers. There's one guy or woman winning each week, there's a lot of people going home with nothing, so you try to make the most of things. Winning is all that matters to me.

For Murray, winning on these courts was proving a difficult task and he had precious little to defend in terms of ranking points having lost in his opening round matches in both Indian Wells and Key Biscayne in 2011. This was a really good time for him to start playing well. There was no Lendl in his group at the event – the pair had agreed they would not stalk each other the entire year – and his pre-tournament interview was as profoundly upbeat as I had ever heard him talk.

Vic Braden, a former player and instructor who pioneered a sports institute for neurological research, taped all the press conferences for his research purposes. It was to Braden that Richard Williams had first sent a tape of his two daughters, asking Vic to run the rule over them, professing them players of the future. There was little about what happened to a player on the court and, more importantly, what went on between his ears that Braden did not know, or wanted to know about.

'I'm a psychologist,' he announced mid conference. The blood rose in Murray's cheeks. 'And I'm very interested to read all the negative pieces about what you haven't done rather than what you have done. I applaud you for what you have done.' 'Thank you, a first!' said Murray before bursting into applause.

'But I still see negative things about you despite all you've achieved,' Braden added.

Murray said that if he stopped playing now, he would have no regrets.

> There's no chance I would have thought that I would get to this level. But I think that once you get there, for me I now want to try and achieve more than I have. I've spoken to many people like yourself to get help and I'm starting to grow up, starting to mature, starting to be calmer on the court.

It was perhaps only to be expected that after such a rosy preliminary, Murray would struggle to live up to his expectations. His loss to Spaniard Guillermo Garcia-López – who played his best match of the year – reopened some old wounds. Away from the press room, Braden talked about the many negative impulses he saw in Murray's character and wondered if he would ever conquer them.

Caroline Wozniacki might have had a happy disposition and a millionaire boyfriend, but her game was replete with negative impulses, too. A crushing straight-sets defeat to Serbia's Ana Ivanovic in the fourth round and she was back in the mental wars. 'It's not easy to lose, I hate to lose and I don't know anything worse than losing,' she said.

> I know I have to break the barrier but if you know the door is open and you just need to put your foot inside the door, it's worth taking that risk. I'm the kind of player who can take risks in a match and if it doesn't work out, I can always go back to my base and try to grind it out.

She grinded on the back courts with her coaches while father Piotr fidgeted on the sidelines. Ricardo Sanchez, the Spaniard who had come and gone as her 'joint-coach' in the space of two months, said that Wozniacki was 'like a machine'. He said he tried to get close enough in an attempt to fix the parts but was not allowed to do what he wanted and so it was best that he left.

'I see the game I want to play, I know I've played the game before but you need to get there step by step and it's all about timing, belief and getting matches under your belt,' Caroline said. 'It is the small improvements. You won't see me serve and volleying or doing drop shots. You shouldn't repair something that isn't broken. I've been in the top five for three years so I must be doing something right.'

In the men's championship, three of the top four reached the semi-finals (Murray's loss to Garcia-López in the second round was the unforeseen hiccup) with Nadal to face Federer and Djokovic up against a John Isner on a sharp upward track. Indeed, the American would reach the world's top ten for the first time if he defeated the No. 1. It was a match of sterling qualities – Isner's drop shots and canny use of angles secured numerous points, his first serve (one of the best in the business) functioned at a 74 per cent success rate and he stunned Djokovic, winning 7–6, 3–6, 7–6 in two hours and forty-four minutes. The ace on his fourth match point sent the crowd as nuts as these folk ever got.

Isner, a late bloomer, was amazed at reaching the top ten, having originally marvelled at breaking into the top fifty after only really starting to excel in college.

I am twenty-six, which isn't exactly young, but I feel like my best tennis is still ahead of me. And I would also say I don't quite have the miles on my body a lot of other players have because I haven't been out here since I was seventeen or eighteen. I did surprise myself, but now that I'm inside the top ten, I feel like I do belong there. I want to try my best to stay here for a while.

It seemed Federer and Nadal had been at the top forever, but in that time neither had experienced what occurred on match point in their semi-final. Light rain had begun to fall as Federer prepared to serve for a place in the final and, on match point, it was decided the lines had become treacherous. Federer circled the court, hands thrust deep into his pockets, until summoned back to serve, when he delivered a crunching ace. 'I didn't expect to play so well tonight,' he said. 'I was creative.' For Nadal, there was a single thought – 'the best one – he was better than me'.

The final was just as tight until a critical misjudgement from Isner at 7-7 in a first-set tie-break that allowed a Federer backhand to fly over his head when he could easily have laid a racket on it. The momentum was now with Federer who went on to land his fourth victory in the desert.

Before he departed eastwards, Federer moved to the table where I was sitting, drew back a metal chair and caught himself flush on the left shin with it. 'Federer out of Miami,' I exclaimed. 'Breaking News', he responded chuckling heartily. Yes, the façade did break. It was terrific to see him like this. A title doubtless helped.

From his semi-final defeat at the 2011 US Open to this title in Indian Wells, his win–loss record was 39–2 in contrast to Djokovic's 20–6, Nadal's 23–7 and Murray's 31–5. In that time he had won the titles in Basel, Paris, London, Rotterdam, Dubai and now once more in the desert. Frankly, he had not looked better for ages. He did not regard himself as an old contemptible yet but there was a lingering sense of frustration with those critics eager to pronounce him past it.

> It was a bit like being pinched all the time, you know how it was, every single question was 'am I going to quit?' I know I come to different places all year and each event wants their answer but sometimes it came from those who know me and after I lost a big match, it was like 'come on you guys'.

He mentioned the phrase 'short-termism' and reflected that too often too much was made of one result without recourse to the grander scheme of things. All players were subject to such vagaries, and he pointed out that Murray lost in the opening rounds of these back-to-back Masters in 2011 and yet reached all four grand slam tournament semi-finals in a year for the first time.

Federer had never fought shy of saying what he thought and while some scoffed at what they presumed was conceit – 'It's nice occasionally to meet other great athletes' he had said during the week – he did not shirk from his duties as the public face of the sport. 'I think I'm the most honest guy to interview out here,' he said, causing eyebrows to rise.

I try to be candid because I don't have to change who I am, people know who they get on and off the court and for me it has worked well. Sometimes people don't like what I say but I don't say anything bad on purpose. I'm being honest with my opinions.

Some players felt that this 'honesty' encroached a little too far. There were occasions when Federer's fluency (he is the only player to give interviews in three languages after each match) ran away with him and privately there was a degree of resentment, even outrage, about some of his statements.

If there is any touchy subject and one says a little bit more than normal, people are like 'wow' so you have to be a bit careful. I've gone through tough periods as well. I remember when I had mononucleosis [in 2010] and I was getting to quarters, semis and finals, I felt I was a step slow and I thought, maybe I should have given myself more time to rest. I'm not afraid of playing and taking losses but then you get a double whammy from the press. I don't like it when the fans start believing that this is the way it is. I'm not how it is being portrayed and actually I am being side-tracked having to think about it.

People want their extremes. Remember Murray winning three back-to-back tournaments last year and he played super consistent in the slams and had chances and now people don't talk about that. Nadal had a great year, he won a grand slam and was in eight finals and that could be a world No. 1 year but it isn't when you have a guy like Novak around. That's why it's important to have perspective and realise where each player is coming from because sometimes a guy is on a hot streak and he's just tough to beat.

Seated a yard from him, I could only marvel at Federer but he had long since perfected the art of keeping himself in peak physical condition by tailoring his schedule to meet the demands required of him. It helped, too, that his style was such that it did not impose superfluous demands on his body. 'I have the odd ache and pain, especially near the end of a long stretch on hard courts, but I am feeling great,' he said.

> I'm happy at how I am managing my health and my schedule and I have to make sure I don't overplay. I had many different scenarios in place in case I would have won Davis Cup but that has gone and it gives me a bit more flexibility. I'm happy with my movement, not just with how I feel after matches and the next morning but also on the court and I feel quick, moving well, reading the play well and I'm just mentally very good right now.

My particular journey to Miami had been the same for many years and never got any easier. Pack, drive from Indian Wells to LA, return the hire car, stay at an airport hotel, half unpack, pack again, toss and turn in preparation for the five o'clock alarm call, queue for the courtesy van, tumble out with bags, trudge along in the monstrously long line for the American Airlines check in and security, grab a Starbucks, squeeze into a window seat and watch the desert disappear, the Gulf of Mexico appear, enjoy the view descending into Miami International Airport and prepare to be blasted by the humidity. To make matters worse, this time I ran straight into Victoria Azarenka at the practice courts the next day and she said: 'We had a spare seat on our private jet, you could have come with us'. I think I said something like 'shit'.

Azarenka, who had been under the weather because of the Indian Wells virus yet somehow won a pulsating opening round match against Mona Barthel, a German of much promise, 8–6 in the third set tie-break, had carried herself with much class to win the title in California. She lost eighteen games against Barthel and only another twenty-one in the entire tournament, which she clinched with a straight sets victory over Maria Sharapova. It was Melbourne revisited. The tests came thick and fast.

Since their dates had been set in stone by an agreement with the ATP that extended for three decades – the arrangement which suited them but made no strategic sense – Miami followed Indian Wells as sure as the beach replaced the desert. The tournament itself – the Sony Ericsson Open – was staged on the island of Key Biscayne, a stunning spot, whose one downside was that all traffic to and fro had to take the Rickenbacker Causeway that linked the island to downtown Miami via the daily bottleneck.

As justifiably proud as Charlie Pasarell and Ray Moore were of how they established their event, so Butch Buchholz was the genial patriarch of the prominent tournament he had persuaded the county of Miami Dade to construct on the site of an old rubbish dump in 1987. Buchholz, seventy-one, but by no means looking it, had stepped down as chairman two years previously – 'I get a seat and a car parking space so I'm okay. For twenty-one years I was the guy who the fans turned to when the beer was too warm or the ice cream was too soft and now it's someone else's turn.'

Few people had a greater appreciation of variants in the sport than Buchholz. He was one of the Handsome Eight troupe of professionals who played on the WCT (World Championship Tennis) pro circuit from the 1960s, had been executive director of the ATP and during his term of office managed to persuade the now defunct Men's Tennis Council to clear two weeks in the calendar so he might try to establish a major tournament in Florida. It became known – and still was despite now being sponsored by Sony Ericsson – as the Lipton, the tea company that backed it in its formative years.

Buchholz had pulled off a remarkable trick in securing the dates of the event for such an extended period, though it made those who had agreed to them at the time appear devoid of foresight. These prime Masters events are a cabal in the loosest sense of the world, acting independently according to their own set of desires, their own geographical and strategic demands, the strength and weakness of where they are in the calendar, and the desire to be declared the best of the group. The players vote on these things – the media would do the same for the first time this year – so there was much to play for.

Essentially, Indian Wells and Miami occupied an entire month-long block of tennis, which was great for them but a curse for many professional players. The problem – and it was a significant one – for those men who failed to qualify or who lost in the first or second rounds of the main draw in Indian Wells was that there was nowhere else for them to go, aside from an ATP Challenger in Dallas, Texas, recently moved from just down the road in Miami. There were a lot of players who wanted to earn money and yet were left to twiddle their thumbs – or just practise, practise, practise, while whittling away their funds. They had to find somewhere to stay between the two events and these were not inexpensive locations. The interests and concerns of those who did not bring a single patron through the turnstiles, however, was some way down the priority list for tournaments of this stature. They had stars to sell.

Back in the time when he was seeking to establish his event, Buchholz knew he had to have a television partner to make his dream become a reality. CBS signed a deal but their involvement handcuffed the event to a set of dates from which it could not move, for the station also televised the NCAA basketball championships, which were a veritable goldmine. The 'Elite Eight' (akin to the quarter-finals) were played the middle weekend of Miami, and the 'Final Four' was decided across its final weekend, the semi-finals on Saturday and the final, one of the biggest sporting events in the nation, on Monday night. If CBS were to stay on the page, the Miami men's final had to be played on the first Sunday in April. If the tournament had wanted to move ahead a week, they were blocked by the Masters golf in Augusta which CBS had the rights to as well. There was nowhere else for Miami to go.

For Buchholz, the need for television to back his venture was paramount. 'We have been fortunate that every year with the exception of one, we have had network TV and for virtually every sponsor we have, that was the prime request,' he said.

> It fits perfectly with CBS. Charlie [Pasarell] got network this past year, on ABC and that's huge for sponsors. Even though ESPN is the sports channel, if you are network it's a bigger deal. If you wanted to change – where would you put Indian Wells and what would you put in between them? What is the alternative? I don't think we have an answer with what to do with it.

'The biggest challenge tennis has is its television ratings,' Buchholz said. He did not believe tennis sold itself well and that it took its stars for granted. Where were the full page advertisements in USA Today for Federer and Nadal promoting his tournament? The Masters golf in Augusta would immediately follow Miami and they were indeed masterful at selling their event. 'The NBA would love to have the demographics of tennis worldwide. We just take tennis for granted and don't do anything about it'. Buchholz believed that combined events were crucial to the future of Indian Wells and Miami.

> The men hate them, I know. Their position is 'we are carrying these girls and they are making all this money and we deserve it, the practice courts are all being used, everything'. But the tournaments will make more money because of combined events. What the consumer sees is the best that tennis has to offer, they don't see men's tennis and women's tennis, they just see tennis. This is the package. When I go in the pro shop, I'm going to buy a shirt, my

wife is going to buy a dress – this is an event, a social gathering. I always think of it as inviting 300,000 people to your wedding and you want everyone to have a good time so you are not going to exclude one or the other. It is men and women together.

Listening to Buchholz has always been time well spent, for very few in the game have experienced more, learned more, known more, nor cared more about tennis. He ought still to be involved at the very top, but tennis does not always embrace these people of quality, with their experience, insight and passion. It is among its many Achilles heels.

Few could have got away with calling 'The Lipton' the fifth slam, but with its initial 128 draw in both men's and women's and best of five-set matches in the men's, it was the closest there was. The bravado of the Miami promoters upset a few people but did not stop a lot of grand slam chairmen from being guests at Buchholz's home in nearby Coral Gables. He forced himself to be content for the tournament to be regarded by his staff as the pick of the Masters. In truth, following Indian Wells was now exposing Miami's limitations, and it was beginning to pale by comparison.

The main stadium was fraying around the edges, paint was peeling, the size of the press room had been halved through lack of numbers and interest. IMG owned the event, one that needed to go well for the group to be taken seriously. Fernando Soler, the head of IMG tennis, was on the scene from day one, and the new chairman and CEO of the group, Mike Dolan, appeared for two days in the second week. This was serious stuff.

Soler was defiant. 'We have spent $1 million on the facility improving the corridors, the dining for the players, we built areas for the players before going on to the court, we improved the locker rooms,' he said.

First of all the tournament is doing better than ever, but it is true that the stadium is fourteen years old and it needs improvements.

My vision is we not only should make improvements in the stadium but real improvements on the rest of the site. We have a temporary grandstand, it's beautiful but temporary. There are lots of temporary courts and we should have more permanent courts and redesign the site. We are working on a plan to make all this happen. This is not related to Indian Wells. It can do whatever it wants. We are not competing with Indian Wells, we are competing with ourselves. It is not only what happens on the site, it is the city, the atmosphere. We have many assets that Indian Wells will never have and they have things we will never have. As a company we are fully behind the Miami tournament.

The Williams sisters were the local catch. This was tantamount to their event. They had skipped Indian Wells for ten years after Richard, their father, insisted the cat-calling of Serena in 2002, after her sister pulled out at the last minute from a semi-final between the two, was racially motivated. Indian Wells had given up trying to persuade them to come back. Their boycott was *sine die*.

They may have been raised on the Californian west coast but, for a long time now, the family home had been Palm Beach Gardens, so Miami was a relatively short hop down I-95. This would be Venus's first tournament since she told the world at the previous year's US Open that she was suffering from Sjögren's syndrome, an autoimmune disease. We were delighted to see Venus back and just as thrilled that the Russian Alisa Kleybanova was at a stage in her battle with Hodgkin's lymphoma that she could compete again.

Venus, like a tigress let off a leash, won four matches, two of them over grand slam champions, Petra Kvitová and Ana Ivanovic, though it was to be the Canadian Alexandra Wozniak who pushed her the furthest, to a third-set tie-break decider. Venus had simply run out of legs by this time and against the canny eventual champion Agnieszka Radwańska of Poland this was not the best state in which to be. 'I know a lot better how to recover and I'm definitely having to cut out a lot of extra-curricular activities,' Venus said. 'I'm not gonna to be the one having fun dinners. I'm gonna be the one stuck in the room. The price to pay is definitely worth it.'

She said that her joints hurt sometimes and the good feelings came and went. The 31-year-old told Greg Bishop of the *New York Times* that it was 'like going to the races. The other cars are ready, the drivers are prepared. But I'm getting used to the fact that I'm not in control.'

Azarenka was not exactly delighted as she struggled badly against Dominika Cibulková, the feisty little Slovak, in the quarter-finals, her 25-match unbeaten record in jeopardy. Azarenka was a set and 5–2 down but Cibulková double-faulted twice serving for the match. She lost her next service game as well and a tie-break loomed in which she saved four set points but lost it 9-7. Azarenka eventually prevailed 1–6, 7–6, 7–5, as gutsy a performance as she had delivered all year. And yet it was something she did in the middle of the second set which provoked a storm. At a change of ends she asked to speak to her coach Sam Sumyk, which was something she very rarely did.

Knowing a microphone was attached to his tracksuit top so that television (and eager writers who preferred to listen to the television broadcast rather than watch the match live) could pick up what he was saying, Sumyk attempted to muffle his words. He couldn't quite manage it. 'You gotta give her some competition,' Sumyk suggested. Then he told her to move forward or come to the net to change things up, and that if she lost, who cared, she was losing anyway. Azarenka did what she was told and it worked that day. She won – though her run of victories ended in the next round when Marion Bartoli produced her best perfor-mance of the year to win 6–3, 6–3.

Sumyk was shocked to receive an official reprimand from the WTA Tour for his attempt to keep what he was saying to his player as much of a secret as possible. Having shown me the WTA's email, Sumyk asked me what I thought he ought to do.

From the WTA

Dear Victoria,

You have brought great excitement to women's tennis as the new World #1 and we want to promote you in the best way possible. Your cooperation, as well as that of your Player Support Team, is vital to this effort. On-court coaching was introduced for the fans watching at home and access to your on-court coaching conversations is a great way for these fans to connect with you.

As you know, the on-court coaching rules (pages 368–372 of the WTA) require coaches to wear microphones when they appear on-court during televised matches to capture their on-court coaching and conversations with their players (Page 369, Section H.2.c). While on-court coaching is optional, players who request on-court coaching and their coaches must follow these rules which apply to all players.

At the 2012 Sony Ericsson Open, your coach, Sam Sumyk, violated this rule on two occasions despite several warnings, when he chose not to attach the microphone properly to his shirt during your televised match against Cibulková on Grandstand Court and again during your televised match against Bartoli on Centre Court. Please see the attached documentation of Sam's microphone violations.

The on-court coaching rules provide that coaches who violate the microphone requirement will not be allowed to participate in on-court coaching at the player's next WTA tournament and the player will not be allowed to designate any other coach for on-court coaching at her next tournament (Page 369, Section H.2.c.ii).

Upon review, Sam had every opportunity to correct his behaviour and not put the two of you in this situation, so he will not be allowed on-court to coach you during Stuttgart. However, as you were not aware of his violations at the time, you will be allowed to designate another coach for on-court coaching in Stuttgart; provided the coach abides by all of the on-court coaching rules.

If you choose to have on-court coaching in the future, please understand that Sam or another coach must wear a microphone and keep it switched on while on court (for televised matches), or he will not be allowed to enter the court and the full penalty for violating the rules will be enforced. We recommend that prior to your matches, you and your coach agree on a solution that allows you optimal coaching benefits while complying with the rules.

If you have any questions about this decision or about how the on-court coaching rules are applied, please let me know.

Regards

Dear Neil.

I just wanted to have your thoughts on how the WTA is handling this matter that obviously concerned myself ... is it right to go through my player??

Thanks for your answer

Sam

I gave Sam my answer, which stays between us, but he remained concerned about what he should do (later in the month in Stuttgart, he entered the WTA office and designated one of the stunned staff members to be Azarenka's on-court coach that week, which, he said 'they were not too happy about').

There was no on-court coaching in the men's game. It was having enough trouble dealing with coaches sitting next to the court, or Bernard Tomic was. On the Grandstand Court in the second round, the Australian teenager was playing David Ferrer of Spain – he had lost the first set and should have been in command in the second. In the fifth game of the set, Robbie Koenig, commentating on television, remarked, as the camera focused on John, that it was 'very difficult to let go when you have nurtured your son' and especially when he was such an incredible talent. Having taken the game to lead 3–2, Tomic waved his racket towards his father in a motion that suggested displeasure. At what should have passed for a routine change of ends, he approached Cedric

Mourier the umpire and said, 'He's annoying me, I know he's my father but he's annoying me. I want him to leave but how is it possible?' Mourier's response, after a brief discourse, was to issue a code violation to Tomic for 'coaching' to which Bernard responded 'thanks'. In all my many years covering the sport, I had never heard of this before. How this situation resolved itself would be one of the must-watch items of the rest of the year.

It was unlikely that this would have been a subject raised at the ATP player meeting during the first week of the tournament. They had more pressing concerns for the sixty attendees who listened attentively to Federer speaking briefly about his meetings with the grand slams during the previous week.

The meeting lasted almost two hours, after which Sergiy Stakhovsky of Ukraine, a player with an innate grasp of figures and an ability to put his views across with clarity and precision, was involved in a lengthy and heated debate with Thomas Schrader, one of the ATP Tour managers whose main responsibility was to ensure, to the best of their ability, the contentment of the players. Neither looked the remotest bit happy. And, on top of this, Rafael Nadal was about to confirm that he had had his fill of politicking and was stepping down as one of the two vice-presidents on the Player Council.

> I have been there for a couple of years, I really don't know how to do things without putting my 100 per cent. If I go to play golf, I try my best every moment. If I go to the player council I try my best in the player council. I put all my energy there. Finally, I believe I put too much energy there. I believe we did a few things well for the sport but I believe it's not enough. So today I believe I am not the right one to keep working there. I think other people can do better than me today.

Nadal was not asked about grand slam prize money, indeed there was no formal press debrief on the meeting in Indian Wells that involved the four grand slam tournaments and the four best male players – no communiqué, no pronouncement, no conference call on one of the most important meetings of the past decade. It was a case of keeping one's nose close to the ground and then going outside of the confines of the normal press conference to catch the players. I liked it that way.

I caught up with Federer and Djokovic in the corridor behind the conference room. Both were keen to emphasise how much they respected the slams, how much trust they had in them, how much they wanted this to work, but how much they believed sincerely in the case for fairer compensation throughout the game. The leading players were now at the fulcrum of the argument.

The women kept their peace because they knew whatever improvement the men might draw out of the negotiations they would pocket exactly the same because of the equal prize money agreements. The men – some more vocally than others – regarded this as demonstrably unfair, the women hanging on to their coat-tails, offering not a squeak and raking in the benefits. Their anger would come to a head later in the year.

♊

The *New York Times* magazine had sent a correspondent to cover the Lendl and Murray story, such was its increasing resonance across all sections of the press. Peter de Jonge, the superb writer, was not a tennis man at all but he probed, was always at practice sessions, matches, conferences and wrote: 'Like stockholders of a beleaguered corporation welcoming the appointment of a ruthless CEO, tennis cognoscenti heralded the appointment of Lendl, who had mysteriously exiled himself from the sport for fifteen years, as exactly what Murray needed.' De Jonge caught the mood perfectly.

According to Murray's trainer, Jez Green, Murray can do twenty-six pull-ups, palms facing out and – this is the key – arms extending fully between reps, yet he trundles onto the court like Woody

Harrelson in *White Men Can't Jump*. Eventually his opponent gets peeved, goes for too much and commits an error or out of weariness offers up an indifferent shot, at which point Murray, brandishing previously unseen power, pounces and puts the ball away. It's fair to wonder why, if Murray can put the ball away at the end of a rally, he doesn't do so earlier. What's intriguing is that Murray is as capable as anyone of playing power tennis. He just doesn't want to. For half a decade, a chorus of voices, on retainer and off, has urged Murray to play more assertively, shorten points and conserve energy. But Murray has refused such advice, or accepted it briefly then promptly reneged.

Behind the scenes, and unknown to de Jonge and anyone else bar those involved, there were vital discussions about Murray's future direction. With the knowledge of XIX but hardly their blessing, two of the leading management companies, IMG and Lagardère Unlimited, had been asked to make their pitches for the Murray contract. He was hot property and many times since he burst onto the scene I had been asked by those management groups he did not work for what I felt their chances were of getting closer to the man (i.e. enticing him to join them).

In truth, I had never talked to him about his management – except asking the occasional question when moves were anticipated and then made – and did not believe it was my place to do so. Octagon, his first management company, had held a grudge against me for writing a piece in *The Times* in 2005 when he was considering a change that he might like to engage with a more personalised company. He decided to sign with Acegroup, led by Patricio Apey, who had been Gabriela Sabatini's manager on her rise to fame and fortune. That arrangement encompassed the time when the LTA was persuaded to part with a small fortune for Brad Gilbert to coach Murray for sixteen months, a highly controversial move.

The XIX deal was signed in 2009 and whether or not Murray's head and the heads of those around him were turned by the fact that the company represented David Beckham and he might piggy-back on such a relationship, we could only guess. Now the big boys were circling once more, hoping they could persuade him that XIX weren't actually doing as good a job for Murray as they could. They spoke to Andy, his mother Judy, his brother Jamie and his girlfriend Kim Sears, which underlined what a significant part she was playing in arranging Andy's life.

It was suggested to both IMG and Lagardère Unlimited that nothing more should be done until after the Olympic Games because Murray did not need to have his mind cluttered with business affairs. All parties agreed but I wondered if one or either would break the accord and try to do something in the interim that would turn the man's head.

XIX were sanguine in response to the big boys trying to muscle in. Matt Gentry, his chief PR man, explained how,

> He had chosen us because of our different ideas, we weren't in tennis, we talked at length about what would happen after tennis, the plans we had for him. We were in there for a reason and while we were aware of what was going on, all along we were optimistic he would stay with us.

Murray's playing week in Miami was seriously curtailed. First Raonic pulled out of their third round match with a knee injury and then Nadal withdrew before their appointed semi-final. 'I want to arrive to the clay court with the right conditions, but also I want to arrive in a semi-final here with the right conditions and I could not,' Nadal said. It was felt that Murray, having had two walkovers, might be fresher than Djokovic in the final yet, on the other hand, the Serbian was seriously match tough; he had not dropped a set all week and against Juan Mónaco in the semi-final had played one of his finest opening sets. The crowd, predominantly Argentine, began trying to lift their man from his sense of helplessness. Mónaco perked up. 'I'm losing 6–0 and I'm a little bit upset,' Mónaco said. 'All the crowd start to sing my name and it was a great feeling for me. In the second set I was happy because I started believing a little bit in my game. But he played like a real No. 1 today, just too good.'

And Djokovic was too good in the final as well, though Murray allowed too many games to slip by early in the match, which gave him too much work to do to peg it back. From the side of the court Murray looked a little sluggish but he said it was a false impression and, if it was true, it showed how well his game measured up against the No. 1 in the world. Djokovic defended his title with a 6–1, 7–6 victory and Buchholz was full of admiration.

Buchholz was more concerned – as we all were because he was clearly trying to put on a brave face – about the real state of Nadal's knees and whether they could take much more of a pounding. 'My doctor, Mr Hernandez, does my elbows and knees and is a consultant for the Spanish football team and knows another doctor on the team who knows Rafa. Tendinitis is a tough thing to fix. They think Rafa is in the fourth quarter of his career.'

Chapter 6

Spring

THERE ARE TWENTY-TWO stops on the ATP World Tour on clay between February and July. One year, I promised myself I would go to Acapulco where the main court was an adjunct to the beach. The same was true of Umag in Croatia, where play began in the early evening and it was – the seriousness of the tennis aside – perennial party time. I have not been to São Paulo or Bastad either and hope one day to tick those boxes.

For the twenty-second time in my case, the trail led to Monte Carlo Country Club which, by a geographical quirk, was not quite in Monte Carlo but Roquebrune-Cap-Martin, a dot in the south-east corner of France. Whatever the precise location, the splendour of the place never ceases to amaze. It was a tennis club fit for Cézanne or Renoir: the courts the colour of red pepper, radiant skies, sea that appeared half dark and half light blue, terracotta roofs, beautiful people – a tennis tournament that reeked of prestige.

Yet, it was not that many years ago that the event had a single sponsor, Algerian airline Khalifa, and was on its knees. The turning point came in 2007 when the ATP Tour management decided to downgrade it from its favoured Masters level to become a secondary tournament. The locals responded with a diabolical ferocity. Roger Federer and Rafael Nadal spoke in unprecedented unity and denounced the move. I will never forget that conference.

The giants having flexed their muscles and with a spider's web of legal complexities that threatened (Monte Carlo had friends in royal palaces), the decision was revoked and the tournament remained on the Masters rota as the 'ninth' event without the mandatory status required of its eight fellow Masters 1000s.

Dropping Monte Carlo from the schedule would not invoke the punitive penalties that accrued if you didn't go, for example, to Shanghai, Madrid or Indian Wells, which a player of distinguished repute could only forfeit if they had a substantial playing record, longevity as a tour member or a valid medical excuse.

The Americans invariably chose to give the tournament a miss (their last singles champion was Jimmy Connors in 1981, though the doubles team of Bob and Mike Bryan were a notable exception and won it for the third time in six years and had been runners-up twice). Federer preferred to rest but wild horses would not have kept Nadal, who had an eighth successive title in sight, away from the club; Djokovic was also now a resident of the principality. For a host of Europeans and South Americans, Monte Carlo was an annual magnet.

For those not blessed with transportation the entire week in Monte Carlo, it was a fine time to keep the blood pumping with steep and unrelenting walks. The press tribune was on the top floor, affording unbeatable views. The courts were on four levels, the second lowest of which was the Court Central, with its Royal Box, where the victors' names were carved into the stone walls and you felt the ghosts of Suzanne Lenglen and Les Mousquetaires in every nook and cranny.

Good dispositions abounded – with room and board at the famous Monte-Carlo Bay Hotel how could they not? There were complaints that the outside courts were ropey and that Central was not playing as true as it had. The French had chosen to play their world group Davis Cup tie against the United States at the club a week before and it was taking some time to heal. The top brass of the USTA had stayed at the Hotel de Paris that week which raised some eyebrows as to whether they could not have found somewhere less extortionate to lay their heads. The presidential parties did like their little luxuries.

Željko Franulović, a former top ten player and ex-ATP board member, was tournament director and carried the air of a contented man. As for the future of the tournament, the bad old days of prospective relegation had long been banished. Rolex had become the major sponsor and were the kind of blue-riband associate with which Monte Carlo ought to rub shoulders. He knew that there would be a few no-shows but that the event had an aura which made it irresistible to all but a rare few. Winning Monte Carlo – though only Nadal had known how that felt in the past seven years – had a real cachet. It was much the same when Formula 1 came to the principality. Franulović explained:

> With the tournaments, goes the lifestyle, the glamour, it is the perfect blend, players love it, they feel at home, there is quality and substance in the title you win. It is cherished and respected more. The only tournament in the world that is forever is Wimbledon.

Had it not been for the Federer–Nadal axis of 2007, Monte Carlo would have been seriously undermined and, quite possibly, gone to the wall with years of heritage threatened. Even Franulović did not realise they were going to speak together before they did and that once they had, his tournament would survive and flourish. 'They were not speaking just in their name but in everyone's and that was the turning point,' he said.

> After that [the decision to revoke demotion] we invested a lot, in new stands, new restaurants, we moved the players to the main building, new medical facilities, which was further proof that we were right, to save the category. A Masters [victory] somewhere else doesn't bring them anything, here they know what they are going to get and a prestigious title to win. I think they prefer to continue like this.

Franulović had won his particular battle but many more were being fought out behind the scenes. Sergiy Stakhovsky gestured me to a quiet corner away from prying eyes, for he was in a tricky position, not wanting to become the leader of a 'revolution' though seen as one who could explain their position as players. He had said some rather outrageous things but everyone was after a quote now and he wanted time away from the heat.

Stakhovsky said he would not want his children to play tennis. He said he spent €170,000 last year on 'game expenses', €85,000 on plane tickets alone. The total accounted for a fitness trainer, a coach and his share of a physiotherapist. 'I'm in the negative at Indian Wells and Miami,' he said, providing more examples: €1,200 to fly from London to Dubai and back; taxes (38 per cent in California, 30 per cent on average); and coaching expenses (salary, food, hotel included). 'Federer, Nadal, Djokovic, Murray – that's simply another world,' he said. 'What those four earn isn't comparable to all the rest. We simply don't exist in comparison to them. The earnings of most players are, really, laughable. Even the 100th soccer player in Ukraine earns more than I do.'

Stakhovsky had parted from his coach this week, he was ranked No. 70 and had not had more than one win at any of ten tournaments he had played this year and said he needed to be the priority again. Rather than speaking up for others, he needed to do right by himself.

The kernel of his case was how much a player needed to make from prize money to be able to offer decent competition in an era of brutal competitiveness. 'When I started playing tennis, I thought that 100 guys could make a living and that would grow to 200 or 250 but it is getting smaller and we have all the issues from that,' he said.

> To be competitive with Federer, Nadal and these guys, you have to have a coach, a fitness coach and a physiotherapist which means spending around $400,000 on travel, paying cheques, accommodation, but no one from 100 to 60 in the rankings is making this money. We are not even saying that by hiring these people you are going to be competitive, but just to give you a chance.

There was real threat of a boycott, but still he stressed their unity.

All the guys I have talked to have the same opinion and none would have a problem with skipping one of the grand slams. I cannot guarantee it and I seriously doubt someone would care that Sergiy Stakhovsky from Ukraine is skipping a grand slam, except Ukrainian fans. But the point is it is getting awkward.

On Twitter, fans have been exploding saying players don't deserve paying for losing in the first round. The fans don't realise how much effort is put year round to get into these main draws. I had quite a good start to the season last year but this year has been a disaster and I might drop out of the top 100, who knows. I'm doing everything I can not to but I don't have fewer expenses because I'm playing badly.

This year I have an extra fitness coach who I took on board to get better which isn't happening but you cannot fire everybody and travel alone because that's not going to get you anywhere. This is a lonely sport. You play against other guys and there are no real friends because as soon as you step onto the court no one gives you anything.

Stakhovsky said he communicated regularly with Federer, the president, but echoing the sentiments expressed by Nadal at the Australian Open, felt he was 'too neutral for my taste' and 'too Swiss'.

ATP board member Justin Gimelstob was a fast-rising star in the game, having been a fine player who was making a name for himself both as a political animal and as an analyst and reporter for the Tennis Channel. He was being pulled from pillar to post. 'We need to remove emotion and look at this in a business sense,' he said. 'What is the player's market value? Is Ashton Kutcher worth $1 million for each episode of *Two and a Half Men*? The market says so, so why not Federer and Djokovic? How much of that money do they bring in?'

Gimelstob was heartened by the involvement of the top four

(though Nadal was taking more of a back seat). 'I can't imagine there's ever been a period where the top four have been more engaged,' Gimelstob said. 'And that's power. That's leverage.'

As the new Tour chairman and president, Brad Drewett spent February traversing the globe, meeting with players from every level. He acknowledged that their issues, while not new, merited his undivided attention. At Indian Wells, he held separate meetings with top players and officials from each of the four grand slams. There were a number of gripes and grudges. The players did not want the blue clay at the Madrid tournament on which they would be asked to perform. Nadal even mentioned a boycott.

Ivan Ljubičić knew all about these pressures but now he was facing another one. At thirty-three, he had decided to retire after the Monte Carlo event but could not know how hard it would be to make the decision and then to walk on court knowing any match may be his last. He could barely raise a racket in what was to be his final match on Centre court, trying to play through the tears. He lost 6–0, 6–3 to Ivan Dodig, his fellow Croatian. 'I tried all the tricks to stop myself crying but nothing worked,' Ljubičić said.

He would not know his last few days as a player and those immediately beyond would be laced with controversy. The smart money was on him running for a position on the ATP Board, having been a one-term president of the Player Council who had refused a second spell because the weight of the responsibility interfered so much with his tennis.

Ljubičić, who spent much of the rest of the week thanking old friends in the press room for their support down the years, came quickly to the point, as was his wont.

There is this [ATP] European Board Representative position up for election. [But] there are a couple of issues there. I did that already and it really creates all kinds of conflicts. You can't work with the tournaments, it's still conflicted. I know some of the guys are still doing it, Justin Gimelstob's doing TV, David Egdes is co-owner

or director of the Tennis Channel. I just don't feel comfortable
[with that].

Nadal was asked in a conference by a Croatian journalist to say
a few words about Ljubičić on his retirement and was lost for
them instead. He had not forgotten comments made after their
French Open semi-final in 2006 when Ljubičić said that the time
the Spaniard took between points was ridiculous and that he
would love to see Federer win the final, adding that 'everyone in
the locker room would'.

Asked later in the year whether there was any locker room
joke he most regretted, he said: 'I'd actually say I regret certain
press conferences. Rafa is still mad about it, six years later. I still
don't know what I could have said for him to still be so upset
even today and still hold it against me. But, that's Rafa, that's just
how he is.'

I was becoming pickier about which press conferences I
attended and those I did not. Professionally, this could be considered poor judgment. It depended what you wanted to get out of
them. Some you could not attend because you were on deadline;
obviously you could not get to those when you were elsewhere
watching or networking, but sometimes the thought of the sheer
agony of sitting through ten minutes of ludicrous questions or,
more often than not, statement making and grandstanding, was
a distinct turn–off.

There were times when you had a specific question you
wanted to ask but, with the transcript service at more and more
events and so many appearing online almost as quickly as the
stenographers took down the words, this was nonsensical and
counter-productive. Why not wait and try to catch a word with
the player later when they were a little less guarded and, in many
cases, happier to engage?

Then there were those conferences called when you were at
your desk which, if you did attend them, could end up causing
you more trouble than they were worth. Bernard Tomic had

beaten Denis Istomin of Uzbekistan in straight sets in the first round and I was curious as to his mood. 'I'll laugh if I win a clay court tournament one day,' he said. 'That would be funny.'

I wondered, as a new resident of Monte Carlo, how long it took Tomic to get to the club from his new apartment 700 yards away. '*You* could walk it in ten minutes,' Tomic replied, enjoying a bit of a laugh at my expense.

'It's near the L'Annonciade behind where the Maserati car factory is,' he added. So you have somewhere you can pop into, I joked. 'Right there, drive the car. I know the guy already at the dealership there. No police here in Monaco [laughter].' A couple of journalists asked him about his cars, we left to get on with the rest of the day and I didn't give the exchange another thought.

The next day I received a message from his father saying that Bernard was disturbed that I had asked him how much his apartment in Monte Carlo had cost (no such question was asked) and that friendships could quite easily be ruined as quickly as they had begun. Armed with the official transcript, I tried to find John Tomic for the next couple of days, but couldn't and decided it wasn't worth pursuing. The next time we met, in one of the corridors of the Foro Italico in Rome, it was a brief and frosty encounter.

But this was a mere trifle compared to the loss of a family member. The day after he had taken the microphone at the annual players party, as he always did, Novak Djokovic was midway through a practice session when he was informed that his beloved grandfather, Vladimir, had passed away at the age of eighty-five. His grandson went out that day and defeated Alexandr Dolgopolov 2–6, 6–1, 6–4, a major trial of his resolve. He declined to come into press and we all understood.

The next day, still awash with conflicting emotions, Novak decided to speak. In these circumstances, it was important to couch the first question properly and, perhaps just as important, was that it was asked by a familiar face. I decided I'd be first to speak up. You could tell Nole's heart was breaking but he spoke, as ever, lucidly and frankly.

'My grandfather went through a lot in his life,' he said in an interview with Simon Briggs of the *Daily Telegraph*.

He came from Montenegro, but in the Second World War he went through two or three different countries to get away from the danger. Then he moved to Serbia with my father and the whole family, and they lived in Belgrade, which is where I was born. He was eighty-five years old when he died, and he remembered a much simpler life.

He was telling me how they lived, how they survived, what they did in their free time when they were young. His advice was always to keep grounded, and look at the basics of life: you need to be happy, you need to be healthy, you need to have a good family and a good relationship with your close ones. In my childhood when I was in Serbia he took me a lot of times to practice, we went together in the trams in public transportation. Whenever I would lose he would say, 'You're not sad, right?' I'd say, 'No, no I'm not sad,' even though I was. He would say, 'Don't be sad. Come on, it's just one match. You play so many matches. Life goes on.'

Novak chose to play on in Monte Carlo, missing his grandfather's funeral on semi-final day and playing above and beyond the call of duty to come from a set down to defeat Tomáš Berdych of the Czech Republic (who had put paid to Andy Murray's chances in a stunning quarter-final), later describing it as the most difficult conditions he had played in but that he held his nerve.

The entire trauma had to catch up with Novak, and it did so in an anti-climactic final against Nadal. Djokovic could offer little but pride and was beaten 6–3, 6–1 as the left-hander from Spain triumphed and the chords of the Spanish national anthem drifted across the Mediterranean for the eighth year in a row.

Perhaps Nadal might consider purchasing a home here one day.

Ion Tiriac, who had represented his native Romania at ice hockey at the 1964 Winter Olympics in Innsbruck, had learned more than anyone in the last forty years how to manoeuvre his way around the world of tennis. As a player (performing in 150 Davis Cup rubbers), manager, promoter and entrepreneur, his wealth of knowledge and his dealings with some of the most exacting people was unparalleled. He had lived through the Nicolae Ceaușescu regime in Romania and come out on the other side in a position of high repute. I recall him staging a Davis Cup against Great Britain in Bucharest in 1990 in the febrile weeks after Ceaușescu's death when he entertained us all to a lavish dinner, which included the finest Black Sea caviar, and was mortally offended when the British team said they were going to stay in their hotel and eat the baked beans they had brought with them from London.

He had managed Boris Becker at the German's zenith, played the rebellious promoter with his tournament in Stuttgart in the 1980s, was the man who sat in the most prominent box on Court Philippe Chatrier at Roland Garros, paying €50,000 a year for the privilege, piloted his own Boeing 737, opened his own bank (Banca Tiriac founded in the post Ceaușescu period) and leasing group, had enticed the city of Madrid to invest millions in tennis and was now the mastermind behind the introduction of blue clay. Anyone who could sell Mercedes cars to the Germans could not possibly be underestimated.

The Mutua Madrid Open was going to be a tricky week though and Tiriac, now seventy-three but still the shrewdest cookie in the sport, knew it. Five years ago, the event had moved from the Crystal Pavilion (indoors on hard court) to the Caja Magica (outdoors on clay) to mixed reviews. For a start, the new stadium had been expected to cost €150 million when first touted but that rose to nearer twice the sum through miscalculations about the state of the soil and the cost of the retractable roofs.

There was little that was aesthetically pleasing about the site, it was like tennis being housed in several large aluminium tins, the tournament was played at altitude three weeks before the French Open – which did not help in preparation – and now there was the additional and, to some people, intractable decision to play on blue clay.

Roger Federer was ready to give the blue surface a chance, even though he was as outraged as anyone that it was introduced at the event in the manner of a *fait accompli*. 'I have no idea how this will be,' he said.

> We're against it, Nadal said so vehemently and I support him. He fears that a tradition is getting broken and that one tournament director wants to have blue clay, the other one grey, green or red. I'm also for traditions but I can understand it that new things have to get tested. The clay in Madrid has to be perfect though otherwise it will be a debacle for the tournament.
>
> I'm against it because Nadal is against it and we would have other options. But the tournament director [Tiriac] has insisted *ad nauseam* that it will happen. In the end we said: 'He does a lot of good things for tennis so we let him go with this one. But it isn't good that he has such things in his hands.'

Djokovic was equally sceptical. 'I understand that we all want to see certain change and improvement in our tennis world but on the other hand, you need to hear out what the players say, especially the top players because we need to feel our opinion matters. That was not the case this time.'

The rumblings of discontent were profound. Gerard Tsobanian, Tiriac's right-hand man and the tournament's executive manager, called for good faith from the players.

> Is it clay? It is. The colour is different? Yes. Do you see the ball better? Yes. Is it a better experience for us all? Yes. Then what arguments can you have against it? Rafael Nadal has revolutionised tennis, he is a revolutionary, an innovator in his physical game, the rotation of the ball and the sleeveless shirts. We are a young and

innovative tournament – he is a young and innovative player. We
are identical. Nadal could be our icon.

The trouble was, Nadal did not want to be Madrid's icon – indeed
he did not really want to be within a hundred miles of the place.
'Why block us?' Tsobanian argued. '[Bernie] Ecclestone changes
the rules every week in F1, he adapts to whatever his clients
demand. This reminds me of the controversy over using models
as ball-girls eight years ago. Eight years later we are still doing it
because from the start we did it professionally.'

Tiriac added that with a prize packet of in excess of
$10 million at the combined ATP–WTA event, competitors had
a duty as professionals to get on with matches. 'That kind of
money does not come from Mother Teresa,' he said. 'The players
have to give back as well.' Tiriac and his tournament director
Manuel Santana, the 1966 Wimbledon champion, promised the
court would slowly improve, explaining that an excess of caution
at the construction stage in order to prevent injuries resulted in
producing a surface that was too slick.

'The court is slippery and I apologise,' Tiriac said.

We wanted to make sure that we had no player injuries, no ankle
problems. As a result, the court experts rolled the base with too
much pressure. When the blue sand was put on top it was unable
to mix with the base; that created the slippery conditions. On TV
the pictures are unbelievable. We are working hard to fix everything else.

Before Federer had been able to familiarise himself with the
blue [I had to confess it did make following the flight of
the ball an awful lot easier than on red clay], he was almost
out of the event. The Swiss was heavily challenged before rally-
ing past Canada's Raonic 4–6, 7–5, 7–6, having to save seven
of eight break points, and withstand twenty-one aces in two
hours and fourteen minutes. 'I felt I was on top the whole match

doing all the right things,' Raonic said. 'I'll probably be happier with the whole outcome in a few days' time but now is not the moment.'

Federer, who captured the title three years before when the tournament transitioned from indoor hard to clay, was seeking his first clay title since completing his career grand slam in Paris in 2009. 'Right now, I'm just playing good tennis and it's a big win because wins like this can create great things,' said Federer. 'It was pretty much a big struggle for me tonight but the level was pretty good and I'm happy where I am in the season.'

Madrid was one of the combined events on the tour, so that the women were hosted with equal celebrity, but they needed something quite outstanding to deny the men their usual dominance of the headlines, interest and crowds (very often there was barely a quorum to watch what would be considered a very decent women's match). Ricardo Sanchez, a veteran Spanish coach on the women's tour who had taken charge of Russian Nadia Petrova after his short spell working for Caroline Wozniacki ended abruptly, had some rather fanciful things to say to *El Pais*, the most respected of journals, which was perhaps not quite what the WTA would have wanted to hear.

'The thing about Venus and Serena [Williams] is they do not want to play [tennis],' Sanchez said. 'They compete now just to make the London [Olympic] Games. They are more into celebrity and fashion. If Serena [played consistently] she would be the best in the world. The Williams are like sprinters – they cannot stand the long rallies, and if you get four balls back, they can't play. When you go from there, they die.'

Sanchez, obviously getting well into his stride, added that Victoria Azarenka's No. 1 ranking was in danger – 'even though she has improved her forehand' – and that Maria Sharapova 'hasn't improved anything in the last five years'. Sanchez was a loose-cannon but what he said made headlines for a day.

Though he would undoubtedly have given Sanchez a piece of his mind had he read his comment, Tiriac was grateful at least that the women did not kick up any kind of fuss about the court, whatever its shade.

'Women are much tougher than men, so we have children. Men are *flojitos*,' Serena Williams said. 'That's why we have the babies, you guys could never handle kids. We ladies don't complain – we just do our best. On the WTA, we are real performers, we are not about going out there and being weenies.'

Serena had dropped one set all week, 6–1 to Caroline Wozniacki in the third round, which suggested the Dane might be putting something together, though the American clearly took affront and won the second and third sets comfortably. In the next round Serena dropped only four games to Maria Sharapova and then, having been given a bit of a test in the semi-finals by Lucie Hradecká of the Czech Republic, she positively gorged on Victoria Azarenka in the final. 'My place is on a tennis court, that's where I'm amazing,' she said.

The non-appearance of Murray citing a back injury and the lack of a complete desire on the part of Djokovic and Nadal to play at all (Rafa's performance in his three-set loss to Fernando Verdasco bordered on a tank) left the field open for someone who might grab this particular Spanish bull by the horns. Roger Federer, as only he could, stepped forward.

After the fright against Raonic, he had played with consummate flair and reached the final where he would face Tomáš Berdych, the Czech who had lost only twelve games in reaching the semi-final, where he had the edge in two tie-breaks against Juan Martin del Potro of Argentina. The final tested both men to the limit. Berdych can rarely have played as well as he did and not won a match. Federer squeaked it 3–6, 7–5, 7–5, emerging from an unsettling backdrop to take the title he had now won on hard courts, red clay and blue in the Spanish capital.

Unlike Serena, the three American men in the draw had hardly pulled up any trees. There were three, John Isner, Donald Young and the wild card Ryan Harrison; the recently retired Ivan Ljubičić was prompted to tweet: 'Wonder how our tour would look if European players were skipping American tourneys the way Americans are skipping European tournamets [sic]'.

Not everyone was aware that Mardy Fish had been taken to hospital after the Sony Ericsson Open in Miami in March, having woken in the middle of the night with his heart almost leaping out of his body, and was considered a serious doubt for the French Open. Fish had played only one match since he had been first taken ill, a listless loss in Houston to 136th-ranked Michael Russell.

Fish responded to Ljubičić with a tweet he deleted soon after, sending: '@IvanLjubicic1 Some of us aren't skipping tournaments bc we want to. Do ur homework before u make dumb generalized comments.' When he heard about the Ljubičić tweet, Andy Roddick chimed in with two of his own: 'I know for a fact that @MardyFish is going through some serious physical issues right now... Irresponsible tweet by @IvanLjubicic1'; '@IvanLjubicic1 also I definitely always respect the choices of ATP tour veterans because I know all of us do what's in the best interest of.... our health and our careers ..... I expect the same in return ..... @IvanLjubicic1.'

Ljubičić re-tweeted all of the Americans' responses (even using the one Fish had deleted), and offered a clarification. 'My tweet regarding American & European players was to open the discussion rather then offend somebody. But I see some people got offended,' Ljubičić wrote, 'and i am sorry for that. Wasn't the plan. And I definitely wish @MardyFish fast recovery!'

As did we all, in the hope that he would be in the pink at this time next year and perhaps well enough to try Madrid for himself. In 2013, the courts would be red again. That much was clear.

For the final Masters stop before the French Open, we decamped to Rome and the glorious Foro Italico, where tinkering with court colour had never entered their heads. The Italian championships had long been staged at a venue constructed in the pre-Second World War years and first called the Foro Mussolini for the country's fascist dictator. Next door to the tennis courts was the aquatic centre, built as part of the city's successful campaign to host the 1960 Olympic Games. This year, a new court had been added, the Super Tennis Arena, and a new press centre, located in a youth hostel located about as far away from the tennis as it was possible to be without being in the next town. It was a vivid demonstration of how little the tournament regarded the importance of telling their story.

The courts with the greatest mystique were those in the shadow of the Stadio Olympico and were now as far distant as it was possible to be from the main centre and so, given time constraints, fewer of us were venturing to where so much of the richness of the event was played out. This was a crying shame and one that required rectifying.

The tournament director was Sergio Palmieri, once John McEnroe's agent and IMG acolyte, a player of limited achievement and former captain of the Fed Cup team. He had done most things in the game but it is safe to say that he was never bosom buddies with those who wrote about it. This was at least the fifth time in the past six years that the facilities had been moved somewhere different.

The players – those who were expected to give press conferences after each match – were not ecstatic either at having to be ferried on golf carts through the throng separating their facilities in the main stadium from ours 500 yards away. More than one of them, including Federer, kicked up a stink about it and wanted to see us on their patch rather than having to be dragged across to ours. My own mood was not helped by the fact that this was an exceedingly bad week for hayfever sufferers.

I was not alone. Caroline Wozniacki's face was deathly white and her eyes looked like red corn circles when she played Anabel Medina Garrigues of Spain on one of the corner courts. I wanted to see how she was faring so made the trek and found myself sitting on the stone steps behind Rory McIlroy (still her boyfriend) and Darren Cahill, who was offering support as a member of the Adidas coaching team. Rory was as charming as I had expected him to be: open, inquisitive and obviously besotted with Caroline. I wondered if there might be the chance of an interview with the pair of them at some stage, Rome being just the place for young lovers. He said he was certainly up for the idea and would check with Caroline later. She retired at 6–4, 4–0 down to Medina Garrigues and that was the last I saw of them that week.

There were two reasons why Ivan Lendl did not make the trip to Rome, the last event before a grand slam. The charity that bore his name and raised funds for 'The Hospital for Special Care', which supported junior wheelchair athletes and other disabled competitors, had its largest annual fundraiser in Hartford, Connecticut that week and Lendl also suffered from precisely the same allergies that so badly affected Wozniacki.

'My allergies from those pines are so bad; they used to affect me all the way through Wimbledon,' he said.

> It is brutal there. Do you know, because of my allergies that once I arrived on the grass at Queen's I used not to touch any balls with my right hand. The only balls I picked up were with my left hand so I could scratch my eyes. If both of my hands go in my eyes I am done for the day. For six weeks, I had to pay attention that I didn't touch anything. Going back this year, I played golf a few times and if somebody hits a ball into the woods I can't go and look for it because it kicks up in my eyes and I'm done. It is that bad.

His fundraiser was in its twenty-sixth year. It had started when, at a Hartford Whalers ice hockey match, he had been introduced to a nine-year-old boy Jonathan Slifka, who suffered from spina bifida and was confined to a wheelchair. When Lendl asked Jonathan if he played tennis, the initial reaction was of horror that he could say such a thing, but he explained about Brad Parks, the

wheelchair tennis pioneer, and Jonathan's mother immediately
had the idea of setting up a camp for kids. It had gone from
strength to strength. Lendl said:

> This year Jonathan, who has much the same sense of humour
> as me, took the microphone and said, 'Did you know that Andy
> Murray and I have the same coach? The difference is that I can't
> walk before practice and he can't walk after practice.' He got a
> standing ovation.

There was no such adulation for Murray on the new Super
Tennis court, for his play was far from super. He won the first set
on a tie-break against Richard Gasquet of France but thereafter
performed wanly and had no real complaints at his three set loss.
Clay, it seemed, still remained far from his thing. And so this time,
the interloper (if we could call him that) in the semi-finals was
David Ferrer, who faded after taking Nadal to a first set tie-break
and forfeited the second without winning a game. Djokovic and
Federer contested for a place against Nadal and it was Djokovic,
all in black on a lovely evening, who demonstrated once more
that he was conspicuous in every department, second serve to the
fore, and won in straight sets.

Medina Garrigues, Wozniacki's conqueror, lost to Serena
Williams in the following round; Williams led Flavia Pennetta
when the Italian retired after four games in the quarter-finals and
then Williams herself said she had hurt her back and withdrew
before a ball was struck against China's Li Na in the semis. You
could tell we were getting close to a grand slam because it was
imperative to protect any niggle with two weeks of grand slam
competition on clay on the horizon. On the opposite side of the
draw, Victoria Azarenka, the top seed, had pulled out before her
third round match against Slovakia's Dominika Cibulková. A
right shoulder injury was given as the official reason but there
was no indication as to how Azarenka had picked up the injury,
nor how long it might keep her out.

This prompted feverish speculation and one forum suggested Azarenka's withdrawal was a fit of pique because her match was scheduled less than twenty-four hours after a late second-round victory and was to be played on Court No. 2, not one of the 'show courts' at the Foro. Azarenka absolutely denied it and said she had a legitimate injury. The only player who seemed to be really up for the event was Maria Sharapova, who was in murderous form. In the final, after Williams had pulled out, Sharapova faced Li Na.

Whereas in Madrid, the women had shown their mettle and the men had complained, a week later it was the other way around. The men's field was as good as it could be and the locals had their match to savour when Andreas Seppi, the Italian No. 1, performed heroically on Court Nicola Pietrangeli to defeat Switzerland's Stanislas Wawrinka, 6–7, 7–6, 7–6, a three-hour-and-twenty-one minute match that had to rank as one of the finest three setters of the year. Seppi saved six match points in all, each consecutive moment drawing the crowd further to the edge of frenzy. It was the first time since tie-breaks were introduced that a match at this event had been decided in three tie-breaks.

The men's final was due to be played on Sunday as normal but the elements were closing in. The sense of frustration only mounted during a women's final as stunning as any in the year. Li Na, hot out of the blocks, led Sharapova by a set and 4–0. But the one facet of her game that concerned those close to Li Na was an inability to see out the win. Eight consecutive games (amid twenty-four unforced errors) slipped away and Sharapova led 4–1 in the final set only for Li, whose husband and coach used the changeover to implore his wife to believe in herself, to regain a foothold. At 5–5, 30–30, play was suspended, though the rain was not heavy enough to drive the players from court. They resumed, Li had a match point at 6–5, only for Sharapova to deliver a crunching forehand for 6–6.

The rains intensified and there was a two-hour hiatus before the pair returned for their sudden-death finish. Sharapova prevailed.

Two hours and fifty-two minutes of tennis had absorbed six hours of the day. Now a decision had to be taken about whether the men's final could start at 8 p.m. The two coaches, Toni Nadal and Marián Vajda, tested the court and were not happy, but happier than those who were still in their seats when Palmieri, the tournament director, announced that we would all have to come back tomorrow. They pelted him with cushions and popcorn containers. Good riddance.

The sun finally popped out on Monday afternoon and Nadal was back at his feisty best. Some of the rallies were a joy to behold, both players crunching the skin off the ball, Nadal's forehand at first losing its rangefinder and then landing where he wanted it to with telling routine. There were some spectacular exhibitions too, not least the backhand lob in the eighth game of the second set, delivered when he appeared so far off balance it would require a miracle to control the two-hander.

Djokovic pointed to an errant line call when his forehand clipped the outside of the line during an eye-popping rally which seemed to be going his way; he was leading 5–4 and Nadal was 30–30 on his serve. The point had to be replayed, Djokovic lost it and the two minutes it took to regain his composure were all Nadal needed. On championship point, Djokovic served a double fault (quite a prescient finale as it happened). Nadal was gnawing away at another clay court trophy. How many more could he possibly sharpen his teeth on?

Chapter 7

Roland Garros

THREE DAYS BEFORE the French championships, Rafael Nadal walked into an art gallery on the Left Bank dressed from head to toe in black. He was giving his blessing to *Les Îles Baléares au rivage de l'expression artistique*, artistic impressions from his home islands. It was a meet-and-greet occasion but more greeters turned up than had been expected. One man ventured very close and would not back off. He could be harmless, he could be trouble. These were the risks you ran with such appearances. Uncle Toni Nadal, Carlos Costa, Rafa's manager, and Benito Perez-Barbadillo, his press attaché, circled, concerned their man was not over-exerted. There are certain hands that needed to be pressed and Nadal was the master at this. The onlooker who was getting too close finally retreated.

Knowing what the next two weeks meant to him, feeling trapped was not a new sensation for Nadal. On clay, more than anywhere else, he was the dominant force, but even with such dominance came periods of self-doubt. There was a detectable jitteriness that suggested Nadal was reflecting on the possible vulnerability of his dominance on clay.

There was not a great deal of time to converse for just around the corner a tournament car with two writers from *L'Équipe* was waiting to whisk him away for the pre-tournament interview that came as part of the champion's package. A distinct bead of sweat formed above Nadal's upper lip but he gave a stunning interview, one of his most revelatory. He initially recalled in 2008, when he had played his finest ever tennis here, dropping three games in the quarter-final against Nicolas Almagro, tearing Novak Djokovic apart in the semis before losing only four games to Roger Federer in the final. 'I have never played that good,' he said, becoming a bit misty-eyed. The first question pointed him ahead one year.

His only loss at the French Open had been to Robin Soderling of Sweden in the fourth round in 2009 and he did not expect to be asked about that particularly stinging reverse. The words came from him in a flood and it was his ability to recall events in detail in a foreign tongue that was most riveting.

'The first thing is that you cannot win always,' he replied.

The second thing is the normal thing is lose, not win, because only one man wins. Third thing: the opponent [he did not mention Soderling by name] played much better than me and if we have to find the reasons, without excuses, is I had a tough year that year. I started with some problems at home [his parents had separated], most important thing, a lot of problems on my knees and, in my opinion, that year I played very bad all the clay court season.

The debate turned to his clay court form in 2012, considering he had won Monte Carlo and Rome, defeating Djokovic in both finals.

I had a few very tough matches in Rome that I didn't have in Monte Carlo. Don't forget Djokovic played much better in Rome than Monte Carlo. When you are able to win the point in two or three balls, the game turns much more easily. Then when the opponent plays more inside, more aggressive, makes fewer mistakes, the match becomes more difficult and it seems like I am playing worse. All my life I worked a lot on court, that's the truth. Outside of [the] court we always worked a lot on the prevention of the injuries and try to compensate my body, try to have my body right to practise as much as I can to play as much as I can.

Today is not the same than ten years ago. Then I was able to go on the court and practise for six hours. When I was nineteen and started fully on the tour when I was not playing for two weeks and I came back, I felt completely out of rhythm. That is because your technique is not fantastic. Today I can be away from tennis for fourteen days, I come back and I don't have a bad feeling. Today I am practising less than before and the important thing is how you practise and what you practise. We go with one goal, perhaps to try to improve the return or to play longer. Toni's style is talking a lot, preparing mentally and that is fine. My knees are there and we are going to try to play here as long as we can in my career.

There had been times when the French people and Nadal did not have the rapport you felt was proper between a nation and someone of his charm and character who had been 'their' champion so many times. This particularly aggrieved Uncle Toni, who felt the French were suspicious of his nephew, consistently recalling and playing over in his mind the jeering of the crowd in the Palais Omnisports in Bercy when Rafa retired hurt after losing the first set to Russia's Nikolay Davydenko in the quarter-final of 2008.

'Seriously, I don't see the problem [with the people],' Rafa said.

That is my feeling. When I go on the street and walk around, they show me the love. I feel that all the time. I understand sometimes, I am on court, I have had a lot of success and the crowd support the other. I respect that. I love this place and this tournament and it is difficult to say anything negative. The situation in 2009 when I lost, was I disappointed? Yes. I don't want to lie. I was having tough moments, even when I was winning but I felt all the stadium not supporting the other but all against me and that was difficult to understand. But I only had that feeling one year. They have never been against me any other time and I am talking with the heart. In last year's final against Roger, I don't feel the crowd against me, I feel it is 50–50. The crowd is free to support everyone and I feel a great support from the French people.

Yet, in 2011, Yannick Noah, the last Frenchman to win the title in Paris, who became the country's Davis Cup captain and who now flitted around the fringes of the sport, wrote an article in the newspaper *Le Monde* alleging that top Spanish athletes were using 'a magic potion', which was tantamount to accusing them of taking illegal drugs to enhance their performance. That prompted vigorous denials and a rebuttal from Rafa. His uncle was incandescent.

In February 2012 *Les Guignols de l'info*, a satirical television show, featured a puppet of Nadal wielding a syringe and then urinating into the gas tank of a car which sped off at the speed of light. He was then turned into a racket-wielding reincarnation of King Kong atop a New York skyscraper after downing another 'magic' potion. A message that read: 'Spanish athletes: they don't win by chance' flashed across the screen, surrounded by the logos of the tennis federation and those of cycling and football.

'This time they have gone way too far,' José Luis Escañuela, the Spanish tennis federation president, said. 'We cannot tolerate the slander and damage to the prestige of our athletes.' The Spanish received support from the ITF, which viewed the 'joke' about Nadal as an attack on its anti-doping programme.

'The ITF condemns the unsubstantiated implications in the Canal Plus video in regard to one of our member national associations, Spain, one of the world's top players, Rafael Nadal, and as a consequence the effectiveness of the Tennis Anti-Doping Programme,' Francesco Ricci Bitti, the federation's president, said. 'We join with the RFET in asking Canal Plus to remove this video, and ask Canal Plus to issue an apology to all Spanish tennis players, who have been unfairly implicated.'

Spanish authorities had threatened legal action against the programme in the past and Nadal, who had never tested positive though under greater scrutiny than anyone in the game, repeatedly declared his innocence and his disappointment. 'I really believe we cannot dope in tennis without being caught,' he said.

I'm the first one to like jokes, but this kind of joke goes too far in that it helps contribute to wrong opinions among people who are far removed from all this, who don't know the system. The 'Guignols' have crossed the line. That's what makes me sad. I'm more motivated than ever to clean up Spain's image, which is characterised by sacrifice, humility, and the spirit of overcoming adversity that all athletes have. You cannot accuse someone of something you have no proof of, even if it is humorous. France is obsessed with us.

Whispers about Nadal were nothing new but there was absolutely no evidence against him. Perez-Barbadillo described the time spent dealing with these malignant rumours as 'crisis management'. It was almost more tiring for him and for Nadal than the competition in a grand slam tournament which was about to begin to the cultured backdrop of Paris's 16th *arrondissement*.

There was more to play for in 2012 in every way. The French Open had raised its prize money by 7 per cent to $24.6 million. Those players who lost in the first round would see their 'take' jump by 20 per cent. For Justin Gimelstob of the ATP, this represented progress but with 'a long way to go'. In *L'Equipe* it was reported that the Open would make €49 million in media rights, €28 million in ticketing, €30 million in public relations and hospitality and €33 million from sponsors (which equated to around $174 million). The figures were not questioned.

As an unreconstructed creature of habit, I had stayed in the same hotel, Hôtel Poussin, in the same room for the fifteenth year in succession and the twentieth in all. It was a ten-minute stroll to the grounds, past the florists on the first corner, where the fragrances lingered, past the smart clientele at the Maison du Thé where cigarette smoke did the same, past the touts – *'Cherche places*, tickets'. The morning walk cleared the senses and the one back in the evening, with my fellow British scribes, was in preparation for a cleansing glass of chilled red wine.

The venue itself is compact and crowded but retains its chic.

The expansion plans were in hand but dogged by political in-fighting of a very French distinction. The surface is invariably characterised as 'red clay' but is actually crushed brick or tiles laid over a surface of white limestone then frosted and coated with a few millimetres of powdered dust that serves three purposes – aesthetics, player comfort and colour.

The court surfaces are then drenched in water, a process repeated several times until a thin, compact layer coats each court. It is deep enough to allow footprints and ball marks, but shallow enough to avoid making the courts spongy or slippery. Before and during matches, workers smooth the surface by dragging rectangular lengths of chain-link across it. The red brick dust is replenished as needed. No two clay courts are precisely the same but the general consensus is that none are better than those at the home of the Fédération Française de Tennis (FFT).

What preoccupies those at Roland Garros is its size, or lack of it. The grounds occupy 8.5 hectares with twenty outside courts and its byways are often seriously over-crowded; it has been decided that the venue will undergo serious renovation. The FFT had hoped the regeneration of the area would be completed by 2016 but later stretched the deadline to 2018, citing the recession. This story has plenty of juice left in it.

The scores at the French Open are delivered in the native tongue, not enforcing translation from French into English, a tendency that tournaments on the ATP and WTA Tours follow that I find irritating. There is something quite lovely about *quinze–zero*, *quinze à*, *égalité*, *avantage*, *jeu*. Lleyton Hewitt said he had to look at the scoreboard because of his lack of French, but he was in a minority.

The French had decided in 2006 to open their tournament on Sunday, based on the desire for one more day's gate money. The stadia were often less than half full at the start of play which did not look good for a grand slam, but this one, more than any other, was run on gastronomic as much as sporting terms. Those in the posh seats on courts Philippe Chatrier and Suzanne Lenglen rarely took to their places before 1 p.m.

On the first day of the event proper, on the steps towards the locker rooms, I bumped into Amer Delic, one of the most thoughtful and decent men on the tour. A Bosnian by birth who had taken American nationality, his ranking was around the 230 mark. He had lost in the first round of qualifying but was hanging around because he was the hitting partner for fellow American Brian Baker and told me I ought to watch his friend, who had won the Nice event the weekend prior to the French.

Delic had become a good friend and we had discussed him putting his considered thoughts in written order. He was forever offering logical and practical ways to advance the plight of the modern player and came up with such informative and heartfelt words I asked if he would mind sharing them with me. He said he would be honoured.

He wrote:

If you have been following me on Twitter (@AmerDelic) you know that there is no shortage of updates of my current doings. Twitter has been a great platform for me to share some of my thoughts, ideas, questions, criticisms and compliments. It all started with an idea to stay involved in tennis while lying at home (on the couch) with my knee wrapped in post-surgery bandages. Most of my followers have been thoughtful and knowledgeable on almost every 'tweet' I send out. In my 5,000+ tweets, topics have been all over the board. From tennis to politics, religion to food, candy to golf and comedy to travel. While these posts may be off the wall, there is always someone in the world that shares a similar thought/opinion. Twitter has been able to bring those similar minds together. Here and there I stumble across some punks who have nothing better to do than write hate messages and annoy people. I either call them out or simply block them. I don't mind a difference of opinion. I welcome it, as long as you provide a legitimate and factual argument.

Also, I am not a fan of tippers/sport gamblers. I automatically block those. In my honest opinion, betting has ruined most sports. It is on the brink of ruining our sport also and I am the last person that wants to contribute to that. If there was a way to make betting on individual sports illegal, I would be the first person to vote for that law. In short, if you are one of those, don't bother following me.

With my public service announcement out of the way, let me go ahead and thank everyone that has been following me throughout my ups and downs in the world of tennis. It has exactly been that. At times it has seemed to be more downs than ups, but just as they say 'that is life'. Injuries suck. I won't sugar-coat it. In my profession absolutely nothing is guaranteed, unlike some other sports (baseball, basketball, etc.).

A few other things that have been on my mind: 1. Money – over the few weeks during/after the Australian Open there have been many rumours of the possible strike by the players. Just to clarify it, they were not just rumours. As much as I love (and I mean LOVE) the Australian Open, it was super close to not happening at all. One of the main reasons was of course the money. Grand slams earn insane amounts of money and share 12.5 per cent of that. For an example, a player ranked fifty in the world and yes, that would be the whole wide world, will get paid just under $20,000 for losing in the first round of a grand slam tournament. It takes my parents about six months to earn that amount, so believe me, I absolutely appreciate every dime of everything I have earned. That is a lot of money where I come from.

However, let's deduct 30 per cent tax from that and now you are already down to around $14,000. That is still a good cheque for just showing up at a tournament. However, you don't just teleport your way to Melbourne from Tampa, Florida. That right there will cost you about $3,000 minimum for a round trip ticket sitting in the coach class for sixteen hours from LAX (Los Angeles airport) alone. (By the way, that always feels great for a 6'5" guy with a surgically repaired knee. Practising the next day when you land feels even better.) Easy math gets us down to eleven grand before I even show up at the courts. In a perfect world, I would take a coach and a trainer with me to a tournament, but since I travel on a budget, let's say I only bring a coach. That's another three grand for a ticket, $1,500 per week (minimum three weeks) so that brings me down to $3,500. Three weeks (two warm-up tournaments plus one week at Melbourne) at a hotel rate $100 per night ($2,100) with food at per diem rates ($60/per person = $120 per day x 21 days = $2,520) leaves me in the minus about $1,120. Years ago I was told that I should incorporate myself because of all the tax purposes. I should change my status to 'non-profit' organisation.

Let me get something clear. No one is asking for charity hand-outs here. I am simply saying that tournaments cannot go on without other players not named Djokovic, Federer, Nadal and Murray. NFL games are not played with just Tom Brady, Peyton Manning and Drew Brees. Soccer games are not played just with Messi, Ronaldo and Dzeko. Golf tournaments are not played just with Tiger Woods, Rory McIlroy and Phil Mickelson. Otherwise they would be called exhibition or practice rounds. You get the point.

No 2. Smurf Clay – I was not in Madrid this year, so I can't talk about the courts from the first-hand experience, however I did spend a couple of hours watching it on TV. As an occasional couch-potato, I was a fan. It's definitely easier to watch. However, the timing of such a drastic change, lack of consistency, safety of the players, bad preparation for the French Open all outweighed the one lonely positive. I am a HUGE fan of progressiveness and improvement of tennis as an overall product, however, let's take a moment and think before we pull any triggers. Adam Helfant, our ex-CEO, should not be the one making the final decision on court surfaces. Leave that up to the players. He was brought in to corral possible sponsorships, TV deals and improve marketing. How did this ever fly with the player council? Probably the same way the 'round robin' was accepted a few years back. We all know that backfired in a hurry. Where is the transparency?

I take a step back. Helfant did bring in a champagne company as a new sponsor. Maybe the plan was to spray the blue clay courts with the Moet to improve its speed and traction? No one really knows. That's another thing. I am willing to bet that if I asked all of the top 100 players, if they ever even met Adam Helfant, at least 50 per cent would say no. How can you represent people that you don't even know? Would that be kosher in any other corporation? My guess is probably not.

My goal is to make all current/future players and fans aware of the situation. Reality is, sooner or later I will hang up the sticks and move on from the tour.[†] However, before I ride off into the sunset (or get a 'real job') I wanted to make people aware that not all tennis players fly on private jets, with entourages while getting massages and eating gluten-free meals. Those who do have certainly earned it and have every right to enjoy it. But for every Roger or Rafa, there are fifty other world class players fighting just as hard only to cover expenses every week. Most guys will continue grinding with the hope that one day they will enjoy the perks at the top. I am one of those guys. I do it for the love of the game. Ironically enough, in this sport, love means nothing.

Delic was speaking not just on behalf of himself, but of a lot more of his contemporaries, struggling to make professional ends meet. His views demand a hearing.

♪

As for love, Andy Roddick's affair with Paris had never been extended beyond a peck on the cheek. He had rarely played on Centre Court, usually despatched to Court Suzanne Lenglen. It was planned that the court would stage more women's matches than men's, so Roddick did not see the funny side of consistently being scheduled there.

Against Nicolas Mahut, one of the 'lesser' local cards given a Sunday start, Roddick was never at home. His distrust of the

---

† Delic retired from the professional tour in August 2012 and is now assistant coach at the University of Florida.

surface was evident as he stumbled, fidgeted and tried unsuccessfully to convince himself that winning the third set might turn the match. He lost in four. At best he was average but, given his weak hamstring, the result was not a real surprise. Roddick's press conferences were usually edgy, contained extremely quotable material and after a stinging defeat, I sensed he might have something more interesting than forehands and backhands on his mind. His relationship with American writers was conspicuously prickly.

In his nine previous appearances at the French Open, Roddick had lost in the first round four times and reached the last sixteen only once. His expectations were low and he lived up to them. 'They probably weren't great, I wasn't playing really well. I move just horrendously out here. My first step is just so bad on this stuff. I feel like I'm always shuffling or hopping or not stopping or something.' He said he would talk no more. He said he made a choice. He played. He was fine. He lost.

If Roddick's departure in the first round was not a shock, Serena Williams had arrived in one of her favoured cities as distinct favourite. Her decision not to play beyond the quarter-final in Rome, citing a back problem, was a subtle piece of brinksmanship and she approached her first round meeting with Virginie Razzano of France in a good mood. The match would become one of the most talked about of recent years. Serena should have won inside two sets, having led the second set tie-break 5–1, but she could not see it through. This was not her. In the third set, Razzano burst from the blocks, won the first seven points and, amid a deluge of errors from the American, led by five games to love. The crowd was animated, engaged, sensing a shock and an emotive storyline.

The atmosphere was further charged in that the umpire was Eva Asderaki, the Greek who had been in the chair for the US Open final the previous September when Serena let rip with her famous 'you're hateful and not very attractive inside' outburst after Asderaki called her for a 'hindrance' as she celebrated what she thought was a certain winner against Samantha Stosur before the ball had landed.

Razzano was making a few high-pitched noises of her own, but nothing too wild and there was a sense that Asderaki may have been evening up the score when she called the French player for 'hindrance' three times, the final admonishment coming at a pivotal point, as the French woman led 5–3 in the third set (from a 5–0 lead) and Williams was getting right back into the match. Clearly cramping, Razzano emitted little more than a yelp at 30–30, but the point penalty gave Serena a break point.

What is and what is not a hindrance? It was a purely subjective call, and a bit confusing to say the least. There are involuntary hindrances and deliberate hindrances but definitions were vague. The appendix of the WTA rulebook stated, for example, that a point should be replayed if 'a player is hindered ... by either an unintentional act of the opponent or something outside the player's own control.'

And why was Asderaki in the chair in the first place? Before each tournament an e-mail is sent to the umpires asking if there are any players upon whom they would prefer not to sit in judgement. Asderaki must have realised that sitting in the chair when Serena played had the potential to provoke the kind of controversy tennis did all it could to steer clear of, especially in a grand slam. It would have been better all around to have kept her away from such a potential conflict, but the decision was taken to give her this particular chair. It rebounded spectacularly and, at the end, she was jeered from the court.

The match itself was spectacular in the sense that it lacked anything resembling tennis. The whittling away of Razzano's lead, the umpiring interventions, Serena's stumbles – all lent it an air of fantasy. Razzano had seven match points and lost them all, either with serving that would not have looked out of place in the 1920s, or nervous net cords from Williams that plopped over the net. The crowd was in danger of falling into an extreme faint until Serena thumped a backhand so far long it almost landed flush on a linesman's leg. The American had been beaten 4–6, 7–6, 6–3 and did not help her cause when, informed that as Razzano's fiancé had passed away a year ago this was an emotional day for her conqueror, she responded: 'We all have our stories.' It was from this defeat, though, that Williams took a decision that turned her, and several others', life around.

◯

What of Novak Djokovic? Here was a man on the edge of destiny, faced with the opportunity to win four grand slams in a row, something that had not happened since the halcyon days of Rod Laver in 1969. His was a fantastic tale to tell and I was invited to join his team for lunch in the players' restaurant next to Centre Court. The area was stuffed with bodies, players milled around and there was a constant clatter of cutlery and chairs. This was a grand slam venue at its most hectic, space at a premium. To celebrate kids' day, as is the norm the Saturday before the championships, the French Federation asked which of the top players would be a part of the show; this was meat and drink to Djokovic who was soon hamming it up for the youngsters on court.

A few yards away, Marián Vajda, his coach, Miljan Amanovic, his physiotherapist, and his physical trainer Gebhard Phil-Gritsch (GG), were talking about their man and what had brought him to this special moment in his life. These were proud men doing an exceptional job. The conversation bounced between us and I captured it as it unravelled.

Phil-Gritsch, who had trained the former world No. 1 Thomas Muster, his fellow Austrian, was the latest addition and had come by the appointment in an unusual way.

I went on a Saturday morning to the flea market in Vienna, a nice atmosphere with all kinds of things to buy and bumped into Gunther Bresnik, who once coached Boris Becker. I worked with him many years ago and he knew I was at the stage where I would really like to go back into tennis and fitness and he told me he would make a call. Two hours later I had a job offer.

They were a little like the Three Musketeers. The sense was that GG was the cerebral one, Amanovic the driven one, Vajda the calm, chummy one. 'We all like the holistic approach,' GG said, explaining that you can only be successful if training is connected to the mind and the brain, promoting self-confidence. To instil confidence and improve his skillset is the coaching team's ultimate goal.

Vajda recalled a conversation with Djokovic after he had become Wimbledon champion and world No. 1 for the first time in 2011 because the coach was anxious that he was committing to too much off the court. They sat down in LA and Vajda was sharp with him.

> I said I don't want any more of this, I want to have a clear mind what you are going to achieve, what is your goal. The US Open is in front of you, if you are going to go on to Jay Leno ten times, I really don't give a shit but the first thing is to practise at eight in the morning – this, this, this and then Jay Leno maybe, maybe, maybe. It's fame but fame is something that isn't real. This is very fragile. Maybe you don't realise it, but it comes into your mind, this contract, that contract, this commitment, this is good for PR. Priority, you might lose it for one or two years.

The conversation became more diverse.

> GG: But he is a smart guy, he knows why he is successful and so far, he never sticks anything in the way. This is fundamental to his success. You cannot short-cut performance.
>
> NH: What has been your greatest satisfaction?
>
> GG: Wimbledon 2011 is the one. He had a huge amount of pressure before that final because everything basically was on the line,

the title, the No. 1 ranking, the dream of his life. To perform in that match the way that he did was incredible.

MV: The cream on the cake, yes. This was amazing, the run he did last year, we couldn't believe it – 'what is going on?' For me, personally, I would say Madrid when he beat Nadal on clay for the first time ever. Then I realised this could be something.

MA: This year, the Australian Open semi-final [against Andy Murray] and final [against Nadal]. Incredible matches. They pushed each other over the limits. You could feel each of them, they are pushing and from a certain moment, you think there is no more ... and there is more.

GG: I didn't believe he could find the energy for the fifth set against Nadal. He was trailing, and where did he find the energy? They have this incredible way to win, without that you cannot push yourself over the limit.

MA: He had bloody socks after the match. Rafa almost collapsed completely. I was shouting to the guy, take a chair, give them a chair otherwise there is no ceremony.

NH: What about his chances at the French Open, this has to be the hardest one.

MV: You have to adjust a little, the sliding, every tournament the clay is a little bit different, a little bit better but basically these guys have changed their technique of running, they are not sliding as we used to in my day. They are making small steps.

NH: Does he pick on you guys? [great laughter]

GG: We laugh more than we cry. If you do your job, you are professional and when the job is done, you try to have fun. You want to enjoy life – in every profession that is very similar. If you want to be successful you have to have real focus.

MV: My feeling was that all those years I had a big stone here [gesturing to his heart] all the time. I blamed myself, what I did wrong. After he became No. 1 last year and I released myself incredibly, a moment of relief because he achieved what he wanted all his life so now I am much more relaxed but even now I have a motivation to see him get better.

[At that moment, our attention was turned to where Djokovic was, on the television screen, play-acting on the court for the kids as part of the build-up to the event.]

MA: He is trying to enjoy every moment out of tennis.

GG: What I really admire is his respect towards people. I have never seen him disrespect anybody and this is amazing. Most people are not like this any more when they achieve this much.

MA: Yes, some change drastically. This is the same guy I met five years ago, he didn't change, he's the same Novak.

MA: He has changed in a good way. Yesterday I set up practice with a kid from Slovakia, Martin Klizan, but Novak couldn't play at that time. Novak went to him in the gym and apologised for not being able to practise. The guy, Klizan, talked all night about it, how humble is this guy. The coach has become humble too. It is amazing that this guy has a real perspective. He could be in the clouds all the time. I say 'why are you writing so many signatures, it takes all your energy' but he says 'No, I give it all'. The public loves him, they admire him, they share with him and this is the best for him.

MA: He gives energy to the public and he takes it from them. It is all natural.

NH: Does he have any terrible habits?

[At this moment, Jelena Ristic, Novak's girlfriend, reintroduced herself to me ('ah yes, you're Neil') and joined the conversation.]

JR: Always late. He is always late.

MV: He doesn't have a sense of time.

NH: What about the ball bouncing?

MA: Thirty-two is the most. They only have to apply the rule.

MV: I wanted to say one thing, which is that nobody believed he could do this [win grand slams and become No. 1] between Federer and Nadal. Now the public recognises he is truly No. 1 and the leader. If you want to be No. 1 you have to change something and it is not a miracle, it is work, it is a mosaic that he gathered piece by piece. But now he knows what to do. We believe in it because he proved it and it is even harder to stay there and he realises this already.

Djokovic had changed a little, in that his attire had changed. In late 2009, having been dropped by Adidas when they signed Murray to a five year contract worth an estimated $15 million – a situation that did not go down at all well with the Djokovic family – he joined Sergio Tacchini, a remarkable coup for a company that had filed for bankruptcy two years earlier. Djokovic was signed to a ten-year deal but as he had delivered victory upon victory in 2011, Tacchini felt the financial pinch. In effect, Nole had become too successful for them to cope with and they were struggling to afford their performance-related end of the deal and said they had better step away. Also, sports goods manufacturers in the United States, the biggest market for high-end tennis clothes, said they could never get enough merchandise to put on the shelves.

The latest brand to clothe him was Uniqlo, a Japanese company that already dressed Kei Nishikori, the Japan No. 1, who was now inside the top twenty. Djokovic signed to a five year deal.

'It is a cool brand with strong roots in Japan, a country whose culture and way of life I respect,' he said.

I have a personal philosophy which I call 'Be Unique', based on my strong passion, drive and eagerness to keep improving myself. I am passionate about being the best possible tennis player, as well as the best possible person, and I have a continuous desire to help people, especially children, who have been less fortunate than I.

Clay court tennis lent itself to heroic performances and if a Frenchman was the hero at Roland Garros, all the better. Paul-Henri Mathieu offered one such remarkable story. Here was a 30-year-old who had been given a second chance at the sport thanks to the total reconstruction of his left knee. He was suffering in 2010 from the crippling effects of arthritis to the extent that he could not even walk down the stairs. He took a decision in March 2011 to have surgery which required breaking two bones in his knee and resetting his leg completely. He was in hospital for a week, in a cast for six weeks more and could only walk again after two months.

'The doctors said I had to have the surgery to walk and live like a normal person. I was not sure if I would play again but I had no choice because I couldn't walk anyway,' Mathieu said. Emmanuel Petit, the former Arsenal, Chelsea and Barcelona footballer, rang Mathieu saying he had been through the same operation [in 2005] and though the call was meant as a fillip, Petit remarked that he had not been able to play again, which was hardly reassuring. Mathieu started his rehabilitation sitting in a chair hitting balls – 'I wanted to have the feeling of the racket, the court in my mind, even for 10–15 minutes, for me it was important. The first racket I touched standing up was in August. It went really slowly.'

In January 2012, he believed he might be able to return to the circuit but every little step forwards became two backwards as pain grew in his swollen knee. He had been able to move a little better on hard courts but how would he cope on clay, with all the brutal sliding and recoveries required to stay in rallies?

He played a couple of events in North Africa and one in Monte Carlo, but required more rest. He entered a couple of challenger events in France and, a few days before Roland Garros, though doubtful, he chose to give it a go. In the first round, on Court 2 and with support ringing in his head and pain coursing through his body – 'I didn't even realise I was playing in the French Open,' he said – Mathieu defeated Bjorn Phau of Germany from two sets down, winning the final set 6–0. His second round opponent was John Isner and, as one might expect, it was scheduled for Court Philippe Chatrier.

'I did not know how I would react, or how the people would react,' said Mathieu, who had never been allowed to forget that in the 2002 Davis Cup Final against Russia on clay in Paris-Bercy, the then 20-year-old made his debut for his country and in the fifth and final rubber, lost from two sets up to Mikhail Youzhny. This was one of those matches that could torment a player and he still felt the hurt.

The match against Isner was a classic as Mathieu, his yellow shirt increasingly flecked with brown clay stains, lost the first set, won the next two, lost the fourth and then contested a series of astonishing games in the fifth set. He had three match points at 11–10 – 'Allez Paul-o, Allez Paul-o' the crowd responded – but Isner dug exceptionally deep and saved them. The American managed to secure only two break points in the fifth set, his forty-one aces in the end counting for nothing as Mathieu won 6–7, 6–4, 6–4, 3–6, 18–16 in five hours and forty-one minutes. The final point was an epic in itself, a series of floated forehand cross-court 'gets' from both men before Isner's last effort spun wide.

Mathieu was shattered emotionally and physically. Unsure he could even play two hours on a reconstructed and untested joint, he had lasted almost six.

> I wanted to give it the best I could. I felt it was the final for me. I knew the crowd were curious to see me again but they supported me, even the match I lost [to Marcel Granollers of Spain, also in five sets in the third round]. I was thinking of the match between Isner and Nicolas Mahut, my best friend at Wimbledon. In the end, mentally I was dead but it was a victory just to play again. I worried about the day after and I woke up and I was fine, the leg a little bit heavy but nothing special. I would like to say I am going to play for sure a few more years but I cannot tell you. I wish, of course I wish.

On the second Monday, in the fourth round, Jo-Wilfried Tsonga was playing Stanislas Wawrinka. The Swiss is twenty-six, blessed with one of the great one-handed backhands of his time and can debate the whys and wherefores of tennis in a gentle, but battle-hardened manner. He is a very good player who wants to become much better. We take a coffee, chat about life, the game, *his* game. His match against Tsonga started late, in the rain and wind, because Djokovic had come from two sets down to defeat Andreas Seppi of Italy, and eventually was suspended in near darkness at 9.30 p.m. with Tsonga leading 4–2 in the fifth set. Djokovic said 'nothing was working and I was just fighting'. The fight would have to resume between Tsonga and Wawrinka.

Stan texted me the next morning and asked if I'd like to have a coffee in the players' lounge. He was sitting with Nate Ferguson who strung the rackets for both players and, considering the implications of what might happen in the next couple of hours, he was remarkably relaxed. I wished him the best, though my professional independence and regard for Tsonga meant I had to be circumspect. But I knew how much this meant for Stan. Though he responded with an immediate break of serve and got the match back to 4–4, Tsonga rallied and won in five sets. He would now play Djokovic.

It was the match of the tournament, full of acrobatic twists of storyline and very much in the Frenchman's mould. Djokovic started beautifully, taking the first set for the loss of a single game and winning fifteen of the first twenty points, but through the wondrous ebbs and flows it was the Frenchman who built himself into a winning position. The crowd on Court Philippe Chatrier was beside itself.

But this is where Djokovic played as we were beginning to think only he could. On the first match point against him, he volleyed cross-court from the 'ad' side and then moved to the middle, one foot positioned on either side of the centre line, when Tsonga chose to hit his backhand down the line as it looked more open. But it was an illusion as Djokovic was leaning that way and cut it off for a forehand volley winner cross court. On the very next point at 4–5, 30–40, Djokovic nailed a first serve down the T and moved instinctively forward to nail a cross-court forehand winner off a half-hit return. Tsonga had a much better chance of victory on his third match point at 5–6, 30–40 when he controlled the baseline rally with his forehand, but once again lost it going down the line. On Tsonga's fourth match point at 5–6, Djokovic found his way to the net and was able to put away a regulation overhead after controlling the point with a big first serve out wide to the advantage court. Tsonga said it was the toughest loss of his life and in the circumstances one could see why.

Roger Federer was plugging away, and in the fourth round faced one of the discoveries of the year, the impish Belgian qualifier David Goffin. It was wondrous tennis. Goffin won the first set and had Federer at sixes and sevens until the Swiss found his touch and won in four sets. At the end of the match, the court announcer strode on and talked to both players at the net. Goffin revealed that he had had Federer's poster on his bedroom wall; Federer put an arm around his shoulder and thanked him for being such a prescient youth. I was forced to wonder if Federer would have joined in such friendly talk had he been on the losing side but it did not seem to bother Goffin at all.

$$\mathcal{O}$$

Andy Murray had his business head on in the days leading up to the tournament. At Ivan Lendl's behest, he had played a warm-up at the Racing Club de Paris and it was there that he posed for a picture with an executive from Rado, the Swiss watch maker, to celebrate a seven-figure deal that had been brokered by IMG. What was a group that had nothing to do with Murray doing putting together a potentially breakthrough contract for him? After all, it was well known that Federer had a multi-million pound deal with Rolex, Nadal had signed with Richard Mille, Djokovic wore Audemars Piguet and Murray needed some kind of watch contract to measure up, but should IMG have been actively engaged on his behalf? Was this the first subtle move in a bid to represent him lock, stock and barrel? They had long harboured designs on Murray and I wrote that their interest was burgeoning when one of their senior representatives told me: 'I cannot believe that Andy will go through his playing career without wanting to work with us once.'

If not said for the purpose, such a comment was going to irritate certain people immensely. XIX Entertainment were a branch of Simon Fuller's Creative Artists Agency, the company that masterminded the careers of the very rich and exceedingly famous across the sports and entertainment world, and they did not take too kindly to suggestions they might be vulnerable to the loss of someone whose contract was coming up for renegotiation at the end of the year. Amit Naor, one of CAA's leading tennis figures, said to me straight out that the story linking IMG with Murray was 'absolute bullshit'. Given that IMG had already pitched for Murray in Miami, it was hard to accept that they had given up the ghost already. But Naor was not a man to argue with for long.

I had always considered Murray a potential French Open champion – much to certain people's humour. He had been to the semi-final in 2011 and though he lost in straight sets to Nadal, all the sets had been tightly fought. His clay record this year had not been particularly proficient but he defeated Tatsuma Ito of Japan in the first round without the alarms of previous years and met Jarkko Nieminen, a veteran Finn, on Court Philippe Chatrier in the second.

Within minutes, it was evident that this would be another markedly eventful day. Murray had woken with a back spasm and was unable to put any weight on his left leg. At the first sit down when he trailed 0–3, he felt terrible. After almost every point, Murray reached for the small of his back and soon beckoned for the trainer, who rolled him into all manner of contortions. A default was on the cards. 'This is killing me inside,' he screamed. At 4–4 in the second set, Nieminen had three break points and a two-set lead may have been enough, but he faltered and Murray, whose body had been loosened as well as his mind, began to seriously flow. Murray won 1–6, 6–4, 6–1, 6–2.

Virginia Wade, the 1977 Wimbledon champion, commentating from London, said that Murray had a tendency to act like a drama queen. This was not music to his ears. 'Maybe people should ask me a question first before commenting on it,' he said. 'She has no idea what I was feeling on the court, she doesn't know what was happening twenty minutes before I went out on the court.'

Murray's former coach Brad Gilbert was in another commentary box: 'Getting through a slam can be a bit like a game of poker: you don't want to let on to others too much of what is going on,' he said.

> If I was Andy I'd be inclined just to say that my back is fine, despite what might be going on. The guys he is measuring himself against are Djokovic, Nadal and Federer and you don't really want them to know more than you have to if your back is not great.

Nonetheless the running commentary was at the heart of the Murray psyche. Even if Lendl had suggested he tone it down, he liked to let everyone in on his attitude. A relatively calm victory over Santiago Giraldo of Colombia was followed by a fourth round date with Richard Gasquet that was bound to raise the temperature of a cold spring day. I discussed the pressure on a British player at Wimbledon and tried to equate it to that on a Frenchman in Paris. 'I have had pressure since I was being pushed in a pram,' Gasquet told me. 'But the sensation I feel now playing in front of my public gives me wings.' Murray was jeered onto court and broke into an impish grin. Then he clipped Gasquet's wings, though not until after a first set in which the Frenchman flew. What was incredible was that the score-line, 1–6, 6–4, 6–1, 6–2, was a copy of that against Nieminen. Murray, eventually, played well indeed and it was a match without dramas. (On a nearby court, Nadal was beating Juan Mónaco of Argentina, a huge talent, 6–2, 6–0, 6–0, which was a ridiculous score-line.)

The quarter-final pitted Murray with David Ferrer, a match that turned out to be another of the fumble-and-curse matches Murray often endured on Court Suzanne Lenglen. His rhythm suffered because of two rain delays, and ten breaks of the Murray serve rendered his challenge impossible. The little man from Spain was driving Murray off his head. 'I'm trying my tits off!' he screamed at one stage, which was a touch difficult to translate to my French and Spanish colleagues in the press seats, but as Kevin

Mitchell wrote in *The Guardian*, 'even as Murray raged at the ground, the sky and every inanimate object from his towel to his racket, he knew he had nobody to blame but himself'.

In the women's draw, it was beginning to look as if Maria Sharapova would be feeling the same if she did not win. These were liberating times for her on clay, her mistrust of the surface had gone, her self-deprecating description as 'a cow on ice' seemed ever more ironic. Williams was out of the way, as was Victoria Azarenka, for the No. 1 had lost to Dominika Cibulková of Slovakia 6–2, 7–6, with a warning for racket abuse along the way. What would she do to recover from the loss, she was asked. 'I'll kill myself,' she answered. 'The tournament is over. What is there to recover from?'

By the quarter-finals, there was no one left in the field who had won the title. In the round of sixteen, Li Na had been beaten by Yaroslava Shvedova of Kazakhstan and Svetlana Kuznetsova, the Russian, lost in straight sets to the Italian Sara Errani, the first of them to love. Indeed, Sharapova would have the hardest fourth round match, dropping a set to Klára Zakopalová of the Czech Republic before squeaking through.

Sharapova was asked if she minded being described as both glamorous and a diva. Her reaction is telling and gave a glimpse of the steely resolve that lurks within her catwalk frame.

> Glamour and a diva. Hmm, yes, that's me. I think a lot of it is perception, and the visual that people have of you – it's understandable, because what the outside world sees is you playing and doing press conferences. And being on the red carpet and everything is just so glam and beautiful. But at the end of the day, it's all one big illusion, and then reality sets in. And I don't go to sleep with my make-up on or wear make-up on the court. I'm sure divas do that, right?

A few days later Mme Sharapova was in the final, to play the other talk of the women's draw, Errani. The Italian was following in the footprints of Francesca Schiavone, who had won this title from nowhere two years earlier. There were marked differences, in technique and flair, though Schiavone was the more expressive and Errani quiet and thoughtful. She was playing with a different racket as well, for which she had to pay a $30,000 forfeit when she changed companies. It came with a handle a couple of centimetres longer than the norm. She called it Excalibur. 'It makes me more powerful,' she said. 'A bit like a person who has longer arms. Of course, you have more speed and more power for that also. But you also need to control it.'

She managed superb control in her semi-final against Stosur, to whom she had lost in Rome two weeks earlier, winning in three sets despite times when it looked as if nerves might devour her. She managed to control them and the scene was now set for Sharapova, who had defeated Petra Kvitová in the other semi-final quite comprehensively. Remarkably, the pair were born within two weeks of each other and both had once boarded at the same Nick Bollettieri IMG academy in Florida.

In the final, Excalibur's magic powers faded. Errani was edgy at the start and once Sharapova was in the ascendancy she was not to be halted, winning 6–3, 6–2 and sinking to her knees, her visor slipping down across her eyes, at the climax. The only interruption to the day's dominance was when there was an error in the on-court announcement and Errani was called forward as 'la vainqueur' – the winner. Maria was able to see the funny side in that.

We spoke a couple of days later. 'It is so crazy,' she said.

Such a nice feeling. The other three grand slams, the days after I had that excitement where you almost want to scream but this one, I've just been happily content with what I have achieved. I still want to scream a bit but it has been a case of walking around with this huge smile on my face.

You can never exactly tell when something is going to happen. I did doubt. You also have to be realistic and have a very clear head.

It is one thing to believe that I'm so good at what I do I'm bound to achieve this or that but you always have to find a way to get to that place. It doesn't happen because you believe. My motivation was based on the fact that it was the French Open and I wanted to win it, how much more motivation does a person need?

I wondered if she had spoken to Yuri, her father, who had borne her from the unforgiving hopelessness of Siberia and been alongside her for so many years but had since chosen to take a back seat and let others – in the current case Thomas Hogstedt, the Swede, in partnership with Russian hitting partner Vladimir Voltchkov, a former Wimbledon semi-finalist – steer his daughter's career.

'I called him about six hours after the match and he was like "oh you are the French champion and the No. 1 so you don't call me" – that was his reaction and he said don't forget about me, I'm over here [in California, where he lives] all alone,' Maria said.

He is enjoying life, he deserves it, he's been such a big influence and sacrificed so much to get me where I am and for that alone he deserves to be on permanent vacation and there's no other person that deserves it more.

I don't think anyone can have all good moments, there will be times when you don't agree on things, especially in that transition period when you go from your Dad being very influential to getting to an age when you feel you know a lot more than they do and raise your opinion, and so there is no perfect relationship with your parents especially in a career like this. That image of me in my head when I won Wimbledon is the image I still see today with him in my life. He gives me that hug like I'm still seventeen years old and to have that at twenty-five is a really nice feeling and even more so with my Mum, so I think that is one of the biggest gifts you can ask for. Now I'm living in a culture in America where so many kids that I see get to a point at seventeen and eighteen and the first thing they want to do is live on their own and have their own way and get away from their parents and it's scary for me because when I come home all I want to do is spend time with my family.

The men's competition had reached its denouement. Nadal thrashed Ferrer without so much as a sliver of compassion for a compatriot – Ferrer got the grand total of five games – while Djokovic was a break down in the first set and 3–0 adrift in the second against Federer, but on a gusty afternoon, he summoned all the energy and character that had epitomised his recent performances in all manner of tournaments. 'Had I won the second set it could have been a different match but I didn't, so it's not,' said Federer at the conclusion of Djokovic's 6–4, 7–5, 6–3 victory.

What better match could we have to set before an expectant audience? The best clay-court player of all time against the man on the cusp of owning all four grand slam titles at once; this was absolute tennis heaven. Behind the scenes, contingency plans were being made for a Tuesday finale to the competition, for the Sunday forecast was miserable and the most important pieces of equipment to bring to the stadium were a raincoat and an umbrella. The final, as usual, would start at 3 p.m. local time and every forecast we saw in the press room suggested rain from five. Could the French not have brought the final forward one hour, or even two?

Nadal started eagerly, breaking the first two twitchy Serbian service games and then appearing to relax, as if he was too easily in command. It was 3–3 but Djokovic double-faulted his next service game away, lost the set and was 2–0 down in the second. He recovered that position, but the first interruption for rain came and Djokovic was in the middle of a real wobble, a massive one, losing three consecutive service games by which time he was two sets and 2–0 adrift and was reduced to making a shrugging crucifixion gesture to his corner as if to say 'what can I do about this fellow?'

Djokovic came alive and suddenly discovered that he was able to perform blindingly brilliant clay court tennis. He won eight games in a row. Against Nadal. On clay! The Spaniard was visibly shaken, and rocking. Now it was two sets to one and Djokovic led 2–0 in the third. Nadal was all over the place, though he countered to bring the score to 2–1. Now it was spitting rain hard and onto court came Stefan Fransson, the referee, to confer (mostly with Nadal, who complained that the balls were heavy and wet). And we all knew what he wanted to do.

Before Djokovic had time to come to his senses, Nadal was off the court and before we had had time to collect ours, the entire Spanish contingent had left the grounds so that even if the weather had cleared – as it did within half an hour – there was no chance of a recall to finish it on the allotted day. At just gone 9 p.m. Djokovic looked up at the skies outside the apartment where he was staying and thought that he ought still to be out on the court. Nadal spent the night reading his favourite comic book *Sengoku* until he fell asleep.

Fransson and Gilbert Ysern, the tournament director, were summoned to talk to the press, who felt they had made a pig's ear of things. It was a meandering conference, in which the pair argued that TV was not in charge of the scheduling, that Roland Garros might have a roof in five years' time, that no one could be entirely sure what the weather would do, that they could have stayed around that evening but forecasters were telling them that there may be a break of half an hour and it would remain very cloudy, and a beauty from Fransson: 'When we stopped the match well, as you all know, Rafa I guess didn't really want to play on, and Novak said that the court was too slippery to play on.'

And so, the final would resume at 1 p.m. on Monday, the dire forecast permitting. It was the first time in forty years that the Open had found itself in this situation. Those who had tickets for Sunday were able to return the next day. As it was, a very decent crowd gathered for the resumption, under forbidding skies.

Djokovic knew he needed to stamp his authority from the outset but a touch of fortune favoured Nadal, who immediately broke serve thanks to a fortuitous net cord that set him up for a ripping winner. The force that had left him on Sunday evening had returned and Djokovic was retreating deeper and deeper against the Spanish tide that eventually broke over his defences, forcing the Serbian to serve a weak double fault on match point, a barely credible end to such a championship. Nadal had won his record seventh French title, 6–4, 6–3, 2–6, 7–5, eclipsing Björn Borg's six.

I had been present at all of Nadal's grand slam triumphs and I had never seen him as elated, or perhaps as relieved, as this. He leapt into the courtside box that contained a phalanx of family members, friends and entourage and was almost swallowed up by the throng. It was as though he was roaring to the gods. He grabbed the trophy with such force that he clouted himself over the left eye with one of its prongs and as he spoke on television, a bruise visibly welled. It was worth the pain, but how much there was in other areas of his body was the story.

'How long will I go on? It is impossible to predict the future,' he said. 'I will be here for as long as my injuries don't stop me playing and until I still have motivation and passion for what I am doing – hopefully for a long time.' Toni Nadal said there were only two paths for a tennis player, either you accepted that you have had enough, or you get ready to suffer and continue.

'The choice is between giving up and enduring.'

Rafa had endured this time, and my mind went back to our conversation three days before the event, in that Left Bank art gallery when I wondered if he saw tennis as art. He said that to him, it was all an amazing picture.

In football, you have time, in golf you have eighteen holes, that makes a difference. In tennis, you don't know when you are going to finish so for example like this year, the final of Australia, that was a crazy match, and to be a part of this confrontation I was seriously enjoying the moment, even if I am suffering mentally because I want to win. I feel very lucky to be here as part of this game.

Did Rafa consider himself to be artistic? 'At art, I was completely terrible at school,' he said.

> I really wouldn't know how to paint a house. With the music and with the art, I was a disaster. I was only ever 'sufficient and border-line' with music and the other things. The best was the physical, I was always good. The thing is that when I was in the school I didn't have a lot of time for school. I went every day but my timing was 9/12 school, 12/3 tennis; 3/5 school and then 5.30 to 7 football and 7/8.30 tennis for another time. I arrive to my home when I should be studying, completely destroyed. But I have the personal satisfaction that I finished the obligatory school and I'm very pleased to do that. The last obligatory year I suffered because it was more difficult, the year [2002] I won my first ATP match in Majorca against [Ramon] Delgado [of Paraguay]. I was supposed to come here to play the juniors but I had to finish the last three months of school, very important.

As of this day, at least, he had passed every test.

Chapter 8

Summer

OF ALL THE lilts and sways of the season, none disturbs the system more abruptly than the switch from clay to grass. The body and mind are used to the slow rhythms, the awesome rallies, the smacking of the soles of the players' feet to remove the gritty remnants. From red (with flashes of blue) to green; tennis returns home.

Its first port of call is the Queen's Club, an institution on the west London landscape for 125 years that, when constructed, was recognised as the world's first multi-purpose sports complex. The first contest of any note staged there was a rugby union match between Oxford and Cambridge in 1886 that finished in a draw. The original club had a cinder track for cycling, a running track, indoor and outdoor tennis courts, real tennis, Eton fives, rackets and a billiards room. Croquet, cricket, ice-skating, baseball (I couldn't fail to tell Andy Roddick that), and football had also been staged there. It was the home of the famous Corinthians FC until 1922.

In 1890, the first London tennis championships had been staged at Queen's, an event which, over the course of time, had become the AEGON Championships, the sponsor that arrived on the scene in 2008 as the LTA's lead partner and was now establishing itself as the name on everything connected with the British game. We may not have known exactly what they did but we knew they did it with a splash.

Away from Britain in Queen's week was its *bête noire*, the

Gerry Weber Open in Halle, Germany, where Rafael Nadal had, controversially, chosen to decamp, as much for financial reasons as anything to do with preference, as his text message the day after the French Open indicated. The British taxman and his sanctions on the global endorsement of performers in individual sports had everything to answer for. Roger Federer had gone to Halle for over a decade, to the extent that they named an avenue near the club after him. That was better than any guarantee.

In any other circumstances, Nadal would have been returning to London W14. I had received a text from him saying how sad he was not to be playing in London. He had been to the club every year bar one since 2005 – usually taking the lunchtime Eurostar from Paris and indulging in an early evening practice session – missing out only in 2009 when tendinitis problems forced the abandonment of his first Wimbledon defence.

'I like to play in all the tournaments where they really want me,' he told me.

It is good for tennis, there is a big change in Halle, they have wanted me to be there for the last few years but [in that time] I really wanted to play in Queen's. The truth is in the UK you have a big regime of tax, it's not about the prize money, it's not a problem of that. They [the Inland Revenue] take from the sponsors, from Babolat, Nike and from my watches [he had just signed a deal with Richard Mille to wear a watch worth a fortune in sponsorship money]. Really, this is something very difficult. I am playing in the UK and losing money. I did a lot for the last four years, but it is more and more difficult to play in the UK. It is too much.

Nadal was reminded that headlines were suggesting he was going to Germany for the sake of a guaranteed windfall simply to show his face. 'That's not the truth,' he said. 'The problem is easy to understand. I'm probably getting a bigger guarantee from Queen's but I am losing a lot more money from sponsors.'

Nobody would surely expect a sportsman to come to Britain

and accept that he was bound to lose money. Only by reaching the Queen's final could he be guaranteed to break even. Though no one wanted to say as much publicly, there were concerns that if this situation persisted, the current deal for the O2 in southeast London to host the Barclays ATP World Tour Finals, which was to expire in 2013, might come under threat. There were sensitive talks behind the scenes to obviate the demands of the taxman; indeed Nadal and others had been led to believe they may have reached a successful conclusion by the time the tournament started – but time was of the essence. He had to let the tournaments know as far in advance as possible where he was going to play and, much to the chagrin of those who so often packed Queen's to the rafters to catch a sight of him, it had to be Germany.

The tax rules had been in place since 1987 and were updated in 1999 'to the disadvantage of sportspeople' with two main effects on tax calculation – a) that 'image' was no longer taken into account and b) that it would be based purely on playing days (not training), whether in competition or exhibitions. The initial test case involved Andre Agassi, the 1992 Wimbledon champion, who discovered that any payments made in connection with activities carried out by a non-resident in the UK as a sportsman were subject to the deduction of UK income tax at source where the payments were made by foreign companies to a foreign company controlled by him.

Agassi played in tournaments in Britain for a limited number of days and using a foreign company, which he set up and controlled, he entered into sponsorship contracts with two non-resident manufacturers of sports and clothing equipment – Nike and Head – and received payments through his company, derived (at least in part) from playing in those tournaments. As a result of monies paid, HMRC (Her Majesty's Revenue and Customs) assessed him for £27,520 of extra tax in 1998/9. Agassi appealed, but lost in both the Special Commissioners' Court and the High Court. He appealed to the Court of Appeal and won, but HMRC appealed to the House of Lords and had the Agassi victory overturned.

To try to explain the complexities, each tennis management company was handed a spiralled pamphlet when they arrived in London that outlined the situation as it stood. It said that foreign sports players were taxed on prize money and appearance fees (usually through a withholding at source) wherever they competed, under local rules. In the UK, foreign sportspeople were taxed on all their income, which applied to all individual sports, and a player's 'income' included winnings, appearance fees, bonuses and a proportion of all their 'on-court' global sponsorship deals. The introduction of the 50 per cent tax rate in 2010 increased the impact of the new rules.

In his March 2012 Budget, Chancellor of the Exchequer George Osborne began to redress the imbalances. The government announced that they would change the apportionment method to include 'training days' in the calculation. The guidance suggested that up to three hours would constitute a training day and that all players should be advised to keep detailed records. Days spent recuperating after injury would count as a training day so long as it included three hours of physical activity. Most professional tennis players trained throughout the year so this could make a substantial difference to the UK tax liability. The change came into force immediately and applied to all open enquiries and future submissions.

It had poured with rain all the way home from Paris and on the last leg of my journey from Waterloo, I caught a glimpse of a spread in the *London Evening Standard*. The headline leapt from the pages STORM CLOUDS GATHER OVER QUEEN'S CLUB. The leading allegation was that the chairman of the club – one of the prime clubs of its kind in the world, where it cost £12,000 to purchase a compulsory share and fees were £1,775 per annum – had been involved in some bad deals, that he was not everyone's favourite and had done some things that not everyone liked, which did not make him exactly unique.

Toby Foxcroft, the 51-year-old 'charismatic businessman known for his easy manner and good looks', had been a board member for four years and it was suggested he was at the centre of a 'whispering campaign' by members loyal to the past regime who did not want him there. This was not the kind of entrée to the grass court season we wanted, especially as, on the face of it, the tournament had its weakest field for years and was having to rely on Andy Murray – who had signed a five year agreement to play – and a couple of old troopers in Roddick and Lleyton Hewitt to give it some gravitas. I asked Foxcroft if he would put the record straight after an article that did little to enhance his image but he declined, saying it was not the right time. He had duties to attend to in the presidential area, where the press had never been welcome.

I like Queen's Club for all its nooks and crannies, for its colourful and chequered history but mostly for the people who run the championship: Chris Kermode, the tournament director who has a terrific rapport with the players, the club staff, the writers, its press team who were the most accommodating folk, the groundstaff and the odd member or two who actually deign to notice that we are there.

I tweeted in the build-up to the event my surprise at the choices of wild cards – Lleyton Hewitt, the four-time champion (no surprise), James Ward, Jamie Baker, Oliver Golding and Liam Broady. Golding wanted to know if I was 'pleasantly surprised or horribly surprised'. My response was simply that I was 'surprised'. The tournament had had a habit of offering help to younger players but perhaps it had been a touch too indulgent with its aid to British players this time around. Kermode wanted to sign as many future stars as the LTA would allow him to sign on long-term contracts. Though several were playing in Halle this year, he had to move because the Germans had, by comparison it seemed, lots of money and were not afraid to throw it around.

Ivan Lendl, holding court in the players' lounge, said the wild cards should all be given to juniors, to see if they could stand up to the test. He did not agree with my contention that they should have earned the right. 'Just throw them in to see if they survive,' he said. 'That's the only way to learn about them.'

The tournament had always been a conundrum as far as British representation was concerned. Murray had signed to a long-term deal so it was not surprising the tournament director-ship felt a little like the cat that got the cream. I remembered a time when his former management group considered playing him in Halle that week and asked what I thought of the idea. I said it would be tantamount to suicide. Imagine anti-Murray sentiment rising should he have decided to play on a crappy grass court in Germany.

How would Murray, the champion at Queen's in 2010, contend with his first match on grass? He had drawn Nicolas Mahut, the Frenchman who had quite possibly spent more time on the surface than any other player in recent times, not least the eleven hours and five minutes over three days it took to separate him and John Isner in 2010 at Wimbledon in what became the world's longest match. Mahut had been the 2007 runner-up at Queen's, with match points that day against Roddick, so this was not a match for Murray to particularly relish. As it turned out, Mahut was just that little bit sharper in every context on a court that was more suited to his preference to move forward. It came down to a couple of tie-breaks, Murray playing the first one well, Mahut the second serenely to win 6–3, 6–7, 7–6. Murray's response to a question about how much it would affect his Wimbledon preparations was to be a lot drier than the weather. 'Oh, it's panic stations, I've got no chance to be ready for Wimbledon now. It's going to be impossible,' he said.

In days gone by, the loss of a home personality like Murray – the British wild cards had all gone too – might have sent the tournament directorship into a panic, but Kermode remained relaxed. Despite the awful weather of preceding weeks hinder-ing attempts to construct seating and advertising, and a line-up deprived of some of its usual members of the tennis firmament, he knew that the tournament would turn out a success because of its global reputation and renown. 'It [the tournament] sells out because the event is bigger than the players.'

> You would like the better players to get through but that is life and you expect stuff to happen. This is sport. If we all knew who was going to win it wouldn't be that interesting.

The presentation of the event was just that – 'The Event'. There were no player images on the tickets, because there was no guarantee that the player who might figure would show up. Instead, the sales pitch was that the ATP World Tour was coming to town, there would be a collection of the world's finest players, and Queen's was a place to be seen. It was very different from Wimbledon, it had its own specific sales points of intimacy, heritage, quality and, quite simply, a really good day out.

The player budget, though not officially revealed, had been trimmed from what it had been in years past. The LTA was not as generous as InBev (the previous owners of the event) had been so the cloth had to be cut accordingly. Kermode could not invite everyone he would have liked. Murray's five-year deal was a part of the overall pot, not an add-on. The loss of Nadal was a blow, of course, for he ticked all the boxes a tournament director would want from a star player: he was there, on time, he wanted to play, he was brilliant with the spectators, and he gave a performance every time, come what may, win or lose.

The 2012 quarter-finals did look a bit thin on real personality. Dimitrov would play South African Kevin Anderson, David Nalbandian of Argentina met Xavier Malisse of Belgium, Ivan Dodig of Croatia who had defeated Jo-Wilfried Tsonga in a third set tie-break was to face American Sam Querrey and Marin Čilić of Croatia would meet Yen-Hsun Lu of Taiwan. The pulses did not exactly race. The final was between Čilić and Nalbandian; decent in the circumstances.

After all the tribulations, it looked as if the tournament was going to get through on time. The crowd poured in, the weather looked set fair and if a British tennis writer wondered quite how much the office would be interested in the two protagonists, it was still a final on home soil a week before Wimbledon started so it had a resonance. Nalbandian had been decidedly relaxed all week. When Harrison Smith, a boy who was suffering from Duchenne Muscular Dystrophy, was invited into the players' lounge to meet the players [tears flowed when we heard his story and the fact he did not have many years to live], it was the Argentine who took him under his wing. Nalbandian's native polo team had been in town during the week and watched a number of his matches, which lifted the player's mood immensely.

I liked Nalbandian, though he had a reputation for being a difficult person to get to know well. In 2002, I had written extensively about him reaching his first Wimbledon final and he remembered that. He liked you to be straight with him, to stand your ground. I did. Čilić was a terrific young man, who had found trying to break from the shadow of Goran Ivanisevic and Ivan Ljubičić rather difficult but, under the tutelage of Bob Brett, the Australian, he was making strides. And they could both play on grass.

Nalbandian clinched the first set of quality grass-court tennis in a tie-break, but Čilić was offering stiffer resistance in the second and broke to lead 4–3 and you could sense the Argentine's frustrations mounting. He was trying to respond to a deep ground-stroke attack but missed long with a running forehand. His momentum carried him towards the baseline official and, obviously mad, he kicked at the wooden advertising surround which splintered and gashed the shin of Andrew McDougall, the linesman.

The abruptness and severity of the attack took McDougall by surprise. Initially stunned, he looked down at the blood coming through his trousers and leapt out of the box. Nalbandian, too, seemed staggered at what he had done. In the tribune, Roger Draper, the chief executive of the LTA, was sandwiched between John Bercow, Speaker of the House of Commons, and Alastair Campbell, communications director at 10 Downing Street when

Tony Blair was Prime Minister. Bercow barely said a word, which was unusual for him. Campbell could not see what had happened on court and retired to the president's room to encounter a sense of panic because no one could find the actual trophy at that moment.

Before he knew it, Kermode was at the side of the court. He can't remember quite how he got down, probably three steps at a time. Tom Barnes, the ATP supervisor, beat him to it, was looking down at McDougall's shin, had a quick word with Nalbandian and immediately informed Fergus Murphy, the umpire, that this was a disqualification. Murphy called: 'Default Mr Nalbandian. Game, set and match Čilić.'

The last time I had been present at a default was the infamous incident involving John McEnroe in the 1990 Australian Open when the American – playing Sweden's Mikael Pernfors on Rod Laver Arena – had forgotten that the ITF had introduced a 'three strikes and you're out' penalty process, though his final act, a crude remark to the supervisor Ken Farrar, would have merited an instant default anyway. The same was true of Nalbandian.

The ATP code states: 'Players shall not at any time physically abuse any official, opponent, spectator or other person within the precincts of the tournament site. For purposes of this rule, physical abuse is the unauthorized touching of an official, opponent, and spectator or other person.'

Barnes was the senior official on the tour, a former US marine who had seen active service between 1960 and 1964. He started playing tennis in his home town of Oxnard, California when his mother gave him a racket with a sawn-off handle. He played junior events in which, as soon as you lost, you had to umpire.

Barnes's official title was Senior Manager of Officiating Operations at the ATP. He had seen a lot in his years working through the ranks and I had asked him earlier in the year if much surprised him. 'I wouldn't say nothing would surprise me but I'm prepared for most things. I'd like to think that was the case.' When he approached Nalbandian on Centre Court, he knew exactly what to do, but he was one of the few on the grounds who did.

'We had had our usual crisis-management debriefs about all the things you could think of, fire, evacuation, terrorist alert, tube derailment and you knew how to set the wheels in motion, but this one took us all by surprise,' Kermode said.

> Of course, we think about what might happen if someone turns an ankle in a final, you go, 'I'm sorry, that is it just the way it can be', a bit like a first round knockout punch in a heavyweight title fight, you want a fifteen-round epic but it doesn't always happen that way.

The presentation party that had formed at the side of the court was now reluctant to walk on. Normally, they couldn't wait to be introduced. There was a serious lack of communication. An incident that was already viral on YouTube had remained oblivious to most of the people in the crowd. 'Why aren't they playing on?'

> You are conscious of what's going on, and all these people milling around and we have to have a presentation, we have a trophy, there has to be a trophy moment, do it quickly, get the photos. I said David needs to speak so I told him 'this is what you need to say' and it came out slightly different. I think it affected him big time, the whole thing escalated so out of control. One word could have been taken out of context. I was thinking player, crowd, sponsor, Queen's, LTA.

The perversity of the occasion was intensified when the on-court announcer asked the crowd to show their appreciation for Nalbandian. Mrs Malaprop, eat your heart out.

Having accepted Kermode's request to 'say a few words', Nalbandian said plenty more than he was expected to say. Indeed, rather than use the opportunity to apologise profusely, he turned the story into a rant about the ATP and its rules, which was completely lost on most people in the crowd. In the BBC Five Live commentary box, summariser David Felgate, a former ATP Board member, couldn't believe what he was hearing.

> Nalbandian has got it all wrong. It wasn't a sincere enough apology. To go off on some political rant had no bearing on what he did. I wonder if there could be a bigger fine for bringing the game into disrepute for that speech. He didn't even apologise to the touch judge or Marin Čilić. It was a poor show.

For the second time this year, a Nalbandian press conference promised to be unmissable; he did not let us down.

> In the beginning of the year you have to sign that you agree with everything that the ATP says, right? And sometimes you don't. And if you don't want to sign, you cannot play ATP tournaments. So you don't have a chance to ask, to tell, to change something, nothing. So if you don't sign, you don't play and you have to agree 100 per cent what the ATP says. Sometimes the ATP puts a lot of pressure on the players, and sometimes you get injured because you play on a dangerous surface and nothing happens. Keep rolling. Keep rolling all the time.
>
> There are a lot of rules and if I have to pay for what I did and it's like that, it's perfect, I agree. I do a mistake and I apologise, and I feel very sorry to the guy. I didn't want to do that. But sometimes you get angry. Sometimes you cannot control that moment that happens many times. Well, to me. Maybe you throw a racket or maybe you scream or maybe you do something like that. So many times it happens at that kind of moment.

Nalbandian had to forfeit his prize money and was fined for unsportsmanlike conduct a total of £44,500. He also lost his 150 ranking points but was not docked any more for the comments against his own organisation. The tournament was keen not to martyr him. 'He intended to kick the box, but he did not intend to hurt the guy,' Barnes said. 'When he realised what he had done, he felt really bad. And when he realised the consequences, he felt even worse.'

As for Marin Čilić, somewhere he was cradling an extremely big trophy and had to console himself with the fact that he was actually the champion, because no one was paying him the slightest bit of attention after Nalbandian's little performance.

Chapter 9

Wimbledon

THERE IS TENNIS and there is the All England Lawn Tennis and Croquet Club – or, more simply, Wimbledon. It is where tennis in its current form originated, is showcased to a gold standard, where great champions are glorified by virtue of winning the event which is watched by millions across the planet and yet precisely how it is run, by whom, who the members are and how they become members is something very few know a great deal about.

It was not until 2010 that anyone other than those who sat on the Membership Committee knew who their fellow members were. It had been Wimbledon's little trade secret, of which there were many. It was what made the place so intriguing.

The application process is open to all but it requires a club member to propose the applicant; a seconder is needed as are two 'supporters', all of whom need to be members. The very few who meet strict criteria can be granted immediate full membership privileges but most will become temporary members until such time as they are deemed worthy of the status of full membership. Temporary members are not allowed to wear the club's purple and green tie during the Championships and if they do, a reprimand is on the cards. The number of members at any one time cannot exceed 500.

One expects all these fortunate folk to be in their places at the Championships, for this is a national institution, a time to be seen in the best suit and the gold-embossed club badge that is the mark of the member. To be invited to join this institution is the dream of many and reality for the chosen few. It enjoys royal benediction: HRH the Duke of Kent is the honorary president and the majors and the minors in his family clamour for the front row seats during 'The Fortnight'.

The former Governor of the Bank of England, Sir Mervyn King, a member of the management committee, is in charge of the seating arrangements in the Royal Box and discharges his responsibilities in this role every bit as diligently as he did his task of keeping the British economy in check. It is the tennis correspondent's dream event, the one occasion in the year when you are top of everyone's 'need-to-know' list. The requests for tickets pile, and yet you have to explain that you can only accommodate six people.

Ian Ritchie, the former chief executive, describes the Championships as 'a few friends having a bit of a do'. To this 'bit of a do' is attached television contracts, ticket sales, sponsorship arrangements and unquantifiable amounts of goodwill that bring in countless millions of pounds of revenue, though no one but those who need to know, know exactly how much that revenue is.

We in the press ranks pull on our best suits and ties, sharpen our pencils and our act, make believe we are quite important, talk in chintzy tones and become a bit la-di-da. I remember my 1982 debut and Laurie Pignon, the venerable *Mail* correspondent, telling me in no uncertain terms that this is 'his fortnight'. In other words, you do what you are told and you do it dressed smartly, with panache, in *Daily Mail* style and never miss an edition.

Thirty years later – much to Pignon's posthumous disapproval I am sure – I could not be in more than one place at any one time, and so had to miss the Wimbledon qualifying competition. It is an event that has its own magic, the only one of its kind in the grand slams not played on the tournament site, but at the Bank of England Ground in Roehampton, where England had prepared for their successful World Cup football campaign in 1966. I retain this enduring image of England's captain Bobby Moore relaxing on the grassy knoll where those now desperate to be a part of the greatest tennis event in the world are sitting, fretting, anxiously awaiting their turn to play.

()

The week before the Championships is the maddest for a British writer. It does not pay to be in the wrong place at the wrong time but the chances are that something will happen of great importance miles from where you have chosen to disembark. I felt it important this year to spend a couple of days at the AEGON International in Eastbourne since the leading British women were playing. They had a decent chance of a bit of space in the paper and that did not happen too often.

Gavin Fletcher, the tournament director, had assembled an appealing field. Petra Kvitová, who would defend her Wimbledon title the following week, was No. 1 seed, topping a list that included world No. 3 Agnieszka Radwańska from Poland and Caroline Wozniacki which meant – optimism mounting – there was every chance of a reacquaintance with Rory McIlroy.

And there he was, sitting unobtrusively at a net post as Wozniacki hit with Thomas Johansson, the immensely likeable Swede who had won the Australian Open in 2002 and was the latest addition/game-changer to her coaching set-up. McIlroy happily acted as ball boy, lolling across the court to retrieve balls that landed in the net.

Once more, there hope sprung that an interview with Wozniacki and McIlroy might be possible, so I intercepted Rory before Caroline's match in the opening round against America's Christina McHale. 'Sure, no problem Neil we can do that, just let her know,' he said. A positive outcome would almost certainly require Caroline to win and so – with half an eye on Laura Robson's handsome victory over Spain's Maria Jose Martinez Sanchez – I watched the score tick over on Centre for an increasingly unsettling hour.

Wozniacki trailed 0–5, lost the first set 6–1, but fought back monumentally to win the second on a tie-break, only to falter again in the third. McHale won 6–1, 6–7, 6–4. There was my bloody interview gone up in smoke. The questions to her in the press room afterwards were the usual routine, most of them starting with the word 'why?' – I asked one that began that way, too – until 'last question' was called.

> Obviously, both yourself and your boyfriend have incredibly demanding schedules at the moment. I know he was here again today. Is there any difficulty for either of you seeing as much of each other as you're able to devote to your practice in terms of balancing your sort of personal and professional commitments?

Wozniacki stared the questioner down as much as she could stare any questioner down. Answer: 'No'.

I slipped out of the press tent to apprehend Caroline on her way back to the locker room to ask what my chances were of some time with her and Rory. 'Oh I'll speak to him and I'm sure it will be fine,' she said. 'Let's try and arrange it for tomorrow.' 'I'll be here,' I said. The next morning Wozniacki texted to say Rory was on his way to Ireland for a golf tournament and she had to leave for London because it was the WTA's pre-Wimbledon party the next night and she couldn't miss that. 'Sorry, we can't do it this time,' she said. I quietly cursed.

For the mainstream British writers, however, there was nowhere else to be at the close of this fretful week but the place where Andy Murray was going to wind down his Championship preparations. Over a decade, 'The Boodles', an exhibition event staged at Stoke Park in Buckinghamshire, had become to Wimbledon what Kooyong was to the Australian Open: an opportunity to flex and refresh, to have a couple of gentle knock-ups and get ready for the ultimate in the lawn game.

The event was organised and managed by Acegroup, which once represented Murray and was run by his former manager, Patricio Apey, on behalf of the bespoke jewellery company. The tidiest pieces in the Boodles shop on the site regularly went for five figures, which was a mere bagatelle to those landing their private jets at the nearby airfields and quaffing champagne until nightfall in between viewing a bit of tennis.

Apey had assembled a cast of players to keep his sponsors in clover, the Queen's Club finalists Marin Čilić and David Nalbandian (we ribbed the tournament director about making sure he had enough protective shin pads for his linesmen), Juan Martin del Potro, Alexandr Dolgopolov and, topping the bill, Novak Djokovic and Murray. After playing his first and only match in the event, Nalbandian slipped through a side door so as not to have to revisit his Queen's Club shenanigans.

Stoke Park was the location Murray and XIX Entertainment had agreed for his pre-Wimbledon interviews, the moment of the year when British tennis writers were at their most frazzled. The pressure on us to deliver something special about Murray led to rising stress levels and nobody wanted to let anyone else out of their sight. There were no international papers present, just 'The Brits' and our man. Trying to get Ivan Lendl to say a few words proved to be impossible, he said he was leaving it to Andy to speak for himself.

There is a time-honoured tradition that we decided between ourselves on what future day the Murray material would be printed and what, if anything, should be used on the day of the interview, or if all of his gems would be saved until later. To complicate matters – at this stage of the season voices are invariably raised and egos more pronounced – the daily writers (who agreed to use the output from their interviews on Monday morning, the first day of the Championships) were scheduled to interview Murray on Thursday, twenty-four hours *before* the Sunday boys who would be using their articles the day before us.

This was a risky strategy, but one we were prepared to countenance despite it causing a sleepless night or two. There was the added complication in that a certain number of my colleagues worked for both daily and Sunday newspapers and a notable few were 'Sundays only' – which remains a very British phenomenon our foreign counterparts cannot get their heads around.

The concern was that quotes might slip into pieces where they ought not to slip, that people would forget which interview went where. The ritual edginess of pre-Wimbledon week was seriously compounded on Murray interview day, though thankfully it did not descend into the shouting match of 2010 in a Surrey pub where we had gathered for a relaxed evening that ended with one writer accused of letting everyone else do the work and lapping up all the quotes himself. Heckles were raised and a perplexed Murray sensed the wine had hit the spot.

In the twenty-minute 'dailies' interview, Murray was open, engaging and forthright. I pressed him on his on-court manner and whether he thought it was counterproductive and he responded in profound terms. Yes, perhaps he had not done himself many favours but it was him being him, he answered. Goaded by the Sundays, he was asked repeatedly about lingering frailties in his back and in answer to the final question, he gave them the piece they had been striving to get out of him – saying those who doubted he was really suffering from back pain that had dogged him since December and been exacerbated in Paris should see the eight needle incisions in his back. This was manna from heaven.

We were all reconciled that these were tennis writers only forums. When we finally descended on the All England Club (Murray had done his bit at the Boodles, playing a couple of matches and giving the event the kind of coverage it craved), the terms changed. There are elements of Wimbledon coverage like no other grand slam in that it is regarded as much a social as a sporting occasion and therefore news reporters – largely present to report on who was there to see and be seen – are granted a level of access uncommon at the other grand slams. This can be a particular torment for the specialist sports writer, who tends to eye the news hound with suspicion. They, in turn, think we are snobby fans.

In the 1980s, the Wimbledon news reporters included such

famous Fleet Street legends as John Jackson, James Whitaker and Hugh Whittow, who were tagged 'The Rotters' because of their incessant interest in the love lives of John McEnroe, Jimmy Connors, Chris Evert and Martina Navratilova.

After his first round victory over Nikolay Davydenko, Murray made a gesture to the sky with both of his index fingers. It was something I had not seen before in hundreds of Murray matches and there was an edgy keenness to know what inspired him to do something so out of the ordinary. 'What is the gesture you did in celebration?' a newsman asked. 'Well, it's something for me and the guys that I work with. I don't really want to go into too much detail because I'll end up getting asked about it every single day.' Murray replied. Q: 'Nothing to do with pointing to heaven and God is it?' A: 'Whether it is or not, I'm not going to tell anyone.'

The draw presented Murray with a string of daunting prospects. If the seeds landed into their supposed spots he would play South African Kevin Anderson in the third round, either Čilić or Milos Raonic in the fourth, David Ferrer in the quarter-finals and Nadal in the semis. And all of this presumed he would navigate his second round meeting with Ivo Karlovic, the Croatian who stood 6ft 10in. in his stockings and served from another couple of feet higher than that. Playing Karlovic was a horrible prospect.

Murray proved up to the task, though the match took an awful lot out of him. Knowing that you may have one chance per set to break his serve meant that the mental pressure was immense and intense. I marvelled at the manner Murray contended with his opponent and a hushed crowd because the way Karlovic plays sucks so much of the atmosphere from a court. It was a victory not without controversy because the Croat, who suffered from a stammer that becomes a lot worse in interviews, wanted to make official representations after being called for what he said were eleven foot faults (I counted eight). He suggested it was part of some 'Murray Must Win' conspiracy. Wimbledon recoiled. Those sent out to watch the Croat play doubles the next day said that he was not foot-faulted once, which probably meant he was making doubly sure of the location of his size sixteens.

On the second day the last of the Australian men departed the event, the worst result for the country on English grass since 1938. 'Welcome to our world,' I texted Craig Gabriel, an Aussie colleague who liked to lay it on thick when the British were tumbling like ninepins. The loss of Bernard Tomic, the 2011 quarter-finalist, to David Goffin of Belgium in the first round was not unexpected given their recent form. Lleyton Hewitt, champion in 2002, was drawn against Jo-Wilfried Tsonga, a daunting and, as it turned out, excessive ask for a thirty-year-old with ankles and toes held together by plates and screws, and young Matt Ebden, notionally the next in line, was beaten by Benoit Paire of France.

Paul McNamee, the former tournament director of the Australian Open, was beaten in a 2011 run-off for the presidency for Tennis Australia by Stephen Healy – regarded as a safe pair of hands – and might have been expected to have an axe to grind. He had been a champion player and administrator for many years and was now coaching Su-Wei Hsieh of Chinese Taipei on the impulse of a friend who had suggested they might be good for each other. Hsieh's reputation and ranking was growing by the week, but McNamee's abiding affection was Australian tennis, something he knew inside-out.

'This day has been coming but it is the worst in living memory,' he said.

The odd player here and there has done themselves justice but they have camouflaged a deeper problem in that we haven't brought enough players through and we haven't had the right philosophy for a few years. On the boys' side, Aussie Rules Football has been very aggressive [in recruitment]. I don't believe we have the right coaching philosophy. Tennis Australia takes them [the young players] away from their own coaches and effectively imposes coaches and it becomes a merry-go-round. I've seen Ebden with three different coaches this year. We have to go back to when we were great. Charlie Hollis looked after Rod Laver; Ian Barclay was with Pat Cash. You need a mentor, one on one to bring them through the transition period.

This day of reckoning was coming.

Whether they like it or not – and they most assuredly do not – the success or otherwise of British tennis tends to be judged on its performance at The Championships. It is nonsense but that is the way it has been for years and the LTA's response is always so startled that they simply invite criticism, decent results or bad. What the performances of British players at Wimbledon (as in Davis Cup) unequivocally tell us is how they respond under the suffocating scrutiny they do not receive at any other time of the year. The British public can see what all the fuss is about, where the investment is going, whether the players are truly deserving of the plentiful funding they receive.

The first few days of Wimbledon historically tend to end in tears and recriminations, but this year the LTA thanked its lucky stars as no inquest was required. Heather Watson's name was on the first day order of play against Czech Iveta Benešová 'not before 5 p.m.' on an unspecified court. As the three matches on the Centre Court schedule were completed quickly, Watson was summoned to play and, with no time for nerves and an infusion of positive energy, the twenty-year-old produced a performance to savour.

'I kept getting the tingles,' she said of a 6–2, 6–1 victory – in which she earned twenty break points and succeeded with six – and if she forgot which way it was to walk off after the match, several of us were in an equally giddy state. No British woman had triumphed on this piece of soil in twenty-seven years. Jo Durie, now a coach and commentator, gladly gave up her record.

Oliver Golding lost his serve only twice against Igor Andreev, the Russian, but they were his first service game and his last, as he suffered a 1–6, 7–6, 7–6, 7–5 defeat; the red rims around his eyes when we spoke later indicated the emotional toll of the outcome. 'He's been God knows how many years on the tour and it's understandable he is going to play the bigger points well. I can be stronger but that will come with age,' Golding said. Laura Robson's first round opponent, the veteran Italian Francesca Schiavone, a grand slam champion in 2010, looked out of sorts in the opening set but used all her wiles and idiosyncrasies to disturb the youngster's rhythm and fought back to win in three. Robson would learn.

> It's a match I should have won. I had the opportunity to break her in the second set and I lost focus for five minutes. She was feeding off the adrenalin then. A disappointing loss for me but it gave me the kick I needed to work harder.

Watson's idyll lasted until the third round where she found the No. 3 seed Radwańska a step up too far, but she was improving, her manner was formidably upbeat and she would be back, stronger and more resilient. The only doubt I had was whether there were enough components in her game to hurt the bigger girls enough.

James Ward, who had been the first British wild card to win a round at Wimbledon in six years, when he defeated Pablo Andujar of Spain in the first round, then faced Mardy Fish, the No. 10 seed. Fish was still playing by sense rather than with total conviction after his heart scare in April. The American had undergone a cardiac catheter ablation in May and had not felt well enough to talk to the media after his first round victory. The second round was to be a fabulous affair on No. 1 Court, one in which Ward took his opponent to five sets, and was crushed in the last because of the ability of Fish to find the mark time and again with his serve. Fish told Ward to go out and enjoy his ovation from the crowd, but the Brit wanted to hear it in victory rather than in commiseration.

There was a roster of noted early casualties. Venus Williams, five times the singles champion, won only four games against

Russian Elena Vesnina in the opening round and sighed: 'I feel like a great player, I am a great player. There's no way I'm going to give up just because I have had a hard time these first five or six freaking tournaments back.'

David Nalbandian, the 2002 runner-up and notorious lines-man's leg-splitter, was out on his ear too, losing 6–4, 7–6, 6–2 to Janko Tipsarević, the No. 8 seed from Serbia. Reminded of his misdemeanour at Queen's he said 'it can happen to anybody'. Except that it had never happened before and it would probably not happen again. Tomáš Berdych, the 2010 runner-up, who had told me in Rome that he seriously fancied his chances on grass this year, was on his way home without a set, beaten 7–6, 7–6, 7–6 by Ernests Gulbis of Latvia, whom I regarded as among the most unfulfilled talents in the sport. I said that night that Gulbis would not win his second round match whoever he was playing. And, sadly, I was right.

$\mathcal{S}$

There were thirty-three players in the men's draw of 128 aged thirty or over and fifty-six topped the age of twenty-eight. Rafael Nadal was only twenty-six but on the fourth day of The Championships the former champion aged as he endured a bone-shaking result. Lukas Rosol, the world No. 100 from the Czech Republic, had lost in the first round of qualifying for each of the last five years but by dint of his workaholic nature and better results, he did not have to endure Roehampton this time around. He thundered at the ball, not very precisely, but here was a man who, on his day, might blow a few holes in the finest of defences. This was his day. The previous evening, he had partnered Mikhail Kukushkin of Kazakhstan to a five-set victory over the British pair of Colin Fleming and Ross Hutchins, who had led by two sets to love. Hutchins in particular was blown away by the sheer strength Rosol generated. 'I hadn't seen anything quite like it,' he said and by 10 p.m. the next day, we understood what he meant.

Victoria Azarenka savours her first grand slam title by planting a kiss on the Daphne Akhurst Trophy in Melbourne. Sam Sumyk, her coach, said that after a hesitant start against Maria Sharapova, Azarenka had seemed as if she was 'strolling through a shopping mall'.

Baring it all. Novak Djokovic shows how much it means to win a grand slam, after a tumultuous victory over Rafael Nadal in the Australian Open final gave him his fifth major. Djokovic had never been in better physical shape and didn't mind showing the world.

The clock on the wall. Djokovic is somehow able to crouch on his haunches as the courtside timepiece shows that he had played 5 hours and 53 minutes to defeat Nadal. It is 2.10 a.m. and the last media bus didn't leave until 4.15 a.m.

At full stretch. Rafael Nadal may have been banished to Court Suzanne Lenglen for his fourth round match against Juan Mónaco of Argentina but dropped only two games, able to sustain rallies like no one else in the game.

Très élégant. Maria Sharapova on her way to completing her personal grand slam, winning the French Open title at Roland Garros. No longer 'the cow on ice' as she once described herself on the surface.

You can just about pick out Rafael Nadal, buried by his family and friends after climbing into the stands on Court Philippe Chatrier to celebrate perhaps the most courageous of his seven victories in the French Open. His coach, Uncle Toni, is in there somewhere.

The bruise is forming under his left eye. Rafa strikes his usual championship-winning pose with his teeth in the trophy but he had struck himself in the face with one of the ornaments on the Coupe des Mousquetaires after raising it too quickly.

The damage is done. Blood trickles down the left leg of linesman Andrew McDougall and David Nalbandian (right) is about to get his marching orders from the men's final of the AEGON Championships at Queen's Club. An incredible finale.

A gesture that said it all. Andy Roddick bids farewell to the Centre Court crowd at Wimbledon. He did not say he knew it at the time but the look on his face suggested that he felt he would not come back. Roddick lost in three Wimbledon finals, all to Roger Federer.

A giant leap for womankind. Serena Williams is ecstatic as she becomes Wimbledon champion for the fifth time, defeating Agnieszka Radwańska of Poland 6–1, 5–7, 6–2 in what became a decent final after a one-sided start.

A kiss and a sigh. Roger Federer plants a smacker on the Wimbledon trophy while, behind him, Richard Lewis, the Wimbledon chief executive, prepares to usher an ashen-faced Andy Murray to the interview where he would break down in sobs.

The vivid Frenchman. Jo-Wilfried Tsonga in full flow is an incredible sight and even when he is flat on his front on court, there is a brilliant animation about him. Tsonga celebrates his astonishing 25–23 third-set victory over Milos Raonic of Canada.

Poetry in motion. Has there ever been a more classical stroke in men's tennis than the Federer forehand, seen here in full flow as the Swiss completes a three-set victory over Juan Martin del Potro of Argentina in the Olympic semi-final? A singles gold would elude him again.

Sisters, sisters, there were never such devoted sisters. The incredible Serena and Venus Williams combine to win the Olympic gold medal in the ladies' doubles. Individually, they are special; together, they are almost unbeatable. Beautiful harmony.

The medal and the flag. Andy Murray's career has been flecked with great deeds but none carried a greater sense of achievement than winning the Olympic gold medal on Centre Court, a month after his shattering loss to Roger Federer in the Wimbledon final.

LEFT Flat on his back. During the US Open, Andy Murray won some rallies from spectacular positions and here, against Tomáš Berdych of the Czech Republic in the semi-final, he finds himself in a ball on the ground. He recovered to win in four sets.

RIGHT 'This means everything to me.' The look on Serena Williams's face says it all after her victory over Victoria Azarenka (who served for the match) to secure the US Open at Flushing Meadows. This took her grand slam title tally to fifteen, a pretty remarkable achievement.

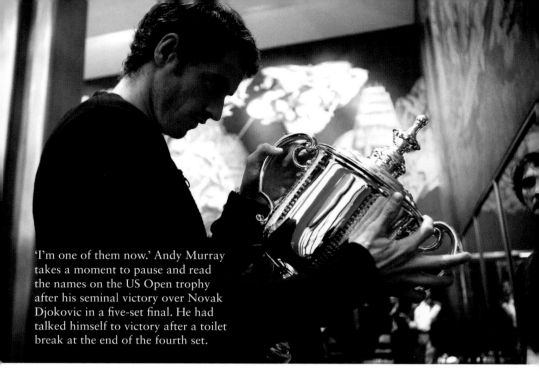

'I'm one of them now.' Andy Murray takes a moment to pause and read the names on the US Open trophy after his seminal victory over Novak Djokovic in a five-set final. He had talked himself to victory after a toilet break at the end of the fourth set.

'The Davis Cup is ours.' Tomáš Berdych, facing, and Radek Štěpánek, back to camera, celebrate success for the Czech Republic over Spain in Prague. The Davis Cup remains a vital part of the sport, but requires modernisation and change.

A very special day for the author. Neil Harman wins the Media Award at the BNP Paribas Open in Indian Wells, California in 2013 and is congratulated by Rafael Nadal, who took the title, his third in four tournaments since his comeback from seven months out with a knee injury.

Rosol was drawn to play the two-time champion and from the outset my Spanish counterparts – who, if possible, watched Nadal more keenly than I did Murray – were commenting on Rafa's lack of an ability to push away, especially off the left side, though he still won the first set in a tie break 11–9. But Rosol came out with thumping intent to take the next two sets. Nadal recovered his poise and won the fourth convincingly and was stunned when Andrew Jarrett, the referee, walked on to tell the players he was closing the roof.

In the locker room, his senses still in a whirl, Nadal raged at the decision and should have made more of the case that as it was only 8.47 when the two were marched off, the conditions remained playable and the printed protocol said that the roof 'will only be used if it is too dark to play on without it'. He had had it his way in Paris, and now the worm had turned. On No. 1 Court, there was twenty minutes more light left for Milos Raonic and Sam Querrey to play on, and that twenty minutes might have made all the difference for Nadal. Instead, it would be a final set shoot-out, except that only one player had brought his pistols. And Nadal's knees were beginning to hurt him badly.

The speed clock on Centre gave up the ghost as Rosol thumped winner upon winner past a groping opponent. A three-ace game completed the rout by a player who lost in the final round of qualifying at Eastbourne the previous week. 'In the fifth set, he played more than unbelievable,' Nadal said. 'I played an inspired opponent and I am out, it is not a tragedy. The decision to close the roof was not the best for me. All I can do is go home and rest which I need to do.' It would turn out to be one heck of a rest and he said later in the year that he was stupid to play in the first place, such was the aggravation of his knees.

The loss of Nadal left the draw somewhat top heavy but that section was not without its perils. Federer was two sets down in the third round to a very able Frenchman, Julien Benneteau, and Wimbledon did not, if it was true to itself, want to lose its six-time champion the day after a plane carrying a wounded Nadal touched down in Palma de Mallorca.

Federer had had these collywobbles in early rounds before and they usually inspired him to great deeds; it was almost as if he needed a kick in the shins to wake him up. Benneteau provided it in decent measure and it was only when the match went into a fifth set, after Federer had played a delicious fourth set tie-break, that the French resistance wilted. It was suggested, with more than an element of truth, that Federer had a lot to prove.

'My God it was brutal,' Federer said after his 4–6, 6–7, 6–2, 7–6, 6–1 success. It was desperately close in all but the closing moments were when the No. 32 seed's body and resolve collapsed. He twice received an on-court massage, needing every bit of help he could to stay upright.

'I was cramping on my quad, so it was tough for me to serve,' Benneteau said. In those cases, it ought to be tough luck. 'A little bit of luck on my side, who knows?' Federer said. 'I fought all the way. The fourth set was so close, Julien was playing amazing tennis. But when you are two sets to love down, you have to stay calm, especially as you can tell by the looks on their faces that your family and friends are freaking out a little.'

Tim Henman, a firm friend of Federer's, was further establishing himself as an integral part of the Championships, a member of the management committee, of the BBC commentary team and the person most reporters turned to for a 'how do you think Andy is going to do?' quote. In times gone by I would have been first in the queue seeking this insight, but we are not on good speaking terms.

During the summer of 2007 I heard from impeccable sources that Tim would announce his retirement during the US Open. The dilemma: should I contact Henman and tell him I had the information (he may well have said 'Yes, you're right but I don't want you to write it', which risked losing a potential scoop) or write the piece, knowing that it would be a bit special. I chose the latter, *The Times* used it on the front page and Tim was unforgiving.

This was a man whose career I had followed ball-by-ball since 1998, whom I had stoutly defended in print when many others condemned him, whom I had shared perhaps half a dozen cross words in nine years. He had never refused an interview or declined a telephone call. My retirement article changed it all. Even five years down the track, though we would shake hands and exchange pleasantries, conversation went no further.

It is easy for me to say he should be bigger than that. After all, so much that had been written about him was visceral and untrue and here was I, someone very much 'on his side', condemned because of a story that was absolutely correct. Paul Annacone, his coach at the time, took me to one side at Flushing Meadows the day my story was confirmed and said how hurt Tim – and he – had been because I didn't call to check it with him first. Annacone's contact with me became as frosty as Henman's. We say hello and that's it. It is, frankly, rather absurd. We're grown men, after all.

Did Henman's initial reaction surprise me? Maybe not. Does the fact that he won't talk to me six years afterwards? Well yes, it does. I had written critically – and probably inaccurately – about people in the past and grudges had been calmed. Sir Alex Ferguson greeted me when we met in London and New York as if nothing I had written about Manchester United in my football reporting days really mattered and there are many things he called me that I had to take on the chin. He had not forgotten but he had forgiven. We were friends.

There was no doubt Henman was building a formidable influence at Wimbledon. Some said he was future chairmanship material. I happen to think he would be a superb choice.

The forecast for the first week of the 2012 event was dreadful. It was likely that the Centre Court roof, its £100 million pride and joy, would be called into use more than it had been since it first trundled into action in 2009. Andre Agassi had been invited to the Club that year to perform in the mixed doubles invitational with his wife Steffi, Henman and the Belgian Kim

Clijsters to mark the unveiling of the new roof. Three years on, he was returning with his wife as the chairman's special guests and thoughts turned in conversation to the impact the roof had had.

'Change is hard, let's face it, especially here,' Agassi said.

Some things you don't want to change but some things are that good that they evolve. I think we are in that grey area with the roof. The spectators benefit by it, the game benefits by it, I think the players have to adjust to it. It's different. Any time you close the roof elements change, more humidity, it looks to me like the ball can get somewhat heavier but at the same time you can play more aggressively because there is nothing else to worry about but ball striking. The grass is so good these days that these guys can be so aggressive and count on these bounces. It looks like the points are shortened.

The key is to block out the stuff that might be distracting about it and embrace the way the dynamic changes. I always liked playing in a little bit of the elements. I could use it as an advantage. Too many elements was an equaliser and no elements became about who is playing better that day, so guys and the girls are really letting it go. Serena being the athlete she is and the strength she has in her game she is going to let the ball fly and the match is on her racket. It is hard to believe anyone can match her. She canes the ball and in full flight she is the standard out there for the women's game.

But this was a testing fortnight for Jarrett, in his seventh year as referee, and Richard Lewis, his first as Ritchie's replacement as chief executive. Lewis, a Davis Cup player for Britain, had then taken a leading role in the LTA men's department before the crushing defeat to Ecuador on No. 1 Court in 2001, after which Henman's call resulted in Lewis tendering his resignation. He had then been appointed chief executive of the Rugby Football League, where in ten years he instigated dramatic and consistently applauded change. When the headhunting group employed by the club to specify candidates to replace Ritchie came calling, Lewis simply could not say 'no'.

Within five days of informing the RFL board that he was leaving, Lewis was behind his desk in SW19. 'It was a whirlwind,' he said. Three days later at the Club's spring press conference, chairman Philip Brook was announcing the measures to respond to the recent drought, after which it hardly stopped raining. 'So I solved the drought problem,' Lewis said.

Throughout the first week of the Championships, various people were shuttling in and out of Lewis's office to discuss the prospect of a three-week gap between Roland Garros and Wimbledon, something that had been on the agenda ever since Brook and Henman underlined their plans to the four leading men in Indian Wells. In the past, conversation began and ended with the BBC and the preservation of its summer schedule, but since it no longer had a contract to cover the Scottish Open golf championship the week before the Open Championship itself and the rights to the Royal Ascot race meeting had been lost to Channel 4 from 2013, a window emerged and Wimbledon climbed through it. The case was put to various European clay court events that, should the voice of grass court reason be heard, they should seek to change surfaces. If they chose to remain on clay, their future would undoubtedly be bleaker than it had been for some time.

*

There were the usual startling incidents to keep the Championships' pot boiling. Rosol, conqueror of Nadal, did not win a set in his next round against Philipp Kohlschreiber of Germany; Yaroslava Shvedova achieved the first golden set in the Championships' history, not dropping a single point in the opening set to Sara Errani, who had played the French final just over two weeks earlier; a pigeon could not find its way out when the roof was closed during the match between Victoria Azarenka and Ana

Ivanovic, which had to be halted because the feathers the poor thing lost trying to find some fresh air were floating gently down on to the court; Rufus, the hawk that guarded Centre Court from unwelcome intruders, was stolen from the boot of its carer's car but returned a day later with an unexplained damaged talon; and there was the match between Agnieszka Radwańska and Maria Kirilenko of Russia of four rain delays that began on No. 1 Court but, because the programme sped by on Centre, was moved and the players were told that, with a resumption at 9.30 p.m., they had until eleven to get the job done. 'My God, you want us to play till eleven?' Radwańska said. Who complained that Wimbledon was not embracing night-time tennis? Around 500 fans stayed behind to see Radwańska finish the job in eighteen minutes.

And it was still raining, just enough to have everyone on edge. The ground-staff were definitely earning their corn. Players sat at the side of the courts draped in towels, players dashed for their courtesy cars, risked injury as they slipped and slid around on the Club's shiny brick walkways. The decision to replace the real grass on the players' lawn with an artificial surface was a masterstroke because by the end of the first week, it would have been a quagmire.

On the middle Saturday, as was the Championships' wont, we celebrated the Armed Forces who manned the courts and were the best stewards in the tennis world with a litany of stars from the world of sport in the best seats, including Jack Nicklaus, Sir Bobby Charlton and the soon-to retire England cricket captain, Andrew Strauss, with his heir apparent, the remarkable Alastair Cook.

There were more recognisable faces in the Royal Box than on the schedule. There were only three men's seeds left in the bottom half, Kohlschreiber, Fish and Tsonga, whereas there was still hope for the prospects of Goffin, Lukas Lacko, Brian Baker or Benoit Paire. It had begun to look like a particularly open Wimbledon.

Murray would play Marcos Baghdatis of Cyprus, entailing another reacquaintance, the second of the year after Brisbane, with his former coach Miles Maclagan. For over two years the pair had worked together, an assiduous relationship of trust and the knowledge that Maclagan would never say anything out of place.

Even now, though he was on the 'other' side, he did not want to offer much in the way of comment, though he did admit that,

> The questions keep coming about when is Andy going to win a slam and with Nadal out, I suppose a lot of people think he's going to cruise to the final which is just not the case, regardless of what happens when he plays Marcos. Rosol has shown that you can't beat these guys if you just go out and play a decent match, it has to be done in a style that can really topple them.

And we all knew that, if he was in the mood, 'Baggy' could do that. But Baggy didn't. Instead, Murray won in four sets and would play Marin Čilić, the Croatian having defeated Querrey in an astonishing match, 18–16 in the final set.

But it was how Murray won, the circumstances, the sheer riveting drama of another finish way past the kiddies' bedtime that kept us all locked in our seats. The day had been tough enough anyway, for Serena Williams, who only managed to hold off a spirited Jie Zheng of China 9–7 in the third, and then for Andy Roddick who, at the conclusion of his defeat to Ferrer, offered one of those gestures to the crowd which did not look much like 'see you guys next year'. Roddick had been through the wars and though his game was picking up, it was nowhere near where he wanted it to be. Pressed, he stopped short of saying what a lot of people were thinking but liked the position he had reached with the Wimbledon crowds.

> I walk around. I have a lot of conversations with people I've never met before throughout the day. It's almost as if I've been accepted

here. It's a different relationship maybe as opposed to some of
the guys who are the absolute superstars, I'm one of the guys that
they've seen on TV that they can say 'what's up?' to. It's a different
level than Roger or Rafa. Maybe it's more comfortable. I certainly
enjoy that.

All of this meant that Murray and Baghdatis did not walk out
until 7.12 p.m. and they would not disappear for another four
hours. Not only was it a race to the last sixteen but, as the brilliance of the match was extended, and the rallies grew impossibly
impressive, it became a race against the clock. The match was
running closer and closer to the 11 p.m. cut-off time at which
time it had been agreed with Merton Borough Council that play
would cease so as not to disturb the slumber patterns of local
residents. When Baghdatis won the third set it seemed as if there
was no way the match would be finished on time and would thus
have to be restarted on Monday morning – an inevitable and
unwelcome delay to the order of play.

What happened then was remarkable as the two combatants
began to play as if the match was in fast forward. Murray was
hardly sitting down at changeovers as he took control of the
fourth set, the umpire having told him they were getting close to
'downing tools'. Murray 'technically' started his motion to serve
for the match at 11 p.m. precisely. Richard Lewis, the chief executive, found himself in delicate situation.

The previous three or four games were very quick. What kind of
protocol do you have for that? Two minutes later it was over. On
nine of the thirteen days, the roof was used and there were argu-
ments and debates but what can you do with a radar that says there
is a 70 per cent chance of it raining and it doesn't rain and other days
when they guarantee it will be raining in twenty minutes, there's a
big blue blob approaching on the radar and it doesn't rain. It is the
referee's decision but the chief executive needs to be there to explain
and take the criticism when it comes. So that was pretty lively.

And we were constantly talking about the Olympic Games and the final details of the handover. One of the discussions about the roof being used so much during the Championships was how the court was standing up to it because it can only take a limited amount of wear. It really was getting marginal but Eddie [Seaward, the head groundsman] and Neil [Stubley, his deputy] were fantastic.

The second week was barely any better, weather wise, than the first. The second Monday of any grand slam (Wimbledon still eschewed playing on the middle Sunday; thank God for that) had long been the best of prospects, with sixteen singles matches to choose from, any of which might be a barnstormer. There was sadness at the departure of Kim Clijsters, not the first player to dream of winning Wimbledon and not make it but one we knew would not be back, having made clear that this was her final year on tour. 'When I first saw the event on television I thought it was how Disneyland would be to another child,' she said. 'I was able to go to the champions' dinner once because I won the doubles.'

Clijsters was beaten by Angelique Kerber of Germany as another German, Sabine Lisicki, put paid to the prospects of Maria Sharapova in straight sets, completing matters with a second service ace. 'She did a lot of things a lot better than me today,' Sharapova admitted.

There was the unusual, and troubling, sight of Roger Federer being escorted from Centre Court with a bad back. Never had Federer retired from a match, but the chill in the day could not have helped and had Xavier Malisse, the veteran Belgian, approached his chances with more conviction there could have been a real shock, but Federer regained his composure and played with untroubled movement in the fourth set.

On a day of perpetual cloud and drizzle, Murray had been moved to No. 1 Court to play Čilić, which may not have helped the home player but at least showed that Wimbledon were giving him no favours. Play ended at 7.55 p.m. with the British player leading by a set and a break, earning him a good night's sleep.

The front two rows of the Royal Box on Wednesday 4 July were about as 'wow' as could be. The Duke and Duchess of Cambridge were on the right hand side of chairman Brook, with Agassi and Graf on his left. Rod Laver was seated on the far right and behind him were Tony and Jane Henman, Tim's parents, and Roy Hodgson, the England football manager. It was men's quarter-finals day and though Federer was playing first against Mikhail Youzhny (a match the Swiss strolled), the match between Murray and Ferrer was occupying most minds, Agassi included. 'Andy is a reactor but he doesn't have to be,' Agassi said. 'He has options. He has a big game. His movement is world class and his ability to handle pace is remarkable. He has a sneaky first serve and when it gets hot, he can save himself a lot of drama on the court by using it.'

Agassi said he didn't have the luxury of a great defence and required tremendous conviction 'because I didn't have an alternative.' He believed Murray was hesitant on some of the bigger moments 'to play as he can'.

The tussles were becoming just as intense off the court. In the middle of the second week I received an invitation from Lagardère Unlimited's team of John Tobias, Sam Duvall, Stuart Duguid and Drew LeMesurier to join them for coffee at their rented home in the village. This was not something that happened to a journalist very often, but the group was refreshing, candid and straightforward. I liked the earnestness and vibrancy of their approach and if they perhaps seemed a bit boy-band-like to a fifty-plus writer, their desire to state their company's case, to stand up for their own talents, was to be admired. Essentially, the discussion covered one subject: Andy Murray.

They had presented to the Murrays in Miami, had heard nothing about any moves since and wondered what was on my radar. Which way did I think he was going to plunge? I offered as much insight as I could without trying to queer anyone's pitch. I did not say whether I thought Murray might leave XIX or not because I really didn't know. There were those who seemed to think it was a certainty he would go, others who said he would definitely stay. At the very least, Lagardère hoped that XIX might sub-contract some of Murray's tennis work their way as they did to CAA. This was one of their bargaining chips. I was impressed with their plans, what they wanted to do for Murray, the breadth of the work they had done on him.

By the time of the semi-finals, the lads from Lagardère were very excited. Not only was Murray still going great guns (inevitably they were torn between wanting him to win and presuming that if he did, XIX would be in a much stronger bargaining position) but the company represented both Radwańska and Azarenka in the women's championship.

They enthused that there would be no IMG client on either side of the draw at this stage of a grand slam for the first time in quite a number of years. 'I don't think we're exaggerating by suggesting that this represents a changing of the guard,' I was told.

Tiger [Woods], Roger, their entire football business [including clients such as Manchester City's Argentine striker Sergio Aguero] as well as their highest profile agents, Tony Godsick, Mark Steinberg and Jon Wagner [Luke Donald's agent, among others] have all left in the last twelve months. To add to their apparent woes, the rumours are that Rafa and his agent Carlos Costa's combined exit is imminent. At a higher level, all the signs point to their increased involvement and investment in US college sports [chiefly marketing and licensing rights], with a marked withdrawal and decline in representation. It is no secret that the company is being set up to be sold within a year.

Lagardère were itching to get on with trying to secure as many clients as possible but there was no doubt as to who was the one they really wanted. IMG were also in the market for Murray, that much was clear. They may have had 130 players on their books (and sixty-two people in their tennis division) but contrary to the

way other companies may have been trying to present their position, IMG had no desire to rest on their laurels and be content
with their lot. They wanted to remain, indeed to enhance, their
position as the most significant of any of the management groups.

The relationship for which they were most envied was
that with Wimbledon, for whom they had an overarching
responsibility that involved the million-pound sale of TV rights
and sponsorships. No one would ever prise them from that.
Wimbledon are IMG's most loyal, most special partner: unique,
evolved and rewarding.

But elsewhere IMG was losing clients and therefore face.
When Godsick decided to part with them in May 2012, Federer
followed suit. They were going to set up together but IMG were
not fazed, believing that they had made Federer and Godsick
incredibly generous offers for the size of the business involved.

Fernando Soler, head of IMG's tennis division, explained how
the company once lost Sampras and Hingis in a single day because
their agent left, yet survived and prospered.

> We feel honoured that we had the chance to represent Roger all
> these years, it is an amazing story for us. We believe we contrib-
> uted a little bit to his success and the same with Rafa Nadal and
> Maria Sharapova. There is no other company who could manage
> to obtain what we did for these players. Can we blame ourselves?
> Sometimes players have their own idea and their own vision for
> their lives. How many companies would have loved to have repre-
> sented Roger for the number of years we did? Are we going to
> complain? No. We move on. And, I stress, we are more committed
> to player representation than ever before.

But if IMG couldn't keep all their good people, who could? With
the prospect of a women's champion on their books, Lagardère
Unlimited were also keen on the latest developments in the game
concerning whether their female clients should be paid as much
as the males. What had been a simmering undercurrent about

drawing more money from the grand slam tournaments took on a different twist when Gilles Simon, the Frenchman and a recent recruit to the ATP player council, was asked to comment on the subject.

Simon was a soft-spoken advocate but what he said made a loud noise. He was married with a two-year-old son, but had decided he wanted to become a political figure, explaining that the ethical issue of equality was something close to his heart.

But it just doesn't work in entertainment, because entertainment is not about being a man or woman. It's just about, as I have said, the public coming to watch you or not. It's not about how hard you work. You can work hard and be a famous singer. You can work hard and just sing in your bathroom. That's the way it works. It's maybe sad, but this is the way it works.

But you media are doing exactly the same. You write. If I take the newspaper, I will see four pages on the men and one on the women, so that's what you are saying. That's what you said the last four years. You said that women have no No. 1, that men's tennis was amazing. I am pretty sure they [the rest of the men's field] are thinking the same way as me. Maybe they can't say it. Maybe they won't. Maybe they will lose, I don't know, $2 million on the contracts if they say that. I don't know everything. In the conversation – for sure I had it in the locker room – and for sure they agree with me. Trust me.

We have equal prize money because women's tennis was at the moment it was given, exactly the same interest as the men. Just after, unfortunately most of these women stopped. We have Roger, Rafa, Novak, and it was a huge difference. And it is not just me saying it. It's the public, too. It's just everybody.

Roddick, who never fought shy of an interesting quote, said: 'Let's not make this a gender issue. I don't know what the numbers are. I don't know what we're dealing with. I've gone about my business. I'm sure there's a way to figure out who people are coming to watch. I'm sure there are TV ratings to look at. I'm sure there are ample numbers out there to dissect.'

There was no doubt that these ample numbers were being dissected.

$$\textcircled{\text{\small ∫}}$$

The doubles competition did not tend to start forming on the writer's radar until late in the second week and sometimes not at all. When Jonny Marray and Freddie Nielsen had appeared in two minor tournaments in consecutive weeks in Nottingham in June, first as a pair and then with different partners, it barely registered in the local *Evening Post*.

A wild card for Wimbledon had come as a shock to a pair contemplating signing-in for qualifying. Nielsen was worried about making a fool of himself and Marray into the bargain. In British terms, more emphasis had been placed on the Davis Cup pair of Ross Hutchins and Colin Fleming, but they had gone down in the opening round to Kukushkin and Rosol in a crushing five-set reverse.

Marray and Nielsen defeated the Spanish No. 9 seeds Marcel Granollers and Marc Lopez in five sets, skipped through round two and then lost a two set lead to eight-seeded Aisam-ul-Haq Qureshi of Pakistan and Jean-Julien Rojer of the Netherlands before pulling that one out of the fire, 7–5 in the fifth (Nielsen recalled especially a short angled forehand winner of his that stunned Qureshi on a break point, which would have meant they trailed 5–3 in the decider).

Remarkably, in the quarter-final, they were two tie-break sets to the good against James Cerretani of the United States and Frenchman Edouard Roger-Vasselin who then won the third, also on a tie-break, and the fourth. Nielsen recalled: 'We were 1-2 down in the fifth, love-40 on Jonny's serve, Roger-Vasselin belts a return and I thought 'oh shit' and Jonny played the volley of the tournament and I could see the look of disbelief on Roger-Vasselin's face. That was the game-changer.'

The run of five setters was broken in the semi-finals but this was a four-set victory of enormous relevance against the Bryan twins, one of the finest teams of all time. Nielsen felt the difference in that match was how well he struck his forehand down the line, though he had been initially reluctant to go for it. Excitement was growing.

The same feeling was mounting at the sharp end of both singles tournaments, a lot of which centred on Serena Williams. The distracted, disconsolate player from Paris had been replaced by a vibrant zestful competitor in London. On the second Thursday, she smacked the No. 1 seed Victoria Azarenka in the semi-final (serving twenty-four aces, an entire set of tennis with a single shot) and just for good measure returned later in the afternoon to whip through a ladies' doubles with Venus, her sister. There would be a classic clash of styles in the women's singles final, for the first Pole to reach such a stage in a grand slam since 1939 arrived in the slighter shape of Agniezska Radwańska. 'I thought my serve was off,' Serena said. She had to be kidding.

The loss of Nadal from the men's singles led to speculation about who would fill his shoes. It proved to be Jo-Wilfried Tsonga, playing without a coach but with no small matter of pride and vivacity, who had taken his place in the last four to become one of those rarities, a really nice Frenchman a British crowd did not want to win. The first semi-final was played beneath the roof, with Federer and Djokovic reprising so many of their recent matches at this stage of a grand event; this time it was the grass court impresario who edged the battle 6–3, 3–6, 6–4, 6–3. There were rallies of 24, 25, 26 and 28 strokes, mammoth trials of patience and resolve which, for the most part, Federer edged.

The day before the semi-finals were played, I sat with Tsonga outside the broadcasting area for a ten-minute chat. He was wearing a denim top and trousers with holes where his kneecaps poked through – hardly Wimbledon attire! He said he was going to give Murray a real battle. Of course I wished him well and he thanked me the next day in a note for the positive piece I had written about him. In truth, he knew I hoped he would lose.

The decision was taken to part the roof for the second match, a contest that did not let us down. Playing Tsonga means an opponent is forced to play many unorthodox strokes; strokes that would normally come off the middle of the racket often fly wildly away from the target area; it means bending and stretching and groaning and striving to make the most of the chances when they arrive. Often, Tsonga seems as amazed by his own strength as his opponent and the crowd are. Murray looked sharp and agile from the very start.

It is never comfortable watching these matches, as brilliant as the player in your colours was. Even when things briefly fell apart for Murray in the third set, his volcanic personality barely rumbled: Murray won the match 6–3, 6–4, 3–6, 7–5. He said that the match had not been that tough physically, it was more a mental trial to become the first British player since Bunny Austin, who first trialled shorts on Centre Court a couple of aeons earlier, to reach the men's singles final.

Lagardère Unlimited had made it to a Wimbledon final, thanks to Agnieszka Radwańska, who would meet Serena Williams. For the first hour (twenty-five minutes of which were spent under cover) Stuart Duguid, Aggy's agent, was very uncomfortable. Serena led by a set and four games to two, she was in pulverising form and Radwańska – who was suffering from a head cold – was gasping for air. There had been too many one-sided women's major finals of late and one could hear the 'equal prize money' brigade forming at the gates.

Radwańska then decided to play, or Williams let her back in. The free flow floundered, Serena got tight and, in these circumstances, the Pole is a match for anyone. Radwańska won the second set and the crowd began to murmur. A rare glimpse of the sun greeted the start of the third set in which Radwańska saved break points in her first two service games and Williams produced another perfect game of four aces to hold for 2–2. Then, inevitably, came the break and Serena, swinging freely now, raced through the last four games, taking her ace tally for the Championship to 102 (more than any male player) and completing her fifth Wimbledon singles title with a succession of on-court bounds that would have done credit to Skippy the Bush Kangaroo. 'This win is super special, I have wanted this so badly,' she said.

If there were a few empty seats to greet the oncoming men's doubles finalists, by the end of the match there was none. Though Robert Lindstedt of Sweden and Romania's Horia Tecau were playing their third consecutive final, Centre Court largely had eyes only for their opponents, the jokers in the pack, Marray and Nielsen.

'It never crossed my mind that we might *win* the actual thing until we won the second set, Jonny hit a return and Tecau missed a simple volley and then I thought, here we go,' Nielsen said.

Then I got injured [he hurt his left wrist] and was mentally down because I couldn't play a proper backhand, but in the third set, in my first service game, we were 15–30 and I pulled out a backhand down-the-line winner. That pass gave me a lift and that was the moment.

When I *knew* we were going to win was when we won the game for 4–1 in the fifth. Jonny hit a good serve, Tecau hit a great return and I played a reflex volley which hit the tape and went over and all we had to do was put the ball in play from there. I had goose-bumps several times from that moment.

Marray recalls that at almost every changeover his partner would say how much he was loving the experience. The final shot, a crisp backhand volley at a delicate angle by the Dane was a glorious moment, greeted by an explosion of sound under the roof, Nielsen leapt into Marray's embrace and in the Royal Box there were tears (oh yes there were) as a story so daft and yet so uplifting was completed. Would there be another one tomorrow?

Between the wondrous sights of Serena's purple knickers and a Yorkshireman trying to a catch a Dane, it was time to see how Mr Murray was before his big day. Over the Aorangi Park, the practice courts, he was striking balls and Ivan Lendl was tetchy. The coach did not relish the suffocating presence of the cameras; the Sunday papers wanted something juicy for their previews and Lendl was revealing nothing. He conferred with Matt Gentry, Murray's PR man, and it was clear Lendl did not want his player constrained by a hundred cameras and notebooks. He did stop to comment on my attire (jacket and tie as always at Wimbledon). 'Obviously someone else dressed you this morning, you look almost human,' he said, Ivan being Ivan. Murray said he would sleep well that night, probably better than a few of us. 'It is not beneficial to think about winning it,' he said.

Sunday morning was drizzly, dark and foreboding. The roof was bound to play its part again. I joined Henman and Mark Petchey in the BBC studios at eight to talk to Garry Richardson on his award-winning *Sportsweek* programme. We were all upbeat. It was done by 9.30 a.m. and so there were hours to kill before the final. I don't think I'd ever drunk so much coffee in one morning. According to the official 'Slam Tracker' from IBM, the statistical gurus, Murray had to have a first service per cent of 68 or better and an aggressive ratio of 1.6. Federer had to win 26 per cent of first service return points and more than 57 per cent of points in rallies of nine strokes or more. I wish I hadn't known that.

Prime Minister David Cameron, who had flown a Saltire over No. 10, was front centre in the Royal Box, as was Boris Johnson and David and Victoria Beckham (though the latter looked totally uninterested). The men's final at Wimbledon did not lack for a certain star presence. Into this cauldron – the court uncovered – walked Murray, a pace or two behind Federer, challenger behind champion. Federer looked like a model, Murray was a touch sheepish in his wake but not at the outset, as Federer slashed at an overhead on break point and lost his first service game.

Although Murray lost that advantage in the fourth game, he was more than a match for the former champion and the final was already producing tennis of the highest order, stunning levels of thrust and riposte. In the ninth game Murray almost took Federer's head off with one pass [Lendl enjoyed that] and so shook up was the Swiss that during a chasing on break point, he netted. Murray served out the set with an ace and a service winner.

The second set was pivotal. Murray was in forceful mode and gave himself two opportunities to break in the fifth game, but Federer's own response was to come forward and it paid off. In the ninth game, Federer mis-hit the final shots in consecutive rallies from 30–15 and it was 30–40. Murray had a double-hander down the line, his staple, but snatched at it. Federer stormed back to win the second 7–5.

In time, as memories became fuzzy, many people would believe that Murray was well on top when the rain interrupted the final, but they were wrong. Federer was in the better fettle at 1–1 in the third. But now the roof was closed. In the corridors beneath Centre Court, where the rain was pouring through, I bumped into the man who paid my bills, Rupert Murdoch, the chairman of News Corporation, parent company of *The Times*. I met Mr Murdoch in his office in New York three years earlier, while talking tennis with Robert Thomson, the managing director of the *Wall Street Journal* and my first editor at *The Times*. Thomson said how much he felt I had engaged Mr Murdoch. I was pretty pleased with that.

Mr Murdoch and his wife Wendi had been treated to the finals tickets by Federer to whom, it was clear from our conversation, he was in thrall. He wondered whether coaches were allowed into the locker rooms during rain delays to talk to their players and what Lendl might be saying to Murray and, inevitably, who I felt would win. I answered as best I could, knowing how much he admired Federer and that it paid not to upset the boss too much.

The players returned after half an hour, the rain thudding

against the roof, almost deadening the sense of ball on racket string. In the sixth game of the third set, the deal was done. Murray led 40–0 with an eighth ace. In the rally at 40–30, he slipped over, and slid into the net, hurting his left arm. From that initial deuce, it took twenty minutes for Federer to finally break serve and, at the end of it, Lendl shuffled a little nervously in his seat.

At 5–4 on a second championship point, Murray's forehand whistled across court and landed an inch inside the tramlines and Federer was collapsing onto the grass, the champion for a seventh time.

The phrase 'runner-up' is not natural for a competitor like Murray. With a funereal atmosphere that showed in the compere's voice and the committee's faces, Murray had to address the world – and especially the 16.9 million watching at home on television in Britain.

It is the microphone under the nose that does it. Sue Barker, bless her, can do no more than say what a wonderful chap Andy is and how well he can play, the crowd applauds, there is much blowing out of cheeks, many misty eyes are wiped. 'I'm getting closer,' he said; more applause. He took the microphone and drew another huge breath. Poor bugger I thought. 'Take your time,' Barker said. 'Tough, isn't it?' Lewis whispered to Federer. 'I've been through it,' Federer says. 'It's very tough.'

'Right, I'm going to try this and it's not going to be easy,' Murray's voice went from baritone to countertenor in two seconds flat amid sustained raucous applause. Kim covered her face. Lendl remained stoic. 'I was getting asked the other day if this was my best chance, Roger is thirty now and he's not bad for a thirty-year-old. He played a great tournament and showed what fight he still has left in him.' Murray did not want to look at his corner for fear of welling up. He mentioned the crowd again – 'you guys' – and his voice trembled. 'It's not the people watching who make it tough, the support has been incredible so thank you.' For Federer, he said Andy would 'at least win one

grand slam' and that being a winner 'felt so familiar' and that the
trophy 'had never left me'.

In the players' box, Mirka Federer had brought the twins
Charlene and Myla in matching blue and white outfits to watch
the final stages and the presentation of the trophy. 'I turned
around and there they were,' Roger, who had become the world
No. 1 again, said.

> This is completely different because it is Wimbledon and this is
> where so many of my great victories happened and I felt very
> emotional seeing the family and sharing such an intimate moment
> with them in this craziness that was happening; [it] was unique
> and a legacy for them.
>
> With so much on the line not just for myself but Andy, it would
> either finish in tears for the guy who won or the guy who lost.
> You think you can handle this and 15,000 feel bad for you and
> the next thing you know it's awkward. That's the hard part. You
> would be happy just to stand there, hold the trophy, take pictures,
> sign autographs, but I'm a believer that it's good to get it out and
> I think he won over lots of people and hearts from fans for the
> emotion he showed in Australia and now again here.
>
> It does show that we are human. I know we put on the poker
> face when we play and we try hard and smash serves and balls
> and all of a sudden when everything is said and done we do care
> about losing, we do care about what the crowd thinks, our hearts
> are broken and I do feel bad about Andy in a lot of ways, but he
> has many years left and many opportunities will come if he has a
> good mental focus.

To the Champions' Dinner at the InterContinental Hotel where,
sadly, the press who used to sit with those members of the media
sub-committee with whom we worked so closely had now been
shoved into a corner, as if an afterthought. Neither Roger nor
Serena arrived until we were on the main course, they spoke
briefly and politely, they sat at the table next to chairman Brook,

the loyal toast was delivered, we chatted about this and that, and yet, somehow, there was one image I could not get out of my mind, that of the British player who, at this very moment, was finding sleep very hard to come by.

Chapter 10

Olympic Games

THREE DAYS AFTER the nation wept both for and with Andy Murray, they were laughing with him. That Murray was prepared to appear in the audience for *Mock the Week* spoke volumes for his fortitude. He knew he could expect some gentle and not so gentle ribbing.

Seated with Kim Sears, his girlfriend, he received a standing ovation from the lion's share of those in the cramped studio, attempted a little wave and looked appreciably self-conscious. Dara O'Briain, the presenter, fanned his own face as he admonished the assorted comedians present: 'When you're talking about the final, keep it light, keep it light.'

The comic Andy Parsons had no intention of complying. 'The three biggest tear jerkers in history are *Terms of Endearment*, *Philadelphia* and Andy Murray trying to congratulate Roger Federer without calling him a bastard,' he said. The cameras showed a blushing Murray unsure whether he should applaud or not.

$\int$

The Centre Court from which Murray had departed on Sunday evening with so many contrasting emotions flying through his head remained a hive of activity for it needed to be resurfaced as quickly and competently as time and technology would allow. The Olympic Games waited for no groundsman. And time waited for no chairman.

Though assured that Wimbledon remained the premier event in the sport, Philip Brook knew the grass court tennis season was brief and locked into a tight calendar, and was determined to change that. Brook had been canvassing long and hard for a third week on grass between Roland Garros and the Championships and this was the moment to announce it. Though he wanted to deliver the change for 2014, he had been persuaded that too many parts of the machine would need recalibrating and it might be better to wait a further year. Even Wimbledon, occasionally, had to be prepared to compromise.

This was, however, a momentous shift in the schedule and a reminder of grand slam might. Brook was well pleased but knew he could appear neither arrogant nor self-satisfied. What he had pushed through he had done because he believed it, correctly, to be right for tennis. 'When I became chairman one of the things Ian Ritchie [the former chief executive] and I worked on during our first year was to spend more time looking long term in relation to Wimbledon,' he said.

> Strategic discussions took place in our committee of management about the question of grass court tennis, where is it going, should we be doing more and how did the players view the proximity of Roland Garros to Wimbledon? Going to Indian Wells in March was the opportunity to say to the top four guys [the men only were consulted at that stage], 'this is something we're starting to think again about' and to get their reaction.
>
> Their view was the most important because if they really wanted it – and we believed Wimbledon had been pretty good over the years in being player focused – we should try to make it happen. This was a vitally important player issue. They all said they would love that [three weeks] to recover properly from the French and prepare for Wimbledon and it was that that really encouraged us and we started to take a long hard look at it and talk to a lot of stakeholders.
>
> With their support and that of the ATP Board [Justin Gimelstob

had become one of the most influential forces in the game and got on tremendously well with Brook] we were encouraged to see if we could get it done. There is concern in any calendar change, so we made long lists of people we should consult and that process went through the Championships. It became clear to us that there was a lot of support for doing it from the players, significant support from some areas of the tournament world and understandable concerns from some tournaments. We felt there was enough support, and it was vital for the renaissance of grass court tennis which is not appreciated yet but I think will be in time to come.

Brook had inspired a facelift the like of which tennis had not seen for years. He was right to do so, though it was bound to provoke an unpredictable upheaval. There were immediate indications that the clay tournaments at Gstaad in Switzerland and Stuttgart in Germany were considering the switch to grass for 2015. In a sense, they had to. There had, according to Wimbledon's chief executive Richard Lewis, been some 'bluff and bluster' about the move but it made absolute sense from every perspective, not least because grass is a surface on which almost every player feels at home these days.

As Brook spoke, the Club was shaping up for the Olympics, which brought a dramatic, positive change of mood and outlook – exactly what we hoped the nation would take from the Games' success. Critical to that was how the courts would stand up to the test; after all, they had been torn up and tattered for the best part of three weeks and were in need of repair. It was a task for which the club and its head groundsman-elect Neil Stubley, veteran of eighteen Championships, were uniquely qualified.

Centre Court was the 'worst case scenario court' because it was the last one that had been used and the first one Stubley and his team needed to renovate for the Olympic showpiece and, for the sake of its good name, the Club wanted it to look its best. Not only that, it had just been pounded for eighty-three hours during the Championships, the most in its 126-year history.

'When we explained what we were doing, there was a bit of a "wow" factor,' Stubley said.

We had been trialling for two years different ways of germinating the grass and how we could get it established. We decided to use a rye grass that would normally take seven to ten days to germinate. We got the seed, put it in a dustbin which we filled with hot water – as hot as your hand could bear – left it for two hours to soak, put in a rooting hormone compound, drained the water so the seed was sitting in the hot tub and then put it into an even hotter room for forty-eight hours where it fermented. By the time we took it out of the tub and planted that seed onto the baseline, it was already starting to grow rather than having to wait for seven to ten days. As the courts became available at the end of the Championships, we started our work.

The one thing that really concerned us was the air temperature. If it had been below ten degrees [C], we would struggle. The gods looked down on us because in the ideal world in our twenty day turnaround the first ten days you wanted it not too hot but nice and showery so the seed was not drying out and was drinking what it needed and after that ten days, once the grass turned slightly green it needed the sunlight to develop and hey presto, we had some thirty degree days.

Eight days before the Olympic opening ceremony, Rafael Nadal announced he would not be defending his gold medal, explaining that, though he had tried his utmost, his legs would not carry him through. He said he required 'infiltrations' in his knee, a surgical measure designed to reduce the extent of the patella tendinitis – the inflammation or irritation of the tendon that joins muscle to bone. 'Rafael has gone through bad times, serious injury, but I think this is the worst time of all', Toni, his uncle said. Spain had to choose somebody else to carry its flag at the Opening Ceremony. Their hopes of tennis gold had surely gone.

Roger Federer was thought likely to carry the Swiss flag for the

third time in succession but said he believed twice was enough
and that somebody else should have the privilege. It fell, quite
properly, to Stanislas Wawrinka, a sportsman often overlooked in
his own land because of another's brilliance. Stan was incredibly
proud of the honour. Novak Djokovic carried Serbia's emblem,
Maria Sharapova led in the Russian contingent. Tennis was the
'it' sport in flag-waving terms.

For Federer, the opportunity to play tennis at Wimbledon again
was something to cherish.

> I guess right after the Beijing Games I thought it was going to be
> so incredible to play the Olympics at Wimbledon and that's the
> way I feel now. It is difficult to achieve [the gold] because it is
> best of three sets in the early rounds. Ten weak minutes will be
> enough and everything can be over. I hope I can do so, so well and
> I want to make my country proud and enjoy myself and devour the
> unique experience of playing at the Club. This opportunity is quite
> something for our generation.

The complexity of the qualification for the Olympics meant there
was bound to be conflict and confrontation if not handled with
sensitivity but still, across the world, tennis players were particularly up in arms at the savagery and incompetence of the process
and the dimness of their national federations.

As for global fascination and television audience, India was
often undervalued, and yet here was a nation where the sport
was third behind cricket and field hockey in terms of awareness
and interest. Thousands play it. Mahesh Bhupathi, who had been
at the vanguard of the sport in the nation for two decades, had
built thirty-eight academies across the country, the main centre
in his home city of Bangalore. Because he was seen as something
of a pied piper where Indian tennis was concerned, he was at
constant loggerheads with the governing body AITA (All Indian
Tennis Association). And, as the Olympic Games neared, this
fractious relationship came to a head in mind-boggling fashion.

AITA wanted Leander Paes, who had represented India in five Olympic Games, to appear in a record-breaking sixth. This was a record of sustained excellence that could not be overlooked. Paes, thirty-nine, was a fascinating character, someone who had once walked away from a plane crash at the old Hong Kong airport. He had played the sport for many years, largely with a smile on his face, and had captured one singles and almost fifty doubles titles.

Bhupathi told me that when the pair re-formed after a decade apart at the start of 2011, it was with the Olympics in mind, perhaps a golden crescendo to their careers. They were, after all, the obvious choice to play doubles together. They didn't play a full schedule in 2011 and it was the morning after they had flown home together from the Shanghai Rolex Masters in October that Bhupathi said he received a disturbing phone call from fellow Indian, Rohan Bopanna.

Bhupathi's recollection of the events was both vivid and electrifying.

> Rohan was in Stockholm with Aisam [Ul-Haq Qureshi, the Pakistani player] and he asked 'did Leander speak to you?' and I said 'about what?' and he said that Leander had approached him to play doubles in 2012, saying he wanted a younger partner and he was willing to commit to Rohan to play the Olympics.

Bopanna had played doubles in 2011 with Qureshi (well enough to reach the finals of the Barclays ATP World Tour Finals as the 'Indo-Pak Express') but they decided to part at the end of that year. Bopanna wanted to partner Bhupathi in 2012. 'Rohan had a successful partnership with Aisam but the big dream was to play the Olympics; he used to train at my father's academy and we are good friends.' Bhupathi said.

Bopanna said he told Paes in their October phone conversation that it was important Bhupathi was made aware that they had spoken and, according to Bhupathi: 'Rohan was promised by Leander he would tell me as soon as we finished playing in Shanghai and I'm just calling to make sure he did.'

As far as Bhupathi was concerned, there had been no such conversation.

> I said that this was extremely bizarre. I told Rohan, 'You do what you have to do but do me a favour and don't tell Leander we have had this conversation because I want to hear it from him.' Three days later I met Leander and asked what his plan was for 2012 and he said 'let's plan on playing Queen's, Wimbledon and the Olympics.' I said 'sure, but what about the rest of the season?' and he said he wanted a younger partner and didn't feel we were beating top teams, which was ridiculous because we were 2–2 against the Bryans, 3–1 versus Mirnyi and Nestor and 3–0 versus Llodra and Zimonjic who were one, two and three in the world.

The argument rumbled on, straining relationships, dividing opinion and the nation's allegiances. Bhupathi felt he was paying an unfair price for a long-term dispute with AITA. He explained,

> I've run the world championships doubles in Bangalore for two years, run the ATP event in Bombay for two years, run six WTA events in Calcutta and Hyderabad. I've raised close to $20 million for tennis development, philanthropy for young kids and this is why they don't like me because every time I went to them and said come on bless it, they said no you've raised the money we will fund it and I said 'fuck that', you haven't delivered anything in tennis in India so far, I'm not letting you run this. My [academy] kids don't get wild cards into tournaments even if they are No. 1, to get into an ITF event they need to be nominated by the federation, and they never are.

And then Sania Mirza, India's foremost women player, was dragged into the debate. Mirza was playing mixed doubles with Bhupathi at the French Open but AITA clearly did not want this team to go forward to the Games.

The media in India is saying 'here is our gold medal chance', the mixed doubles is a sixteen-team draw and they have won the French and so he [Anil Khanna, secretary of AITA] is on the back foot. How does he get out of this? I cannot go to the Games only for mixed, I have to be there for the doubles to sign up for mixed, those are the rules.

Bhupathi discovered, through a series of well-placed contacts, that AITA was going to nominate Bopanna and Paes as the doubles team. 'My friends in there were trying to bat for me and told me I had to do something, like write to the sports minister,' Bhupathi said. 'I wrote to him seeking help and he said I had to play with Sania at any cost, so that means I will play doubles and he was going to make it happen. He told me to "play the game" while he did what he had to do.'

Bhupathi sent an e-mail to each member of the appropriate committee telling them that Leander and he (Bhupathi) had not had a dialogue for six months. He told them that when Paes walked past Bopanna, he looked the other way. He said that if the committee thought he and Paes could deliver a medal, they were living in cloud cuckoo land. 'It's not going to happen, we are not miracle workers,' Bhupathi said.

Leander says he doesn't want to play with Sania unless he has it in writing because otherwise he thinks as soon as I got there, I will sign in with her. But we have just won the French mixed, Sania will not give it in writing, so it is publicly announced [that Paes and Mirza will play the mixed]. It is hard to understand but that is the way it operates. Now Sania is bitter, she is upset with me because I didn't play with Leander and I say to her 'I would have considered playing with Leander and asked Rohan to back down if they had told me that you were guaranteed to play with me'. When I ask this question they [AITA] tell me it depends on my Wimbledon performance. I say: 'I have just won the damn French Open, why does it depend on Wimbledon? Why it is me who is constantly made to prove stuff?' I say if they [the federation] are not going to guarantee me a mixed spot with Sania which is a potential medal then I am sticking with Rohan by any means because his Olympic dream can't be shattered.

This was hardly the Olympic spirit the IOC would have wanted to portray. Bhupathi described the whole episode as inexplicable. He had told his parents in 2011 that he and Paes had been back on the same terms as they were at the start of their careers, that he thought it could all end in gold and yet 'the next thing I know he has gone to Rohan behind my back'.

All he had to do was sit me down and say 'Hesh, I would like to play with Rohan'. What am I going to do? Nothing. I have played a lot of tennis but I can never explain how I felt in the Olympics. I was so tight after all that. My wife was with me during Queen's there but I literally slept two or three hours a night because of dealing with ministers, committees, I was caught up in everything and with the time difference, it was an absolute nightmare and when I got to the Olympics believe it or not, Rohan played probably two of his best matches of the year but I couldn't put a ball in the court.

I will never compromise anything for my country, I knew Rohan and I had a legitimate shot if we played well, grass is a fast surface, we play well on fast courts but it all built up to a point where, on Twitter, I got abused by a lot of Indians who don't know the story, they called me a traitor. It was shocking.

As it happened, Bhupathi and Bopanna only won one round before losing in straight sets to the Frenchmen Julien Benneteau and Richard Gasquet while Paes and Vishnu Vardhan, the partner with whom he was eventually tagged, also failed to get beyond the second round where they were defeated by another French tandem, Michael Llodra and Jo-Wilfried Tsonga.

To compete in regular tour events, entry was dependent solely on ranking but the Olympic selection carried the extra burden of meeting the Davis and Fed Cup eligibility requirements and the whim of the national Olympic committees who might favour player x over player y and didn't have to explain themselves. Belgium, for instance, imposed a standard whereby players had to have reached at least the last sixteen of a grand slam, the last eight of an ATP Masters 1,000 or be ranked in the top twenty-four to come into consideration. Some players met all the ITF requirements, but their national committees would only send those they saw as reasonable medal hopes. Players could apply for 'exceptions' but could not be sure they would receive them.

One such was Serena Williams, who only succeeded in securing her eligibility by playing in two ties in World Group II of the Fed Cup in 2012, against Belarus in Worcester, Massachusetts in February (the week after the Australian Open) and then in April, against Ukraine in Kharkiv, which involved flights from Miami to Frankfurt, to Kiev and then the city where her astonished team mates were awaiting her. The stipulation that players had to have participated in (or made themselves available for) the Fed Cup in two separate years between Olympic Games necessitated this crazy travel pattern. 'I just couldn't play last year because of my health issues so I had to do this to make it to the Olympics at the last minute,' Serena said.

As compared to the bitterness seeping through the Indian camp, the British party was relative sweetness and light. Murray had received the Olympic flame on the steps of the club (Djokovic and Tomáš Berdych raced from their practice courts to watch the handing-over ceremony) and in turn strode up St Mary's Walk where he passed it to Venus Williams. He was beaming the entire time. It seemed from everything he said and every movement of his body that the fog of disappointment over Wimbledon had quickly cleared.

On 11 June, the cut-off date on which entry for the Olympic draw was determined, no British woman was in the top fifty-six but Elena Baltacha and Anne Keothavong were awarded ITF 'invitations' (it may have been no coincidence that both the current and a former LTA president were on the committee). As the days ticked down to the event, Watson was called up to take the place of Alona Bondarenko of Ukraine and, at the last minute, as she walked away from practice on a court next to Bill Gates, the billionaire owner of Microsoft, Robson discovered that she too would play singles, courtesy of the withdrawal of Croatia's Petra Martic. From no women involved in the singles, Britain suddenly had four raring to go on 28 July, the opening day of competition.

Team GB was: Murray in the singles and doubles with his brother Jamie, Laura Robson and Heather Watson would play singles and doubles, Baltacha and Keothavong would play singles, Colin Fleming and Ross Hutchins were an improving doubles team and a decision on a mixed pair would be left until the team had spoken among themselves. The team manager was Paul Hutchins, Ross's father and former Davis Cup player and captain.

There was a strong sense of renewal in the British game. For the first time in more than twenty-one years, there were four British women in the top 100 as Watson reached the second round in Stanford, California and rose to No. 71 to become British No. 1 for the first time. Robson had debuted in a WTA Tour semi-final on clay in Palermo, Sicily where, had she been a little steadier in the second set against Barbora Záhlavová Strýcová, she would have gone a step further. Keothavong was No. 2 in the domestic rankings at No. 76, Robson third at No. 91 and Baltacha was hanging on to a spot inside the top 100 at No. 100. On 12 March 1991, Jo Durie (No. 62), Sara Gomer (No. 89), Sarah Loosemore (No. 93) and Monique Javer (No. 100) completed the British representation in the WTA top 100.

Hutchins was a survivor from those days and, though he had undertaken many roles in the meantime, his Olympic responsibilities were vital, for there were as many hoops to jump through as were embroidered on the Games' flag. As he said: 'I can't have an influence on Andy Murray and the team winning gold medals but I can have an influence on them not winning.'

Hutchins had been in the same position for the Beijing Games four years earlier but did not attend in person and realised this had been a mistake. 'I don't think the preparation was right and the attitude wasn't right, either,' he confessed. This time, playing at home intensified the demands and the numbers with which he had to deal. 'I wasn't quite sure how it would work out but thankfully we had tremendous cooperation from the All England Club and we separated ourselves by working at Aorangi Park [the practice centre] and not over in the bubble in the main complex.'

The younger elements in the team obviously wanted to be a part of the Olympic experience, enjoying the association with their fellow competitors, collecting the pins, taking the souvenir pictures and generally pinching skin to make sure it was all real. But getting from Wimbledon, where they were housed, to the Olympic stadium in Stratford was a logistical nightmare, even if there was not a car on the road or the Olympic lanes were doing what they were designed to do.

Hutchins' challenge was that the side contained so many different personalities and family connections – he and Ross; Judy with Andy and Jamie – which could lead to conflict and there were other coaches, parents, the ITF, LOCOG (the London Organising Committee), the British Olympic Association and the All England Club. 'I couldn't take any credit if we won any medals but it could have easily imploded and the whole thing could have got a lot of people pretty fed up,' Hutchins said.

The Olympic Games, in tennis terms, had replaced one alphabet soup of organisations with another. It was the desire of these to be seen to be able to run their own show without cooperation from those in charge in any given, non-Olympic year. The number of shaking heads I would see emerging from various meetings suggested it was not working too well. Even Richard Lewis, the chief executive of the Club and Martin Guntrip, the secretary, were threatened with eviction from their offices during the Games as the Olympic 'family' took over before common sense prevailed and they were allowed to remain at their posts.

Hutchins is firm in his view that a lot of things could have been done better.

> I had a number of discussions with pretty senior people about what it could have been from an organisational point of view. Was the event supposed to be – grand slam status, Masters status, tour status, challenger status? And people say 'challenger?' Was it that bad? I know all about that category of tournaments. And I said well, you know…

He need add no more.

Comparisons between the Olympics and Wimbledon were inevitable, given the proximity of the two events. I lost count of the number of players who said they would never complain about Wimbledon again after their Olympic 'experience'. Hutchins believed that with a little more foresight, LOCOG and the ITF could have left more of the All England structure in place, but that with 26 sports to take care of, they wanted a common leadership strand to run through all the sports. Tennis could not be an exception.

There were only two bones of contention in the British camp. One was the decision not to go to the Opening Ceremony and the other that Murray and Robson should play mixed doubles together rather than Murray and Watson. Hutchins wanted to hear from all sides. It was clear that the common consent about attending the Opening Ceremony, though a once-in-a-lifetime experience, could well have a detrimental effect on professional preparation. They decided not to go.

The British press became agitated about the mixed doubles choice. Murray and Robson had twice played in the season-opening Hopman Cup in Perth, got on tremendously and seemed a natural fit. Watson, though, by virtue of her new status as the British No. 1 singles player, believed she should partner Murray.

To comply with IOC rules, each nation was required have to have a selection committee and Hutchins was the chairman, but he had a clause inserted that if any decision was required that affected his son Ross, he determined it to be a conflict of interest and would recuse himself. Ross Hutchins was in contention for a mixed spot and so his father – having determined from Andy that he would like to play in the competition – stepped aside from the selection process.

Watson and Robson were lower ranked in the doubles than Baltacha and Keothavong and the committee chose the younger pair – who were only eligible for the doubles originally – to represent GB (Baltacha and Keothavong were subsequently given an ITF invitation). There was also the explosive nature of the mixed doubles set-up; matches would be decided in two sets with a champions' tie-break to split them at a set apiece, so there was no time to waste getting to know a new partner.

Murray initially hesitated but came down on the side of Robson. 'Although it was not exclusively his decision, you go with what your No. 1 wants when it comes to a team,' Hutchins said. 'What was the point in me saying to Andy, you want to play with Laura but we want you to play with Anne Keothavong because she's the best volleyer and he is out there moping around on the court? That doesn't do anyone any good.' When she lost to Maria Kirilenko of Russia in the second round of the singles and was stopped in the mixed zone interview area for her views, Watson was clearly choked with emotion. 'I really thought I was going to play with Andy,' she said in the certainty that she would become a stronger person and player for the rejection. For Hutchins, attention was turning to how to draw the best from the No. 1 player without sticking his nose in too much.

I have got to know Andy better in the last three or four years partly because he is very friendly with Ross, he has come to the house, knows the family and he doesn't just see me as this guy who has been around for years. But the most important thing for me was to know his team very well which I did. I don't need to get involved with Andy, I don't need to inspire him before he goes out on court because he has people who do that. My job was to provide an environment he was going to relish. The group management principle is not fussing over Andy and not asking his opinion every minute of the day or how he's playing. The others were confident that I wasn't trying to interfere in their roles. I think we did a pretty good job.

The Spaniards, without Nadal in their ranks, had a strong team but their tolerance was tested as the coach picking them up from Heathrow on their arrival late one evening went the wrong way down the M4, turned around, got lost in the centre of London – 'we went around Piccadilly Circus three times,' according to press attaché Pedro Hernandez – and at one stage Alex Corretja, the team manager, tried to stop the bus and insist that the driver get out and let someone else take the wheel. They finally made it to the Olympic village at two in the morning, exhausted.

Visually, Wimbledon looked strange, the vivid purple backdrops took a lot of getting used to, orange was the predominant colour for the volunteers, security was a notch up from the Championships – there were army personnel everywhere but they made one feel confident and secure. There was barely a soul in the place as practice intensified. Wozniacki was hitting on Court 5 with Laura Robson. Freddie Nielsen was there as her hitting partner as Thomas Johansson, her coach, had struggled to get the proper credential. And who was sitting by the side of the court? Ah, Rory McIlroy.

He was as personable as ever. We chatted for half an hour, he posed for the occasional picture with awe-struck passers-by, the sun beat down on his pale frame, he rather took to my straw hat and we talked about the work on his modified swing plane I'd seen covered extensively during the Open championship the previous weekend. He said how sad he felt for Australian Adam Scott – Ana Ivanovic's boyfriend until they parted earlier in the year – who had blown an apparently unassailable lead in the final round at Royal Lytham & St Annes. Wozniacki, though going through her paces on the court, looked at Rory after every point.

The players' restaurant, to which access was allowed with a certain credential during the Championships, was closed off; staircases which were a journalist's right of way were blocked off to create the 'mixed zone' where players could be interviewed immediately after their matches and to which everyone was mandated to attend.

On the second day, *The Times* had published a fantastic double-page picture spread by Marc Aspland, the chief sports photographer, twin images of Federer at the Championships on one page and Federer at the Olympics on the other. I wanted to point it out to Tony Godsick, Federer's manager, who I knew was in the players' restaurant. Before the tournament began, entry to this area had been permissible but once it had started, access was denied.

I was bending the rules by seeking five minutes with Godsick. I had asked one of the press attachés whether they would mind, told them I was trying to get the Federer image signed for charity and that I'd be up and back in ten minutes and, with no one else in the vicinity, I made a dash for it. Two of the fifty or so tables were occupied. There was no one around.

I had been chatting to Godsick for five minutes when Clare Wood, the tennis event manager, and one of her acolytes approached, demanding to know how I had gained access to the restaurant and who had let me through. Amazed at their off-hand attitude, I said that I would not tell them. 'Yes you will,' Wood said. Godsick explained why we were talking but that did nothing to diminish Wood's anger.

As we walked away from Godsick and his young family who need not have been privy to her outburst, Wood remained insistent that I had no right to be where I was and 'who did I think I was?' At this, I stopped in my tracks and said I would tell her who had let me through as long as nothing would happen to the person, whose reputation I valued. I received Wood's assurance. All of this was a terrible overreaction and grossly out of keeping with the occasion and the surroundings. A quiet word would have done the trick quite nicely, but people were evidently extremely anxious about protocol during the Olympics.

I did not see Wood at all during the rest of the event but I did feel for her when Carl Maes, her ex-fiancé following an acrimonious split, decided to re-tweet me sniping at the organisation of the event.

As ever, the initial stage of the tournament is a mixed bag and you take your chance when picking a match. On Court No. 18, Bernard Tomic was playing Kei Nishikori of Japan. The surface was slippery and it was not a particularly nice day as I sat down next to Lleyton Hewitt. 'C'mon mate, c'mon Bernie,' the Australian corner tried to get to their man but his mind seemed elsewhere. He shot a few choice words at Todd Woodbridge, the Australian team chief, but could not translate this energy into a match-winning performance and Tomic eventually lost in two distracted tie-breaks. It was not good.

Hewitt bound Australian hopes while his own body was being held together. After Samantha Stosur lost in the opening round to the Spaniard Carla Suarez Navarro, a headline appeared in the Melbourne *Herald Sun* exclaiming AUSTRALIAN TENNIS IS A JOKE. Steve Wood, the CEO of Tennis Australia, had just issued his 'Wimbledon wrap' seeking to place a gloss on the results there which had been, to put it mildly, a bitter disappointment.

'As a proud tennis nation, there were a lot of Australians (you and I among them) who were disappointed with our results at Wimbledon and no one was more disappointed than the players themselves,' Wood wrote.

As John McEnroe himself said, the days of the grand slam nations dominating the sport are long gone. We are truly international. Just as Sam Stosur's wonderful victory in New York last year didn't mean that everything was now perfect in tennis in this country, the 2012 Wimbledon result does not mean everything is broken – far from it. There were four men in the main draw at Wimbledon and another five women. Tomic was the youngest in the men's draw [and is the only teenager in the top 100] and [Ashleigh] Barty the youngest player in the women's. It has taken some time to get the right people and facilities in place and begin helping these young athletes find their way in this incredibly competitive sport. But all of the work of many of you and of these players, their coaches, families and support teams is starting to bear fruit.

There was much controversy about the empty spaces around Centre Court, largely where ITF members who had been granted access to tickets had not bothered to show up. It was an embarrassment for the sport to see so many slabs of green and more so when the Royal Box was occupied by people who would not have got past the guard on the door had they been so slovenly dressed at the Championships. Even Ricci Bitti was seen using his mobile phone in the box during one match and I sent a cheeky text to Brook, the chairman, telling him that a chap two rows in front of him was breaking the rules. Brook waved from across the opposite side of the court that he had received the message.

Those forced to watch the television were frustrated at the lack of people in the crowd. It was later said that for the first round match between Novak Djokovic and Fabio Fognini of Italy, only 3 per cent of the tickets were made available to the general public with the rest going to the Olympic 'family' of VIPs, sponsors and media. What was more, only two of the tickets were sold at the low level price of £40, three at £55 and the rest in the higher price bands. So much for the inclusive Games.

As time went on, attendance and fervour did build. The Duke and Duchess of Cambridge were on No. 1 Court to watch Murray dismiss the challenge of Spain's Nicolas Almagro for the loss of five games to reach the semi-final against Djokovic.

In the opposite half of the draw, Federer had Centre Court problems once more with Alejandro Falla of Colombia, who should have beaten him in the opening round of the 2010 Championships, but the Swiss then settled into a decent pattern of play which, while not entirely commanding, was enough to earn a spot in the last four against Juan Martin del Potro, of Argentina. This match was to prove a classic of its kind.

The press benches, that had not always been full even for some of Murray's matches, were suddenly overflowing with Argentines sent from elsewhere to cover some tennis and, from the outset, del Potro was magnificent, with staggering depth to his ground-strokes; when he won the opening set, Federer knew that it could all disappear fast. In the ninth game, the Swiss led 40–0 but after a series of shanks was break point down, which he managed to rescue with one of his special forehands. In the tie-break, he allowed a 4–1 lead to slide but on a second set point, the first of which disappeared when he lost his footing on the now crumbling earth behind the baseline, he sent down an ace. Typical of the man.

The final set was a masterpiece, the flow never faltered. Federer, having broken to lead 10–9, promptly dropped his own serve with his muscles clearly tightening. The two traded mighty blows until the thirty-fifth game of the set when del Potro suddenly unravelled, making a couple of backhand errors to gift a break. Federer, on his second match point, secured a 3–6, 7–6, 19–17 victory in four hours and twenty-six minutes, the longest three-set match in the Open Era and half an hour longer than required to separate Tsonga and Milos Raonic of Canada in their second round match three days earlier which Tsonga won 25–23 in the final set. Del Potro, overcome with emotion, buried his head into Federer's shoulder at the net. The Swiss hardly knew where to look. There was still water in his eyes and huge sniffles when del Potro spoke to the press later. And he had a mixed doubles to come and had to prepare to play in the bronze medal match two days later. Federer had time to rest and watch Murray and Djokovic go about their business.

I could not recall the last time I had seen Murray take a game of such importance by the scruff of the neck and hold it there. On the balmiest of Friday evenings, in front of a delirious crowd whose chanting of 'GB, GB' made the hairs on the back of my neck stand on end, Murray was unrelentingly superb for two hours. Djokovic did not play a bad match either but there was something about Murray that was quite intoxicating. Having won the first set with a delicious forehand winner, he saved break points in his opening two service games of the second set, and another in the ninth with a prodigious serve.

Djokovic was laughing manically at his inability to break through and, of course, the minute he was in trouble on his own serve, he lost sets and then the match, Murray stepping in and thumping away glorious backhand returns to win 7–5, 7–5. He was assured of gold or silver, the Centre Court rocked and Murray wept, this time a different kind of tear. He collapsed into his chair and suddenly, like an uncoiled spring, leapt into the air. We met in the corridor behind the interview room. We had had a conversation before about tennis in the Olympic Games and he knew I was not entirely in favour, seeing it as more a move designed to enhance certain people's political cravings rather than as a necessity for a sport which had its own four magical elements. 'Well, Neil, do you still think tennis shouldn't be in the Olympics?' he said, a big cheesy grin covering his face. I asked him for time to think it over.

The next day Murray and Robson knew that, to reach the mixed doubles final, they would need to win two matches. The first, against Hewitt and Stosur of Australia, was bound to be rigorous with two grand slam champions against a team of grand desires. There were only a smattering of fans inside Centre Court. I was more or less the only occupant of the press box – a point made in a text from Matt Gentry, Murray's PR man, who was in the players' box at the other end. The expectation that Robson would be targeted was evident but it was Stosur, a former No. 1 doubles player, who was faltering and as much as Hewitt attempted to rouse her, the British pair triumphed 6–3, 3–6, 10–8 to secure an afternoon match against the Germans Christopher Kas and Sabine Lisicki.

Once more, Robson stood firm. The British pair rolled the first set as Kas struggled but the Germans fought back, taking the second on a tie-break so that, for the third match in succession, Murray and Robson would need to play a champions' tie-break decider. It was here again that their remarkable resolve was evident and they won 6–1, 6–7, 10–7 to reach the final where they would face the world No. 1 Victoria Azarenka and Max Mirnyi, a former world No. 1 doubles player, of Belarus.

'When you play singles, I'm sore in the same places. When you play doubles, it's a bit different,' Murray said. 'You're trying to be explosive at the net and there are quick points. Yeah, other things hurt a little bit more. But, I'll do everything right tonight to make sure I'm in best possible shape for tomorrow because it's a big day and I want to do well.'

In the women's singles, Serena Williams was scything through the field like a demented thresher, beating Vera Zvonareva of Russia, Wozniacki and Azarenka for the cumulative loss of seven games to reach the final against Maria Sharapova. Serena's mood was terrific and with good reason and she playfully pinched the bottom of Bulgaria's Grigor Dimitrov – a fellow student at the Mouratoglou Tennis Academy – as she tried to get past him in the mixed zone. I could think of a few photographers who would love to have captured that image.

The final was more like an exhibition. Williams defeated Sharapova 6–0, 6–1 in sixty-three minutes, completed with an ace and about as close to perfection as possible. She had been utterly dominant, especially with a serve that consistently thudded into the backstop. Serena was only the second woman behind Steffi Graf to complete the Golden Slam of all four grand slam titles and Olympic gold. Her coach Patrick Mouratoglou was astonished.

'I think she is the best of all time because the tennis level has raised a lot in the last twenty years but she is the woman who plays the best tennis for me that has ever been played,' he said.

Maybe in ten years someone will play better than her, like Federer has been the guy who played the best that had ever been played in the men's game. Serena is capable of everything. It is so motivating. I started twenty years ago and the ultimate goal for a coach is to work with the best players in the world and win the major titles. Even though I loved all the things I did and the players I worked with, with unbelievable joys, this is amazing. At Wimbledon, for me she played very badly and she won with her serve and her mental strength. Here at the Olympics she played incredible tennis, kilometres above everyone really, untouchable, a different game, killing everyone, it was impossible to play against her.

As the strains of 'Star Spangled Banner' played out across Centre Court, a huge gust of wind tore the American flag from its moorings. Serena insisted she had not blown it down.

Murray had watched Britain's Mo Farah win the 10,000 metres gold medal on Saturday evening, and marvelled that the man could run the final 400 metres in fifty-three seconds. He said that when he was completely fresh his personal best was fifty-seven seconds. 'It was incredible, incredible to watch,' he said. Murray went to bed as motivated as he had ever felt in his life. 'I just so much wanted to be a part of the gold medal story,' he said.

He woke to rain on Sunday morning. If the roof was to be closed for the men's final, so the sages said, he would lose to Federer. At just before 2 p.m., the clouds parted and the match started free of cover.

It was an unforgettable match. Murray started hesitantly, saving early break points, but it was when Federer dropped serve in the sixth game that the texture changed completely. The Fed folded. Indeed, Murray won nine games in succession to lead 6–2, 5–0 and even though we were in a best of five-set climax, there seemed no chance of that happening. Though the third set was closer, the full stop came with a blistering ace, Murray's second in succession, that drew chalk on its way to glory. He had won with incredible decisiveness: 6–2, 6–1, 6–4.

It was worth recalling that, four years earlier, when asked

whether Murray might be a major contender one day, Federer dismissed that notion because he believed the Briton waited too long for the opponent to make a mistake; he preferred the grind, stood too far back and that, over a fifteen-year career, you needed to make the point yourself rather than wait for your opponent to make a mistake. The lesson, Professor Federer, had been heeded.

I was told that my match report on the final had moved people to tears. Murray clambered into the box to embrace Kim, his mother and father, his backroom team, then leapt into the air as he returned to the court; even a hardened writer like me could not help but come over a bit sentimental. As Murray made to depart the box, eleven-year-old Henry Caplan from Essex had escaped his father's embrace and wanted one from Murray who, thinking it was one of the children of Tony Godsick, Federer's manager, duly obliged. 'Anything for my fans,' he said.

For the ceremony, Murray was preceded back on to court by del Potro who, amazingly so after his long semi-final duel, had beaten Djokovic in the bronze medal match, followed by Federer. The sun shone. The crowd roared, then stilled. God Save the Queen was played. Murray's knees buckled.

He was a new man, though response to his acclaim was, as ever, a sheepish wave. For too long, that had been the way he played his tennis, as if his talents were not quite good enough for the stages on which they demanded he be set. He had reached four grand slam finals and lost, they had called him a bottler, and if you are a shy guy, that could have an enormous effect on one's esteem. As much as others tried to build him up, it needed Murray to do it on his own. And now he had.

A little later that extraordinary day, Murray and Robson succumbed in the final of the mixed doubles to Azarenka and Mirnyi. They played stunningly at the start but faded and lost 2–6, 6–3, 10–8, unable to maintain their remarkable run in the deciding champions' tie-breaks. 'Initially I was disappointed we didn't win gold and I almost felt it was my fault because I hit two double faults in the final set tie-break,' Robson said. 'But standing on the podium in front of your whole family made it so special.' The next day, when she appeared on BBC television, Robson had to be persuaded to put her medal around her neck. 'I had worn it for the whole of the previous evening and the ribbon does start to get a little itchy so I had it in my pocket,' she said. 'I feel a bit self-conscious wearing it sometimes.'

My mind went back to the previous afternoon and Murray's bolt to the players' box when his heart was filled with nothing but utter joy. Having clambered back down to the grass, he leapt as would a World Cup-winning goal-scorer in what was truly a golden moment. As he tried to capture the defining image of his son's greatest sporting day, Will Murray's heart melted when he saw Andy's head tip forward. 'Who would have thought a skinny wee boy from Dunblane would win an Olympic gold medal?'

Chapter 11

US Open

SO MUCH THAT I loved about New York, at least the bits of New York I knew, had changed since I first reported from the city in 1986. Bill's Gay Nineties, the speakeasy-cum-sports bar in Midtown where I'd had my bachelor party in 1989, and that had often played host to dignitaries from the tennis world in the intervening years, had closed its doors on 25 March 2012.

Bill's piano – where I had sung my heart out many times – was stilled, the lights had been dimmed, its wonderful cast of owner Barbara, door-man Aldo (who told great tales of his 'friend' Rocky Marciano), Maureen, Gerard, Paul, Richie (the world's greatest barman/writer) and those great ivory-tinklers Elliot and Rick were seeking employment elsewhere. When I returned in August, it was a building site.

Barbara had lost her lease and there was to be no stay of execution. The *New York Times* visited on closing night and described the 'same egalitarian scrum that always patronised Bill's: neighbours, friends and regulars'. Barbara revealed in the paper that she had had a call from London saying, 'How can they let this happen?' Yes, I was emotional.

Not only was Bill's gone but Harglo's, the 2nd Avenue establishment the British press frequented in the eighties and nineties, was no more and neither was its erstwhile neighbour, Eamonn Doran's. The extraordinary Hunter no longer played piano at Mimi's on 2nd and 52nd and Doug Quinn, the bow-tied bartender who was the spirit of PJ Clarke's on 3rd and 55th, had departed his post in June.

What was an upstanding member of the fourth estate to do? For what had not changed were the working hours at the US Open, the very length and intensity of which required that, at the end of the day at whatever ungodly hour that was, you simply needed to wind down with a glass of something or the whole thing would do your head in.

For all of these years visiting the great metropolis the bar-room patter had been the same; once the locals found out who you were and what you did, they would offer messages of sympathy for a Brit who had come to watch the tennis and always ended up writing about someone else walking away with the trophy. If I could have bumped into any of my old pals from the past this year, I may well have said to them that, this time, I believed it would be different.

This is by far the most intense of the four grand slams for the British press. Newspaper edition times require that you are up with the lark, take an early bus – never later than nine – through the Manhattan throng into the Midtown tunnel to Queens for our daily quota of updates for print and web, Twitter conversations, match upon match, evening sessions that often drag into the early hours, and then the bus home knowing this would be the way of it for seventeen days straight.

The sense that this might be a US Open like no other formed on the first day I arrived in the city and noticed a story buried in a corner of the paper that an umpire had been arrested on suspicion of murdering her husband. Lois Ann Goodman appeared in criminal court (she was pictured in her Open umpire's tracksuit being led away by detectives) charged with having 'personally used a deadly and dangerous weapon(s), to wit a coffee cup'. Goodman, seventy, was chewing gum in the dock and asked that the judge spoke up because she was hard of hearing. Her husband was found at the foot of the stairs at their home in Woodland Hills, California and LAPD lieutenant David Storaker said 'there was an awful lot of blood. It just didn't match the fact he had just fallen down the stairs.' Goodman was bailed and flew back to the west coast to launch her defence.[†]

The USTA Billie Jean King National Tennis Centre, to give it its full mouthful of a title, was a grand slam site sorely in need of regeneration. And it was going to get it. There was an announcement of a 'strategic vision' – a series of interconnected construction projects, infrastructure upgrades and improvements to site circulation – which aimed to 'preserve its stature as a world-class venue'. The Mayor of New York City, Michael R. Bloomberg, spelled it out: 'The city recognises the crucial need to improve the USTA facility and supports this vision, so that the centre remains a top-ranked tennis venue capable of hosting the US Open, and thereby allowing the tournament to remain in New York City for many decades.'

The Open is New York's largest and most valued annual public sporting event, generating $756 million in 'economic impact'. Attendance regularly tops 700,000, which ranks it as the highest-attended annual sporting event in the world. In 2012, it reached 85 million TV viewers in the United States and was broadcast to 188 countries, with more than 41,000 hours of coverage. But the state of the site indicated that it had fallen on hard times. And the Open could not be seen to be falling too far behind its expansionist grand slam pals.

John Vegosen, the current president and chairman of the board of the USTA, and his executive director Gordon Smith initiated a *tête-à-tête* in the boardroom beneath Arthur Ashe Stadium to discuss the site's future. 'What we are striving to accomplish is to have an absolute first-class centre, the best in the world and we have some challenges,' Vegosen said.

---

† Prosecutors dropped the Lois Goodman murder case on 30 November, saying they had received additional information and were unable to proceed because of insufficient evidence. She was given permission by the USTA to resume as an umpire in 2013.

There is a financing challenge, because we are a mission-based organisation and we have to support the sections with their funding, we have a lot of grass roots and community efforts we support and in terms of our mission, we don't have the kind of Government funding that the other grand slams have, especially Tennis Australia, which has a lot from the state of Victoria.

Vegosen and Smith detailed the plans for the future of Ashe Stadium, with its 23,700 seats, 97 per cent of which were sold each year (a few thousand were unsold for the day sessions in the second week in 2012). The players may seem like ants from the top rows but people want to buy tickets there and that was their prerogative. 'Ashe will be here long past the time any of us are present at the Open', Smith said. 'It just needs a roof'.

The USTA deliberated about building a roof after four consecutive years in which the men's singles final had been moved back a day as wild weather struck the city. It looked to those outside that the USTA reacted to these incidents like a deer in the face of an onrushing truck. The sight of hundreds of ball kids with towels attached to the bottom of their feet scurrying around a stadium trying to wipe lines dry did not sit well with a multi-million-dollar event that trumpeted its own magnificence.

But there were many complex issues to consider. The size of the stadium for one thing – the area that required covering was five times bigger than the Wimbledon roof, the August weather varied enormously in the north-east of the United States and there was the underlying soil condition (the court had been constructed on a garbage dump) and it was not designed to carry any additional weight.

Smith said:

The real problem is that when this stadium was built, given the soil problems, it was not built to hold a roof and the technology to this date indicates the only way to have a roof was to build a building over the current building with new pylons to support the structure. We spent a lot of time and money with the world's best architects, mechanical engineers and structural engineers to see if that was feasible and reasonable. For the last ten years, we've undergone four separate studies dealing with firms who have built cutting edge stadiums around the world, moveable roof stadiums, no-roof stadiums, all sorts. We determined that a building over this building did not make sense.

The refinements to the Armstrong Stadium meant that it would be 'roof ready' once it had been newly-built but there would be one year intervening in which it would be unusable, so the USTA had to get around that sticky problem. So when would we see this roof on Ashe? Five years? Ten? 'I'm not going down that route. I can't give you a time,' Smith said. I wondered whether they may ever reach a point where the whole idea of building a roof would be discarded as economically unfeasible. 'We aren't going to reach that point,' he said.

Andy Murray chose to lose himself in the city. Not exactly go missing but become a part of it. To live it. He had arrived early from Cincinnati, where he had lost in the third round to the Frenchman Jeremy Chardy, which he dismissed as a bad day at the office. The rest of his team had gone their separate ways for a few days. He craved some solitude because, even in this most individual of sports, you needed those 'Dietrich moments'. He wanted to be alone. He walked in the park, he popped into the local grocery store (no bars), he contemplated where his game was and everything about where he went and what he did assured him that he had never been in a better place than this. He dared to dream.

After all, he had won the junior title here in 2004 and had always talked up the city. The place gave him a buzz he could not quite find anywhere else. There was something about the American way that appealed to him and the fact that he, a rather shy lad from Dunblane, could express himself more freely here was reassuring. He decided that he would change hotels this time and as a millionaire he could afford to live like one. He chose the Trump International, a 52-storey hotel with astonishing views across Central Park which boasted not only a three-Michelin-star-rated Jean Georges restaurant but a 55-foot indoor heated pool and a wide array of spa services, including Swedish massage and 'the Liquid Gold Body Wrap'. Well, why not?

He could not escape attention entirely though and a photographer spotted him outside the hotel and shot a question about Prince Harry and the Crown Jewels (the Prince had been in Las Vegas that week and was pictured swimming naked in a hotel pool). Murray evaded answering consummately in a manner that had been groomed over the years. We talked about how he had coped with the spotlight that landed on him at a young age and had intensified as the years passed. 'It slows down the process of growing up because you can't be yourself as you would like,' he said.

> When I had the problems in the beginning of my career it did change me for sure, especially in front of you guys [the press]. When I played Wimbledon for the first time you watch the video of my matches against George Bastl or Radek Štěpánek and I'm jumping around after every point, showing every emotion, 99 per cent of it positive. I was happy and when I was speaking to the press, it was fun and I was answering all the questions. But I changed when I started having 'the problems' [the conversation with Tim Henman when he was teased into saying 'anyone but England' when asked who he would be supporting at the 2006 World Cup].

Murray admitted to insecurity, that he felt increasingly lonely and vulnerable on court.

> You are being judged by everyone. 'Is he a brat, is he spoiled, does he have a bad attitude?' All sorts. That makes it even worse. It was very hard for me and it slowed down my maturing process. But

having come out the other end I believe I will be a lot more mature than I might have been at twenty-five, but for a period it definitely slowed me down. I wasn't really growing up.

These were increasingly emotive times. Murray knew that with the Olympic Gold, though it was tremendously reassuring in many ways, also heaped a little more pressure on him. And when you are trailed everywhere not just by the people you can see (us) but those you can't, it can especially get to someone with Murray's sensitivity. It would have crushed lesser people.

One by one, his friends and associates arrived; Kim Sears was in the city, which always cheered him up immensely. She stayed at the Trump, the rest of the gang were in the Radisson Lexington, the hotel where Murray had stayed before he was not quite so famous. I often took the bus ride out to the site with Dani Vallverdu, Jez Green and Andy Ireland – Team Murray. They would talk about lots of things but it was never Andy-specific. This had always been the way it was and I respected them for that. Ivan Lendl went home to Connecticut where he could be with his family and his golf clubs (he was often either off the tee at seven in the morning or had finished practice so he could be back for a 4 p.m. start).

There was a plaque on the walk of champions at the Unisphere entrance to the grounds that honoured Lendl's 'steely determination, ferocious ground-strokes and unparalleled conditioning' that had steered him towards eight consecutive Open finals from which he gleaned three titles. Lendl had never stayed in New York during his playing days, avoiding what he called 'the chaos'. He had a court laid in his back garden in Greenwich which was, to the last millimetre of cement, precisely the surface of the Louis Armstrong Stadium, the old centre court.

I [Lendl] would practise, go home, take a nap and then go golfing. If you are staying in the city, no matter how quickly you get in and out, you are in the middle of it. A reporter might have wanted to grab me, they will want to grab Andy, asking for this and that and before you know it, you have spent an extra hour here and that is a waste.

Could Murray crash the party? The *New York Times* used as the cover to its Open preview the iconic 1932 black-and-white image of construction workers seated on a girder dangling sixty-nine floors up as they took a lunch break from building the old RCA Building on Rockefeller Plaza, with tennis players transplanted in their place. Murray was second left, seated between Andy Roddick and Roger Federer, so *The Times* obviously considered him to be a legitimate contender. 'But these guys at the top have staked their territory, they aren't just going to let Andy in,' said Darren Cahill, the coach who had grown to know what made Murray tick as well as anyone. Murray felt good enough that he would share his observations with *The Times* in an occasional column during the tournament. Lendl would never have done that.

Meanwhile, Laura Robson bounded onto the practice court. For the first time, she was a direct entry into the main draw of a grand slam by virtue of her ranking and she had a new man at her side, the recently-appointed Croatian coach, Željko Krajan. This was a defining move, for Krajan had coached Dinara Safina, the Russian and younger sister of Marat Safin, to the world No. 1 ranking against many odds. That partnership faded and he tried to instil his beliefs into Dominika Cibulková of Slovakia and though she rose from No. 31 into the top twenty in their time together, she found him too intense, too demanding.

I approached Krajan for an interview and he was initially reluctant. 'Come and see me in a couple of days,' he said. I got the sense that he was anxious not to rock any boats before he had really started in his role. But, true to his word, in a couple of days, he invited me over. He said he saw no limits to Robson's potential, but needed to discover for himself how professional she was, and that he would 'require a lot of discipline' from her.

'It is important for me to know if she feels she lost her way a little bit because there are lots of expectations from people thinking she should be higher up the rankings.'

Krajan looked and sounded like a man to be reckoned with but that was the last we would hear of him at the Open; word came through after my article appeared that he would not be doing any more interviews. That was the way Robson had decided was the best way for the moment. Lendl did not want to do interviews either but a word here or there helped Murray's cause. So be it, we would have to speak to Laura alone, a privilege we had no idea how often we would enjoy in the coming days.

In the opening round, her opponent was Samantha Crawford, a tall American wild card, on a remote outside court where Robson had endured trials and tribulations in the past. Often the tennis was messy but the British player prevailed in straight sets. The next match was not so ordinary, for she would meet Kim Clijsters, the former world No. 1 from Belgium who had won this title three times and was nearing the end of her sunset year on the tour.

*

From Majorca came the message that Rafael Nadal was taking another two months away from the sport, which led to another round of dispiriting claims on the internet of a smokescreen for something a lot worse than protecting his knees, be it burnout, changing his game, or even, the dreaded word, 'doping'.

It was pointed out that, at the time of his announcement – he was suffering from Hoffa's Syndrome, where a fat pad becomes pinched between two bones in the knee – Nadal had competed in a 36-hole Balearic Islands amateur golf championship at the Canyamel course on his home island. He shot rounds of 81 and 85 and finished in thirteenth place. He had been told by his doctors that playing golf would not affect him in any way, yet knee injuries are the second most common injury a golfer can experience. I knew, though, that Rafa would never take stupid risks with his health. He was not the type and, anyway, Uncle Toni wouldn't hear of it.

The loss of Nadal to a grand slam field shifted the emphasis further towards Murray. Former champions Mats Wilander and Boris Becker had pegged him for victory. This was a further cross to bear and it did not look particularly like sound judgement when he stepped out on Arthur Ashe Stadium for his first match against Alex Bogomolov, Jr., who had chosen to play under the Russian banner, the home of his ancestors, rather than the United States, where he lived.

The tail end of a storm that had brushed Flushing Meadows knocked two hours from the schedule and interfered with Murray's routine, and though a 6–2, 6–4, 6–1 victory looked good on paper, he was not particularly satisfied (which was also good). 'I can't do it, this is crap,' he screamed. But he did, even if at times, it was. His second round performance against Ivan Dodig of Croatia in a night session on Arthur Ashe was altogether more the Murray we knew: high octane, high level, almost effortless in its brutality. After two rounds, he had not dropped a set.

As for Andy Roddick, as he counted down the days to the Open, the man who won the title nine years earlier was coming around to a decision he had been pondering for weeks. Roddick defeated Rhynne Williams, an American youngster whom Lendl regarded as such a good worker that he had invited him to Miami earlier in the year to practise with Murray, in straight sets but knew it was only a front.

At around 5.30 p.m. on 30 August we were told we should congregate in the main interview room at six for some news from Roddick. Initially, it was believed he was withdrawing from the event because his hamstring had been tweaked again, but when we walked in and the entire USTA hierarchy occupied half of the front row and the aisles were packed with agents, PR people and his family members, we figured this was more than an update on his well-being.

In Roddick bounced, cap in place as ever, folded his arms across the table and said:

I'll make this short and sweet. I've decided that this is going to be my last tournament. I just feel like it's time. When I was playing the first round I knew. I don't know that I'm healthy enough or committed enough to go another year. I've always wanted to, in a perfect world, finish at this event.

On some big moments this year, I think I've known, walking off at Wimbledon, I felt like I knew. I couldn't imagine myself being there in another year. Whatever my faults have been, I felt like I've never done anything halfway. This is probably the first time in my career that I can sit here and say I'm not sure that I can put everything into it physically and emotionally. I don't know that I want to disrespect the game by coasting home.

On Roddick went, in the manner we had come to expect from him, an honest, direct, shoot-from-the-hip conference in which he bared his soul in such a way that we onlookers felt good to have known him. It had always been that way with me. He once demanded I accompany him into the ATP office in Rome because he was incensed that his withdrawal from the doubles through injury would cost Mardy Fish, his partner, a share of the prize money Roddick thought was rightfully his. The ATP staff were completely taken aback that a journalist should enter such a sanctum but Roddick with a cause was a Roddick worth following. We had engaged many times in his career, largely about the state of the game, about tennis politics, about life in general. I would miss him.

His decision lent proceedings an unreal air. First, he played Bernard Tomic. An hour after Roddick's announcement I passed a growling John Tomic on the stairs. He was not impressed that a match involving his son that may have been played to a less rowdy afternoon audience was now scheduled late at night, with everyone rocking for the American. It was difficult to persuade him that it was unlikely to have been any other way.

Quite by chance, in the hour or so preceding the match, John and I were in the same queue for coffee. I didn't quite have the heart – or the courage – to tell him that I was there because I wanted a word with Rory McIlroy. As such, I was a little disconnected from the conversation with John, which was often hard to follow anyway, because McIlroy was across the lounge and I was trying to catch his eye. I still hoped our interview might happen.

My attention was suddenly taken by John thumping the top of the table so hard that my coffee spilled. He was adamant Bernard should be running in Central Park at seven in the morning but that his son was not up for it. He needed to bring in a new physical trainer. His son had to work, work, work. John was determined to make Bernard better all round and I could only admire him for his passion and commitment. I hoped that Bernard might offer as much that evening.

I managed a quick word with Rory as he left for a tournament in Boston the next day but there was no chance of the interview this week, an outcome compounded by the fact that Caroline, who was suffering with a knee complaint, won only four games against Irina Camelia-Begu of Romania and was out of the championship in the first round.

The Roddick–Tomic affair was largely one-way traffic: the American dropped seven games and Tomic squandered the third set to love. The dreaded word 'choke' was not far from anyone's consideration. He did not move as much as he should have done and whether or not the occasion overwhelmed him, as his father feared it might, we could only guess. The Australians christened him 'Tomic The Tank Engine'. On the same day, the thirty-year-old Lleyton Hewitt, his feet held together by pins, ran for four hours and thirty-five minutes to defeat Gilles Muller of Luxembourg 3–6, 7–6, 6–7, 7–5, 6–4. That was the attitude Tomic needed. In the commentary box, John McEnroe gave voice to what a lot of people courtside had been thinking, words reported to Tomic as he sat in the interview room.

Q: They made a pretty big deal of it on the television, tanking, all that stuff.

Tomic: Really? What do you think?

Q: I'm not sure, I think with your relaxed style sometimes people get the wrong impression.

Tomic: That's how I play. Do you have a problem with that?

Q: No, it was on TV. It was a big deal. Better to give you the opportunity now to talk about it surely.

Tomic: Yeah, no, that's your prediction. I have mine. That's how I play. If you think that's that, it's up to you. What is your name?

Q: Will.

Tomic: Will who?

Q: Will Swanton.

Tomic: From?

Q: Reuters.

Tomic: I'll remember you.

It was an unnecessary overreaction. Swanton had asked the questions quite properly only to receive a flea in his ear. I felt Bernard was being unjust, and had to do better. The next day I saw John and Bernard sitting at a table. John was doing most of the talking and a lot of it animatedly. I did not stop to find out what it was all about. This was family.

There were remarkable exchanges in interview rooms these days and nowhere did they happen more often than the US Open, where some writers (and many non-writers) appeared to hang out all day. Did these people ever watch any tennis? After her second round victory, Maria Sharapova was asked about her condition in Montreal just before the Open. She responded that she had blood tests and 'some ultrasound stuff' and that the doctors said she should rest. Before we knew it, the rumour spread like wildfire that Sharapova was pregnant and yet her engagement to Sasha Vujacic, the Serbian basketball player, had been broken off in the spring.

Max Eisenbud, Sharapova's agent, was inundated with emails and woken at 4.30 a.m. the following morning by the medical editor of ABC News asking if he would come on *Good Morning America* to discuss it. Maria thought it was all terribly funny; Eisenbud less so. 'Hey Harman,' he shouted across the grounds, 'tell those buddies of yours in the press room that Maria isn't pregnant, RIGHT!!' I said I would pass the message down the line.

Sharapova was saddened by the break-up with Vujacic. It was one of those things. He was playing basketball for a team in Turkey, she was travelling the world non-stop. It did not make for harmonious or practical relations. 'It was a challenging decision from both of our ends,' she said. 'He wasn't at home one time during the ten months he was in Turkey, so that made it extremely difficult but we have a tremendous amount of respect for each other. Still would love to call him as a friend.'

Heather Watson had lost in the first round of the tournament to China's Li Na saying, 'Everything I tried, the ball just kept coming back. I don't think she made a single mistake'. Anne Keothavong managed two games against the No. 6 seed Angelique Kerber of Germany but Johanna Konta, recently recruited to British ranks though Hungarian by birth and having lived a long time in Australia, had qualified in fine style and defeated Timea Babos of Hungary – a sweet coincidence – to reach the second round. There, she should really have beaten Olga Govortsova of Belraus, for she won the first set and was on the cusp of victory, leading 5–2 in the third, but it was here that she suddenly seemed to be reminded that there was some British blood in her and lost the last five games and the match.

Perhaps we should not be so cruel but this tended to be the way of things: a British player gets into a good position, gets nervous and falters. Had that happened to Robson against Clijsters on Arthur Ashe stadium, no one would have been terribly shocked.

No one could doubt what the tactics would be, for Clijsters owed everything to her tremendous power, astonishing athleticism and willpower. This was the day she would find someone who could match her in all respects.

Robson played astoundingly well on one of the great courts of the world, it was as if a butterfly had broken from its chrysalis. She flowered, she moved so well, struck the ball so sweetly and in two tie-breaks when the smart money would have been on the player with the greater experience, it was the teenager who flourished. I could not remember the last time I had seen a British girl play with such freedom of expression. She won 7–6, 7–6 and it was as if she had not expected anything less. The chorus of acclaim that swept Clijsters into her retirement from singles tennis was mixed with adulation for the discovery of a new talent. 'I have the next part of my life coming up,' Clijsters said. Robson felt very much the same way.

In the next round she faced Li Na, the queen of Chinese tennis, and this level of competition was good for her. Had Robson subsequently been playing someone of less repute, she might have relaxed, mentally more than anything; it had happened many times before to many players. Krajan pushed her to work harder in practice for, if anything, Li was more solid even than Clijsters and was now coached by Carlos Rodriguez, the dapper Argentine who had been Justine Henin's mentor during her career of seven grand slams. Now there's a player who could punch above her weight.

No British woman had defeated two grand slam champions consecutively at a major since the semi-finals of the 1968 US Open, where Virginia Wade beat Ann Jones (gosh those were the days) and then Billie Jean King, to win the title (gosh, those *really* were the days). The last day of August on Louis Armstrong Stadium was the place to be if you were British and in a 'gosh' mood. The match against Li was stupendous: five service breaks in the first set that culminated in Robson, her forehand pre-eminent, whittling away at Chinese confidence until Li faltered. The second set entered a tie-break in which Robson led 3–1 but Li responded with a crunching forehand winner, delivering another to bring the match back to all-square. Robson needed to steady and so she did, overcoming poor calls from the chair, showing Li that she would not buckle (instead the No. 9 seed did) and the left-hander swung away with increasing conviction to win 6–4, 6–7, 6–2. 'My game is based on being aggressive and if I'm not doing that I shan't do very well,' the winner said. She would need to remain aggressive, for her next opponent was the defending champion, Samantha Stosur of Australia.

There is something of the Brit about Stosur. When it comes to playing in her home grand slam, she seizes up; in New York, the shackles were cast aside. But she knew that Robson would pose a problem, that Laura's hitting would be unfettered and that she had to hold herself together, which was not always her strength. Stosur led by a set and 5–2 and our pens were dipped in ink, ready to suggest that Robson had finally hit the wall, but then she was back again, thumping through the ball, unnerving Stosur and rattling off a couple of games to make things very interesting. The match had the feeling of a siege about it; Stosur had eight match points but Robson saved them, and then came a ninth, but this time, the British forehand missed its spot.

In the space of six remarkable days, though, we had discovered that Robson was a real player. Youthful promise had given way to a maturity that, given her poise off the court, promised so much. Beneath the doe-eyed façade lies a serious competitor and it goes without saying that her performances in New York prompted Robson's stock to rise so quickly they must have felt the tremor on Wall Street.

> I went on court [against Clijsters] planning on enjoying myself because I'd had a tough first round against [Samantha] Crawford where for once I was a higher ranked player in a slam, so going to play a past champion was going to be a lot of fun for me.

Robson said she did not have time to get nervous because the match was so close and that she did not believe for a minute she would lose.

> You have to be clocked in, if you are match point and it's 6–5 in the tie-break, you're not going to go for a crazy shot, just one that gets you into the point and I ended up playing a good serve into her body. I hit the same serve on match point against Li Na. I watched the Clijsters match on the Tennis Channel in my room later that evening and I don't know who was commentating but basically up until the match point they were convinced I was going to lose. It's understandable really but at 5–2 down it was like 'yeah, she's done for' and then at 5–5, they still didn't think it would happen.
>
> Everyone has some crazy win at some point in their life. Usually I look at Željko and he's got his feet up and looks very relaxed. There's not much he can do. I don't rant these days. I used to a lot and it just makes you feel a bit better at the time. I've grown up enough now to realise it doesn't help.

There was not a day off from competition during the US Open but the second Monday is traditionally the third of the Labor Day weekend, when the roads are blissfully clear, Manhattan deserted, tools downed and as many who can get their hands on the gold-dust tickets make their way to the tennis. The order of play for Arthur Ashe Stadium was rock solid: a dash of Ana Ivanovic to get us underway, local tastes catered to with Fish playing Federer and Serena Williams against Andrea Hlaváčková, the Czech. The evening match was Murray (who had hardly been at his best to defeat Feliciano López of Spain in the third round) facing the Canadian, Milos Raonic.

Ivanovic tastily knocked out the Bulgarian Tsvetana Pironkova in straight sets and on walked Serena, looking exceedingly poised. Within an hour she was walking back off again as, for the first time in her sixty-two matches at the Open, she won without dropping a game. Hlaváčková, a lovely girl whose boyfriend is Fabrizio Sestini, an ATP Tour manager, was reeling from the outset. 'The first point of the whole match, I served and she returned a 100mph forehand. That was like: "OK, I know who I am playing. You don't have to prove it to me." But she obviously wanted to prove it to me.'

It was easy to become distracted during the match and the more so when we learned that Fish would not be taking the court against Federer. The man who had required heart surgery in the spring and had been in rugged good spirits suddenly panicked. He did not feel well in the car going to the stadium and, when he arrived, it was clear he couldn't compete. The medical team spoke to him, so did the officials, so did his coach, Mark Knowles, and his agent John Tobias. It was agreed that Mardy should not put himself through the match. A walkover was announced.

At the conclusion of Serena's match, I tweeted: 'GSM Serena 6–0, 6–0. There's a second walkover today'. It was re-tweeted by the Serbian Janko Tipsarević about a minute later with the hashtag '#equalprizemoney' on the end. My Twitter feed went viral, as did his. I was angry and he was getting it in the neck from every side. He could count to ten before he did anything like that again, as robust as his feelings were on the subject. Meanwhile, on Arthur Ashe Stadium, Croatia's Marin Čilić and Martin Klizan of Slovakia were trying to get a New York crowd excited. They did their best.

The night session was not the longest either. And that was because Murray came to play. Raonic was staying in the same hotel as me, the lovely Elysee on East 54th St, with his coaching and management team. He had just been signed by Creative Artists Agency as a response to the likelihood they were going to lose Novak Djokovic to IMG. Raonic was seen as the next best thing, something that his manager Amit Naor constantly told me as I returned to the hotel in the evenings, usually finding him on the opposite side of the street on the steps that once led to Bill's bar enjoying a cigarette. Such was the confidence in Raonic that Austin Nunn had been lured from the ATP as his personal PR.

Murray knew all of this of course and there was something about him that night that made me really believe this was his time. He annihilated the Canadian. I was seated in the must-have press seats on Arthur Ashe, the front row behind the umpire's chair reserved for those in the press who had a representative on the court. Tom Tebbutt from Canada kept us company but he could not get comfortable. Neither could his man.

Seated next to me, Brad Gilbert was summarising for ESPN. What an education! Midway through the first set he was telling me how many aces Murray had served, what his percentages were, his accumulation of passing winners and yet, though he was right on every count, he did not have a notebook and I did. 'It is all here,' he said, showing me the upturned palm of his left hand on which nothing was written. I was interviewed at one of the changes of end and made some silly remark about the perception of Murray at home 'having altered 360 degrees'. My old maths master Jim Harrison would have quivered at that error and suffice to say, almost everyone back in the press centre picked it up. I was duly chastened.

The perception of Murray that evening was of a man at ease with himself and his surroundings. He won 6–4, 6–4, 6–2, simply running Raonic ragged. Later that evening, I encountered Raonic in the lobby of the hotel. What was there to say? Hard luck didn't really cover it.

Two days later on Armstrong, a court that brought out all the negative impulses in him, Murray was having an absolute shocker against Čilić, losing the first set 6–3, beginning the second with successive double faults, missing everything by yards, trailing 5–1 and facing a set point in the next game. Here, Murray played a backhand volley cross-court that was pure instinct. Čilić missed a backhand to go break point down and Murray clipped a forehand winner and was back at 5–3. Now Čilić was nervy and, on a fourth break point in the tenth game, served a double fault. It was 5–5. Čilić led 4–2 at the first change of ends in the tie-break but Murray reeled off a succession of winners and the match was level at a set apiece. He only lost two more games. After the match he was a bit jumpy – perhaps it was the effects of the ice-bath and nothing more than that. 'I will simply have to do a better job in the next round,' he said, adding that his dialogue after the match with Lendl was fairly brief. I bet it was.

Most anticipated that Federer would be Murray's semi-final opponent. But one wondered if four days of rest courtesy of the Fish withdrawal might affect his match fluency, though the Swiss had experienced breaks in tournaments before and this had not been a problem. But then Tomáš Berdych stepped in. I managed to finagle a seat at court level again for another night-time extrava-ganza. Seeing Federer this close really did take the breath away but, on this night, Berdych was too good, noting that he was able to drag Federer from his comfort zone, something he did not like. Berdych crash-landed on the cement surface at one stage, got up and looked me straight in the eye; I could sense that the embar-rassment served only to inspire him. The four-set defeat might have serious implications for Federer's desire to end another year as the world No. 1, something he said was the ultimate achieve-ment. 'I don't know right now if that is the priority for the end of the year. I will have to go back to the drawing board,' he said in answer to my question. 'We'll see where I go from now.'

Roddick had already gone from the event and from tennis on a night of prickly sensations against Juan Martin del Potro, one clubber of the ball too far for the older champ. It was difficult for Roddick to focus on much of what was happening once del Potro had rubbed out his first set lead and began to discover his extensive forehand range. That used to be the way A-Rod treated his opponents. At 4–5, 40–0 in the fourth, Roddick wiped a tear from his right eye as he prepared to receive. Once he had lifted a last forehand long, Roddick made his way to the net, del Potro hugged him and a muted crowd responded kindly to their man. These are never comfortable moments, when you are expected to encapsulate your career with so many emotions flooding through your mind. He had been the champion in 2003, reached world

No. 1 status and helped his country to Davis Cup triumph. The heartache had come for him at Wimbledon, in the immovable shape of Federer. I sent Roddick a note later that day wishing him well. He sent one back thanking me 'for being one of the good guys'. It meant the world. Del Potro played Djokovic in the quarter-finals where, apart from a walkabout at the start of the second set when he lost ten consecutive points, the Serbian was in dazzling control.

The men's semi-finals on Saturday afternoon therefore pitted Murray against Berdych and Djokovic with David Ferrer, who had recovered from 4–1, 0–30 down in the fifth set to beat Tipsarević. This was the final year of the CBS demand that the men's semis should be played the day preceding the final, the crazily indulgent 'Super Saturday'. 'Suffrage Saturday' would have been more like it.

The forecast for the weekend was wicked. Moving up from the south was a storm system scheduled to arrive first with gusty winds, with the prospect of something really nasty in their wake. A tornado warning had been issued for late afternoon. The chances of getting both matches in, should they be played consecutively, were slim to none. Surely, the remedy was to play Djokovic against Ferrer, second on the schedule, on the next door Armstrong, announce the fact to the crowd and cry 'we're doing this for tennis'. Unfortunately, the show had to come first.

How Murray and Berdych were even able to put on said show was a miracle. Control of your body let alone the ball was almost impossible. Almost every time either player threw the ball up to serve, it moved six inches sideways. It called for improvisation, touch and patience: slice and dice tennis. Murray's cap blew off when he was serving with a break in the first set and he volunteered a let when he should have let the umpire make the call. The cap was promptly binned. Berdych, his black cap firmly on, was implacable and won the set.

Murray required rousing and in the first game of the second set, with stunning use of the conditions, he broke to love.

Berdych was rattled and the set flew by, as did the third (once again Berdych lost his opening serve game to love) as Murray raced to a 4–0 lead, eased the set and was 3–0 up in the fourth. He became sloppy only once, but once was all it needed as on his third break point in the fifth game, the Czech responded and the set was settled by a tie-break. As bits of flotsam and jetsam continued to fly across the court, Berdych led it 3–0, then 5–2. Murray responded with a stunning backhand return to level for 5–5. It was 6–6, then 7–7. At this point Berdych was forced to abort two serves in the swirl. Then he missed a forehand, then another which he challenged. It was a foot long and Murray was in the final.

◯

Venus Williams had said something very peculiar after her 6–2, 5–7, 7–5 second round defeat to Angelique Kerber of Germany on the opening Thursday night. Her defeat wasn't a surprise, for Kerber was the No. 6 seed and Venus was unseeded, but this quote was a shock. 'Today I felt American, you know, for the first time at the US Open. I've waited my whole career to have this moment.'

She equated the feeling with the one she had enjoyed winning a doubles gold medal with her sister Serena at the Olympic Games a month earlier, explaining that this one was helped by the late night crowd supporting her all match. 'Come on V' they screamed. She could not quite make it but her comment about playing in a stadium named for a tireless crusader for blacks in sport (Arthur Ashe Stadium) was remarkable and would no doubt lead to much discussion on the subject. Instead, it seemed to be forgotten as soon as it was uttered.

Maybe this was because her sister was crushing the field. In the quarter-finals, Serena dropped four games to Ivanovic; in the semi-finals one fewer to Sara Errani. Victoria Azarenka, in the meantime, had been taken to three sets by Stosur in the quarters and Sharapova in the semi-finals. One had strolled and the other had needed to slog all the way. The duel was hotly anticipated, and the extra day's break for bad weather would help Azarenka. But Serena was on fire and the No. 1 seed knew it.

As it turned out, the final was a classic for its emotional intensity. Serena won the first set in just over half an hour but Azarenka settled and began to find her rhythm, to wit she won the second set and, with a goodly wind in her sails, led 5–3 in the third. The Americans, those Venus felt finally loved her, positively screamed for Serena here and, despite Azarenka's bravado in punching the air after the eighth game, it was the thirty-year-old who responded in champion fashion. Azarenka served for the match, was broken and lost the last four games in a blizzard of winners. Not since Martina Navratilova in 1987 had the Open seen a women's champion aged thirty or older.

Azarenka's coach Sam Sumyk emerged from the stadium, saw me and said: 'Let's go and have a glass of wine Neil, come on.' His assessment of the final was riveting.

I see it as a privilege to play against Serena, to learn from her, to be in her era and it can only be good for Vika. One of the best things that has happened to her is to play Serena. Women's tennis is better and better, I think we owe that to the Williams sisters because they have put the bar so high that we have to work our ass off to try to catch up. That is the case for more than a decade. The best compliment we can give them. You can find people who won't like them, who cares if they are white or black, they are fantastic for the game, for every single other player.

The two important matches for Vika this year were in the Australian Open against Kim Clijsters and this final against Serena. One she won and one she lost. After a loss like this one you don't have a lot of options, either you find the first bridge and you jump and keep going down and sink and never get up or you have that more realistic approach and yes, it hurts, still a little sad, of course but then your brain has that wisdom and says, 'Hey, that was a helluva fight and I was part of it and I'd rather be there than not

be there.' That will give me bigger wings. At the end of the match
I was convinced it was going to help her.

On the way back to the hotel, Sumyk was trying to find the right
words to say. He did not think 'bad luck' fitted the bill, believing
it 'a shitty thing' to say. He told her she had been incredible and
she asked if she could say something. She said, 'Sam, I think I can
be very good at this game.' Sumyk was glad that he was not the
only one who believed that.

For the fifth year in succession, the men's final was delayed but,
as the British had waited for seventy-six years for a champion,
another twenty-four hours did not seem such a hardship. The
coincidences were incredible. Andy Murray and Fred Perry were
born under the star sign of Taurus – their birthdays were 15 and
18 May respectively – their initial first round victory in a grand
slam had come at the US Open, Perry won on 10 September 1933
and this was 10 September 2012, they were both the No. 3 seeds.
Their opponents in the final, Novak Djokovic – who had recovered
to defeat Ferrer comfortably in the second semi-final – and Jack
Crawford, the Australian in Perry's case, were both the No. 2 seeds.
Djokovic and Crawford (who died on 10 September 1991 to give
the anniversary added piquancy) were reigning Australian Open
champions. Any more stats like this and my head would burst.

The wind had died a little but, on the back end of the storm, a
distinct edge had been taken off the heat. Indeed, it was a chilly
but bright morning, the breeze still jerky enough to throw tennis
players off balance. A 4 p.m. start meant 9 p.m. British time and
the chance of getting the story into the first edition had already
passed. The deadline for the second was midnight but that called
for a quick final and these two do not do quick finals. The pages
had to be turned over quickly and it was decided that two pieces
would need to be written for the back page that could be slotted

in whatever the outcome. I was told to write a story on the premise that Djokovic had won while Simon Barnes, our chief sports
writer, could have the glory, glory piece celebrating a Murray
victory. It is not often I write something I hope will never see the
light of day but this piece was it. The match report, to be spread
across two pages, would be my responsibility.

The forecast suggested we would make it this time, though the
wind was still capricious in nature and biting at times. It was
nowhere near the force that had caused Saturday's evacuation, the
first time in my 82 grand slams I'd experienced something quite
as incredible as having to dash for cover. It had also interrupted a
conversation with Sir Alex Ferguson, the manager of Manchester
United, who had watched the semi-final against Berdych from a
private box and been tempted to introduce himself to Murray
(in the company of another Scottish knight, Sir Sean Connery) in
the middle of his press conference. I don't think I had ever seen
Murray leap to his feet as smartly as he did when Sir Alex walked
into the room. And we were old adversaries, from my football-
writing days, a point he made to Murray when he spotted me in
the front row of the interview room. 'There are some pretty rum
people in here,' he said. Murray found it all highly amusing.

I scribbled my number on a piece of paper and handed it to
Sir Alex just as the sirens started to wail and we dashed from
the grounds. I doubted I'd cross paths with him again for quite
a while. I had no idea he had slipped back into the grounds on
Sunday to watch the women's final but he could not stay until
the end because he had an 8 a.m. Amtrak train south on Monday
morning for a rendezvous with an old friend, the racing trainer
Michael Dickinson, famous for landing the first five in the 1983
Cheltenham Gold Cup: Bregawn, Captain John, Wayward Lad,
Silver Buck and Ashley House. Dickinson had retired to the
splendour of Chesapeake Bay in Delaware. As the train rolled
out of New York's Penn Station, Ferguson received a text from
Judy Murray wondering if he might want to sit in Andy's box at
the men's final that afternoon.

The United manager had been in the States since the middle of the previous week, having been to Harvard Business School in Boston where he was to be the subject of a case study – 'Managing Manchester United'. He returned later in September to sit in a classroom there to hear Harvard students discuss his career, to speak to two classes (where it was standing room only for over 200 people on both days) and be questioned by them to 'examine his management philosophy and identify the skills necessary to thrive under the conditions of hysterical stress known as the English Premier League'.

Ferguson, who had bought an apartment in New York's Upper East Side five years earlier – 'the best investment I ever made' – hadn't realised the Open was on during his trip and it was not until his lawyer Martin O'Connor passed on the invitation that Sir Alex decided he would go to the semi-final. As he looked down from his seat, who did he see, but Judy Murray. That set off a remarkable chain of events.

Sir Alex said: 'I texted her [Judy] and said "I'm watching you, so behave yourself. If you want to look up over your right shoulder you might have a surprise."' Judy looked up and there he was. He invited her up for a glass of wine and she asked if he wanted to come down to see Andy.

'I said "I'd love to." I'd never met him you see. We went down, turned a corner and who should we walk into but Connery.' The steward on the locker room door told them that Murray was in the interview room. 'Connery marches straight in,' Sir Alex said. When he received Judy Murray's text, Ferguson called Dickinson to ask if he minded if their meeting was cut short so he could catch the 2 p.m. train from Delaware, which gave him an opportunity to make it back to Ashe Stadium as close to the designated 4 p.m. start as possible. The pair lunched on Dickinson's yacht in the bay and went back to his ranch for an hour. 'Michael has two eagles,' Ferguson said. 'We were sitting up on a hillock and there they were in a tree and around the pond there were a group of vultures. The eagles wait for the vultures to move on the fish, the vultures know the eagles are watching them. It's a matter of patience.'

Three games into the final and here he was back in Queens, taking his seat next to Murray's PR Matt Gentry – a Tottenham Hotspur fan – in the row behind Simon Fuller and Judy Murray. He barely moved for the next five hours. By then he would know what real patience was.

Into a frenzied bowl the young warriors emerged for the final. Murray, breaking to love in the first game, was the more secure, inevitably buoyed by his win over Berdych. Djokovic appeared disconcerted, playing more backhand slices than I had seen from him in months, aggravated by the conditions and the considerable competence in Murray's play. There was a rally of fifty-four shots in the sixth game, every sinew stretched; Murray was 3–2 ahead with a break but, in a captivating eighth game, Djokovic came in behind a first serve, won a single point requiring three smashes, broke back and forced the tie-break. Murray had six set points (imagine if he had lost it), and finally tempted Djokovic into an errant forehand return.

There had been ninety points in the set, forty-six to Murray and forty-four to Djokovic. The second set looked to be a much sharper affair, for Murray raced to a 4–0 lead but, serving for a two-set lead at 5–3, he made a brace of forehand errors and temporarily faltered. We held our breath. To his credit, Murray's response was that of a true and distinctive talent, and he clinched it in the twelfth game. Once more, Murray had defended for his life, nagging away so decisively at Djokovic that the Serb screwed an overhead wide to go two set points down and, on the second, he missed an off-forehand into the sidelines. Not since 1949 had a player recovered from two sets down to win a men's final at the Open. Judy Murray had to dash to the ladies' room. For once, history favoured her younger son.

But this was where the Serb showed his mettle. Djokovic

remained resilient and Murray stumbled. 'My legs feel like jelly right now,' he shouted as he was losing serve and, it seemed, resolve. Sir Alex Ferguson was churning inside.

> Every time he looked up, I gave him a shake of the fist. You can't help yourself, he is this young Scottish lad, you know how much he wants this and there were times when I wanted to give him the Ferguson fucking scowl and get right into his face and say 'for fuck's sake waken yourself up'. All I could do was mouth 'come on son you can get through this'. He focused on me a couple of times and I hope I might have inspired him a wee bit.

Djokovic pocketed that set and led 2–0 in the fourth, by which time he had won thirteen of seventeen games. The rallies were intense, almost numbing in their brutality. Though he was behind throughout the fourth, there was a sense that Murray had stabilised, the certainty had returned to his manner, if the desire for point-scoring had not. The stunner was in the ninth game when a florid backhand on a first set point brought Djokovic level and he served first in the fifth.

Ferguson really wanted to be down at Murray's side. He has urged so many young players through such moments in their careers, with a word here, a gesture there.

> Andy was at a fork in the road. Was he just happy to be there, or did he really want it. I turned to Matt [Gentry] and said, 'This is the biggest moment in his life'. I wondered what he was thinking, because I sensed that if he lost it from here, it would have been a long way back in his career. But then I had this sense that he was going to be all right.

Murray took a toilet break at the end of the fourth set, and remembers talking to his reflection in a mirror in the cubicle next to the players' entrance. There was only room for a sink, a toilet and the mirror. He said there was one set to play and all he could do was leave everything out there. Essentially, he talked to himself for two minutes, his voice rising and falling until he realised he was shouting 'You are not losing this match. You're just not. This is your time.'

He said that he felt a bit silly, but that he believed in himself more utterly than at any other time in his life. Whatever fate had in store, he was prepared to face it. Ferguson would have loved to have heard what was happening but all he could do was to rise from his seat for a few seconds to stretch his limbs. He looked across at Lendl. 'He didn't move a bloody muscle all the match, incredible that,' Sir Alex said. 'The Czechs, they are a bit detached in that way. But he has obviously given Andy that something that brought all his inner determination to the fore.'

At the start of the fifth, Murray was revitalised, the private call to arms had worked. 'He gathered himself brilliantly and that wasn't easy because he was playing a great player and I thought he needed the crowd with him,' Sir Alex said. 'I was looking at them for quite a while and although there were pockets of Scots, the Serbians were all in bunches so they created more volume. Andy doesn't use the crowd and maybe it's something he will learn as he gets older.'

But the Serbians in the crowd were rocked, as was their hero. Whatever Murray had said in the locker room, he really was going to leave it all out there. A superb forehand brought up break point in the first game and Djokovic netted a backhand slice. Murray broke for 3–0 in a game in which the defending champion had two game points, but Djokovic responded to break back for 3–1 and held for 3–2.

We were at our stations now in the press room, deadlines flying by. I wanted to write this piece so badly I could feel my temples pounding. And then I saw the story form. It had to be this time. Murray held to love for 4–2, quite possibly the finest service game of his life. Djokovic must have sensed it too, for he played a careless service game and was broken for 2–5. He called for a trainer. 'Went for his groin didn't he?' said Ferguson, who immediately began to tap his watch, in typical touchline fashion. 'It's natural I suppose,' he said, 'but bloody hell I didn't even know I was doing it. Djokovic made Andy think, I am sure he had that in his mind. It was clever. Andy had to go point by point. If he wins the next one he's in a good position.' In fact, he won the next three.

A first championship point went by when Djokovic floated a high ball, Murray could only get a tip of his racket to it and Djokovic slammed the ball into the open court. Murray went to the wrong side of the court to serve at 40–15. A second championship point: a missed first serve, a pause to still the crowd, a second serve, a Djokovic forehand return a foot long, and the wait was over. Onto his haunches he crouched, a sense of disbelief etched on his face. I pressed the button and sent the copy. I believe I waved a fist in front of a few of my non-British colleagues. This was a truly dizzying moment of fulfilment. The whole place was going mad, on and off the court, but Murray was more in control than anyone. Everyone looked for someone to hug in Murray's box. Ferguson simply rose to applaud, long and hard.

It was a terrific moment. I don't think I could have been happier if I was parading a trophy on the pitch at Old Trafford. This kid had fought so hard and there had been so many people saying he couldn't do it.

He is shy and that comes across so much but as I said to Judy after the semi-final, 'shyness shouldn't be an impediment to being a champion if you have the ability' and it's always been there from this kid right through and is part of his character. I cannot imagine Andy Murray going into a restaurant in New York and high-fiving everybody. He would slip into his seat, eat his meal and then he would go home. I see the shyness come through all the time and many Scots are like that, unless they are in a lot of company. I've said that many times.

The individual element of tennis fascinated the United manager, who was also in the Centre Court crowd for the Wimbledon final, though no one had realised and no camera picked him out. He had always said that a team needed eight players to play well to win a game, the other three might 'work their balls off' and play indifferently, but you needed a decent eight. 'In tennis you don't have that.'

> Even the coach is fifty yards away so there is no communication. Andy Murray is an absolute credit to himself and everyone who works with him. Judy wanted me to come down and see him after the match but there was no way I was going to take any focus away from him. This was his moment. I just hoped they had a good night and relished what they had achieved and I just peeled away.

But Ferguson was aware of the trouble that Murray had landed himself in for his off-the-cuff remark six years earlier about England's football team.

> I do it all the time. He should make a joke of it now. He has matured enough. The press asked me about Scotland independence a few weeks ago and I said: 'Bollocks, do you think we're going to vote for anything that lessens my chances of annoying you bastards? As long as we're still in the United Kingdom, we just annoy you English more. But the rivalry does give a person a certain determination. Andy had that in the final.

The scene in the corridors near the players' locker rooms was controlled pandemonium. Sir Sean Connery was giving interviews, and although I was admonished to 'hug the walls' by a security man, when Murray came past heading to his interview on Sky TV I offered my hand, looked him in the eye and said 'Very well done.' He nodded and said, 'Thanks Neil'. It was the best I could think of at the time. Judy seemed to be in a state of shock, she didn't want to say a thing, at least nothing we could quote. The Djokovic backroom staff passed by, offering hugs and handshakes because, in the despair at their man losing a grand slam final, they said they were genuinely pleased for Andy and I suspected, for me as well. Nole paused to shake hands but didn't stop to say any more.

In the lobby of the Arthur Ashe Stadium, Team Murray was dispensing champagne in plastic cups. I could hardly refuse. I got a hug from Kim; it was that kind of day. Lendl held court, though he still didn't relish the idea of microphones jabbed into his face any more than he had when he was a player. Justin Gimelstob wanted to interview me for 'ATP Tour Uncovered' to talk about what it had been like following Murray across the world all these years. It took fifteen minutes, by which time the champion was more than half-way through a bravura press conference.

What were we to do now? For the last time at this championship, we clambered onto the media bus back into Manhattan, a band of press brothers in a state of shock. We were cheered aboard. In truth, we were shattered but sated, emotions raging. I recall trying to think straight but every thought came out jumbled. Even the bus went the wrong way and was surrounded by a phalanx of heavy-metal bikers making their way to the lower end of Manhattan. What was this about? Suddenly we realised that dawn had broken on 11 September. Our bus was completely hemmed in and knowing how much work we would have to do later that day, a group of us jumped off to walk the dozen blocks back to our hotel. We talked delirious mumbo-jumbo to each other.

The Hakkasan Japanese restaurant on the West Side played host to a delirious Team Murray. Lendl had first gone home and when he joined them, some half an hour later, most were particularly jolly. The bill came to $6,448, though the teetotal Murray sipped a lemon soda that cost six bucks. The restaurant waived all but $1,289.60 and one of the staff posted the bill on the internet to an immense furore. Had it been done without Murray's consent it could have been construed as a breach of confidentiality but nothing could upset the sense of joy in the camp. The expectation for the Open champion was the rounds of the US morning shows – he was on CBS *This Morning* looking extraordinarily fresh and manicured when I stirred from my slumbers at just past seven.

The media tour then took in Central Park, over which Murray

had looked each of the previous twenty-one mornings, for the photo-shoot before he was greeted at the British Consul-General's home on 1st Avenue by a piper wearing the tartan of Macdonald of the Isles, and playing 'Scotland the Brave'. He was presented with some goodies from home, Hobnobs and Irn-Bru. He spoke for almost an hour, with the Open trophy on the polished table in front of him and beneath a portrait of James II and his coat of arms of entwined thistle and roses 'signifying the governance of Scotland and England by a single monarch'.

When Sir Alex Ferguson returned to the States to speak to the students at Harvard Business School later that month he said that what had kept him going throughout his managerial career – one of the most garlanded of all time – had been the relationships developed with young people and the confidence and hope they gave him, that they surprised him and never let him down (though one or two may have done). Up on the board behind him were written the two words 'love' and 'hate'. He spoke about those. 'I said that I don't think any of my players loved me, but I think they respected me.'

Love and hate – Murray could relate to those. He was front page news in *The Times* and a few more newspapers on Wednesday morning and love was in the air. The haters had all but disappeared from view on the online comment pages. A couple of days later, away from the crowds, we spoke about what this had meant, how he had endured, and of the sense of accomplishment he now felt. He was utterly compelling as ever.

I have lost matches before and at home afterwards and it wasn't good, I was very uneasy. After Wimbledon everywhere I went, everyone was so positive and upbeat and supportive and I hadn't necessarily felt that before. It helped me get over Wimbledon quickly. Things have changed. The Olympics had a different crowd, everyone so passionate. I hadn't experienced anything like that before. It wasn't just the tennis, the whole country was so positive. Beforehand the media was saying 'this will be a disaster, the traffic will be bad, the stadiums aren't ready, the ticket situation is a fiasco' and after a few days, it was 'Oh, we don't have any gold medals, when are they going to come?' and then it turned into the best thing I've experienced since I was old enough to understand emotions. Everyone was so pleased and so together and you don't always see that and I hope it will be like that more and more now because it helps, it helps everybody.

He had had to deal with plenty of ambivalence; he had stored up plenty of angst against the press because he felt he was dealing with the same criticisms and that no matter if he won or lost, the negatives outweighed the positives. And it was not always the press.

I got asked the same questions and people said the same things in the street. It wouldn't have mattered how many times I said 'I'm playing against the greatest players of all time,' and how hard it is to win, it didn't stop people thinking 'oh he'll never win' and 'mentally he's not strong enough', whatever. They thought I was just not that good. It took performances like the one at the Olympics and then the Open to change that, to make people finally realise I did have that grit and determination and an ability to win against the best in the world in the biggest matches.

Imagine having to live with the suspicion that, when the matches got tough, Murray would get going. He would not be able to win. I know because I had had these conversations, I had worried that so many people believed it was a matter of 'when' rather than 'if'. That had always made me nervous. For Murray.

For me at times it was really hard that I hadn't won anything major or done what I expected to do and I did get brought up for my attitude and the way I acted on court a lot. When I saw the press there I would feel 'they're judging me, watching my every move, what is he saying, how he is acting, what is he doing, has he improved that shot, why is he not winning?' That can be hard.

But over the last two years I have felt the press that travel to the tournaments have accepted who I am and weren't looking to see whether I had changed because I've stayed pretty much the same. I don't feel now when I see the press that they are hoping I implode here. But it has been a long journey. These feelings now are pretty special.

Humble pie was quaffed in large quantities. *The Independent,* in the manner of the satirical magazine *Private Eye*, printed an editorial headlined 'An Apology to Andy Murray', a piece that also endeavoured to make good any bad blood that may have existed between the paper and Andy's mother, Judy. It had previously been rather unflattering about her tone of voice and occasionally over-eager support; now, alongside a triumphal endorsement of her victorious offspring, the paper saluted her for making the sacrifices necessasry to ensure her son's success.

Earlier editions of the London-based national press may have given the impression over the past few years that Andy Murray is an immature sour-faced, slovenly, Scottish choker who could not win a Grand Slam title even if his opponent were a one-legged, short-sighted octogenarian equipped with a banjo.

We now accept that, on the contrary, Sir Andy (as we hope you may style him come the New Year's Honours list, Ma'am) is a true-born British world-beater in the tradition of Sir Francis Drake and the Duke of Wellington.

When Murray boarded the 9.30 p.m. BA flight home, he entered the first-class compartment, having upgraded himself as a bit of a treat. He was desperate for some rest.

I lay in bed for an hour the night of the match but I couldn't drop off so I went on my computer and read a few things and I knew then that everyone was so happy for me. It was such a long road and worth it in the end but there were times when a lot of people were doubting whether it would happen – and not only me.

When I got on the plane my mind was blank, it is hard to explain. It was weird. I was watching a Rocky movie and I wasn't particularly enjoying it. Kim was asleep, Andy Ireland [his physiotherapist] was asleep and I was so desperate to go to sleep. I ordered four glasses of champagne, drank them one after the other and went numb.

And who would begrudge him those four drinks after becoming the first British man to win a grand slam since Fred Perry in 1936?

Chapter 12

Autumn

IT IS VERY rare for Simon Fuller – the man more attuned to what it might take to get a star on the Hollywood Walk of Fame than win a grand slam tennis tournament but who had decided in 2008 that he wanted to make a play to represent Andy Murray – to speak publicly on the subject. The outcome of the US Open had loosened his tongue just a little.

Fuller and I had spoken initially in the corridor outside the doping control room where the British No. 1 had been escorted after his New York victory – that was the way of it once you had completed a grand slam tournament – even though trying to fill a tube with urine in these circumstances usually took an age. The management guru's assertion was that all he wanted to do was help a young man he had believed 'could make history'. Well, now he had and Fuller was ready to express why he had brought a tennis player onto a portfolio that had largely been the province of singers, dancers, and reality television shows and their stars that garnered him a personal fortune approaching $400 million.

'I became aware that Andy was looking for a new manager and business partner and was intrigued. I love sport and the opportunity to work with someone still so young [twenty-two at the time] and with so much potential was irresistible,' Fuller said.

He had yet to win a major tournament and this gave me the challenge I needed to see if I could help him to achieve his dreams. I had a strong feeling that he had every chance to become a true British icon and we are all about building global icons in their field.

If other tennis management companies looked down their noses at Fuller (and they did, regularly) it did not surprise him. New kids on the block always take a bit of time to be tolerated. The message from those who had been around a lot longer was always the same: 'why don't they bring in more deals for him?' and 'there are no patches on his kit' or, more pertinently, 'what do they know about tennis?' Fuller told me that he hoped his entrance into tennis had gone unnoticed, though I think he was understating his impact about a hundred-fold.

He revelled in his outsider status, allowing him to think more clearly and individually and not be swayed by what the establishment may have expected of him.

I am brave in my decision-making and have no fear, and I have never felt the need to conform. My only interest is doing what is best for the people I work with.

I commit to doing things that I believe in and enjoy. My primary motivation is delivering success and fulfilment for Andy, not just making money or creating fame. It is about helping to make his dreams come true. Every decision I make is based on a clearly defined long-term strategy revolving entirely around what Andy wants to achieve. With Andy it is his passion, dedication and drive that makes him such a remarkable athlete. For me personally it is his honesty, integrity and heartfelt passion that makes him an exceptional person to work with.

As for the sport itself, tennis's potential is absolutely huge. However, I believe there is much to be done to increase its commercial and public standing. It is not a sport that sustains the public interest throughout the year and this must change to fully reach its potential. Each tournament needs to be better connected. It feels very disparate. The ranking system is complex and little understood and it lacks the excitement of a sport that has a proper

season where every match matters. I have many ideas about what
I would do and hopefully one day I will be able to put some of my
theories to the test.

We await that day with much interest.

Murray himself had spent a couple of days resting and was
then heading to Scotland for a walkabout in Dunblane, his home
town. His neighbours in Surrey had attached some balloons to
his front gate but that was about as noisy as they get in Oxshott;
going back to Scotland really opened his eyes. The night before he
had stayed in the home Judy, his mother, had recently purchased
and was still wide awake chatting at three in the morning. Andy
said he had no idea what to expect later that day but 'wouldn't it
be funny if there were just a couple of people outside the butchers'.

There were a couple of people outside the butchers all right,
surrounded by about twenty thousand more. The place had gone
barmy.

[...] a lot I recognised from school, teachers and the people who
worked in the newsagents, still exactly the same, the barber I used
to go to – 'Fuzzy's' – I saw him. I had had mine freshly cut and he
said it was a decent cut 'because it was all over the place in New
York'. Hugh McDonald, the chief sports writer of the *Glasgow
Herald*, had given up his day off to be a member of the audience.
Judy spotted him and invited him inside the ropes. Hugh said he
simply wanted to stay in the crowd and 'applaud, like everyone
else'. It was that kind of day.

'I don't get a chance to go back that much and after we had
walked through the city centre I went to the tennis courts and the
golf club which are right next to each other,' Andy said. 'The golf
club car park was where I used to spend all of my time, I used to
take my bike there and cycle on one wheel with all of my friends.
It was weird going back and seeing so many of my old friends
still there.'

Perhaps the image that will remain most indelibly in my mind from 2012 is that of Murray standing in the middle of the High Street in Dunblane, hands in pockets, shy smile, with crowds ten deep on the pavements all around him. In the background of that image was Gentry, who had moved to XIX Entertainment from Hill & Knowlton, the sports PR agency, six months after they had signed Murray in 2009 and was appointed as his point man, working also with Andy's brother Jamie and his mother. Gentry had been at Murray's side, guiding and guarding for the past three years – 'trying to get people to see what he was really like, rather than what they thought he was like.'

He had had to try to work his way into the tennis fabric, against those who felt that XIX were amateurs in a professional world, hicks who did not know what they were doing.

'But we faced that when we signed David Beckham and then with Lewis Hamilton [in F1], it was a case of "they only know about show-business".' Gentry said. 'But Simon thrives on being an outsider, he isn't someone who is entrenched in the idea that "this is the way it is done, so we just do the same thing."'

Gentry had had to try to iron out the rough-around-the-edges attitude that made Murray an unlikeable figure, especially to females. He did not want to turn Murray into someone he was not but equally, if he were to make the money and win the deals that ought to have been flooding his way after the US Open success, softening him a little was imperative. Getting him to shave more would help. It was widely perceived that Murray was not exactly chomping at the bit to do sponsorship work; indeed it was one of the elements of his personality that was recognised by those management companies who wanted to get more deeply involved. There was a rumour that he had lost a substantial deal with FedEx, who were looking to put a lot of work his way, but his lack of enthusiasm meant they sped off in a different direction.

'His time is so tight,' Gentry responded,

and to get him to work with a brand he has to be really enthused by it. He likes to be involved with technology, something young and cool. But if it becomes a chore he is turned off by it so we have been very selective as to what we put in front of him. Clearly, with his win in New York, his market value has shot up quite a bit. It is hard to put a figure on it but there are a lot of people wanting to get involved. We have to sift through what brands we know he would like to be associated with. There's no point in us agreeing something that would require him to make twenty personal appearances in a year because he doesn't have the time to do it. Andy is extremely wealthy so it is not as if he is desperate to get out and make whatever he can.

Murray, like the rest of the tennis world, now had his eyes on the Orient. He was playing two tournaments in Asia, the Rakuten Japan Open in Tokyo followed by the first of the two Masters 1,000s in the autumn, the Shanghai Rolex Masters he had won in both 2010 and 2011; Djokovic was defending his title at the China Open, while Federer played in a Davis Cup world group qualifier for Switzerland (two wins helped his nation back into the top sixteen nations for 2013), and Shanghai before he would once more highlight the field in his home-town tournament in Basel.

For Murray this would be a tough slog. The event after an inaugural grand slam victory is always a difficult one to approach and the fact he was drawn to play Ivo Karlovic in the first round did not make matters any easier. Murray got through that and two further rounds before he faced Raonic, a repeat of the fourth round meeting in New York where the British player had excelled. Raonic decided that, rather than play possum as he had done at the Open, he would be bolder; even though he stuck to an adventurous game plan, Murray had two chances to win the match only for the Canadian to produce a couple of big serves and push on to win in three sets. Murray was disappointed but not downhearted.

The Shanghai tournament was proud of its tradition as the Masters event most favoured by the players, finishing top of their charts most years because it went that little bit further in its desire to pamper and promote. The one downside to the event was the trial by road that was the journey from the city to Qi Zhong, with its roof of eight petals and a players' lounge that was the envy of the tour. Nothing was ever too much trouble.

Richard Lewis was in China to meet the players before moving on to Istanbul to address the women, who had been largely sidelined as the debate about prize money was dominated by the men. Federer arrived the evening before and, faced with a bizarre death threat issued by 'Blue Cat Polystheistic Religion Founder 07' who said they would assassinate Federer 'for the purpose of tennis extermination', security around the Swiss was tighter than normal. 'With all this happening, there he was, for a long time, engaged totally in the wider interests of the sport,' Lewis said.

> I can think of a number of eras in the game when that didn't happen. Coming back into the sport, one thing that genuinely surprised me was how the lower-ranked players aren't making much money. Their expenses had gone up a lot but their money hardly at all. The sport is going through a golden period and I think it is a perfectly legitimate case the players are making.

Lewis's memory went back to 1973 and the lounge at Queen's Club, where he was based, listening to the political dons of that era: Donald Dell, Arthur Ashe, Cliff Drysdale, Stan Smith, Butch Buchholz, Harold Solomon and Mark Cox, discussing the impending boycott of Wimbledon. The crux was the decision of the Yugoslav tennis federation to suspend Niki Pilić for refusing to play Davis Cup in New Zealand. Wimbledon decided to bar Pilić from playing in the Championships and the ATP called a boycott which seventy-nine of its members joined. The British press said that 'Wimbledon was bigger than a few spoiled players', record crowds turned out, and the stars of the show were Ilie Nastase, Roger Taylor and a teenager from Sweden named Björn

Borg. Lewis, who had failed in his bid to qualify for the main draw, earned a place in the event thanks to the boycott.

In those far off days, Lewis did not remember prize money ever coming up in discussion. It was more the calendar, tournament ownership, conflicts of interest and the lack of computer rankings. The thought of players sitting around a table discussing how they should be ranked seems remarkable considering where the sport is today. Remarkable too, though, is that the debates about calendars and conflicts of interest have not ceased. Lewis regards the desire for a greater share of the prize money as a single thread in a 'whole of sport' issue.

> We [the grand slams] have a role to play and are happy to do that but it is not just a single issue, it is about ranking, point allocation for the tournaments and also the calendar. You cannot look at one element in isolation and this is not something you solve in one year, and that has been the discussion with the players, this is a journey, a several year issue, there is no magic wand and I think a lot of them understand that.
>
> It is not a sport in crisis, but a sport that has things to improve and fix and adjustments that need to be made.

It was a point emphasised by Frenchman Gilles Simon, who had joined the player council at the start of the year and was in the discussions with Lewis. Simon had long felt that politics was a waste of time and energy but now he saw that the men were unified, fighting as an entity rather than individuals, and he was keen to help lead them. 'My first concern was most of the people think guys ranked between fifty and 100 win a lot of money and $500,000 is a lot,' Simon explained.

> But take away the tax which is 30 per cent. When you are in the top 100 it is not possible to decide whether to hire a coach or save some money for the future. These guys are playing Novak or Roger who have the coach, the physical trainer, the physiotherapist,

everything, and the competition is unfair. This is why we wanted to increase significantly the first round prize money in the slams to be sure that these guys have enough money to hire something and not to be scared. This is not money going directly into their pockets but to use for investments to do better.

Those rising to the top in Shanghai were the expected bunch, though Stan Wawrinka had his compatriot Federer wobbling for a bit, Radek Štěpánek was still playing crafty tennis and took a set from Murray, and Tomáš Berdych was pressed for a long time by Sam Querrey. In the semi-finals, Djokovic continued his stately progress against Berdych before Federer and Murray tussled for the first time since the Olympic final. It was a match defined by a phantom rain shower.

Murray won the first set and from 40–0 down in the opening game of the second, had let six break points slide when Federer noticed a few spots on the court. He pointed them out to Ali Nili, the umpire and, though it did not look as if it was raining at all, the call came to close the roof. Murray suggested they play on while the roof was being closed but ultimately six minutes were lost that could have seriously undermined Murray's concentration. At 2–2, Federer led 40–0 but Murray plugged away, breaking with an instinctive forehand return. More rain fell at 5–4, this time enough to thoroughly wet the surface, the eight petals were closed and Murray had to wait around to serve for the match, which he did stylishly.

The final against Djokovic turned out to be the best three-setter of the year, one that turned when Murray, in control by a set, 5–4 and 30–0, played a backhand lob that should have delivered him the first of three match points. There was nothing Djokovic could do but retreat, attempt an audacious 'through the legs' shot and swallow his medicine. He accomplished the first two parts superbly but was not willing to accede to the third. Murray should have chased the lob in, but did not and it was this momentary hesitation on which, no doubt, he would come to reflect for a while.

Djokovic not only managed to keep the ball in play in that

seminal rally, but before Murray had gathered his thoughts in the proper order, he was shattered by the most perfect of drop shots. Djokovic grinned from ear to ear. He was reprieved and though Murray would stand five times within a point of collecting his first Masters 1,000 title of the year, he could not quite get the job done and was beaten 5–7, 7–6, 6–3 in the longest ATP final of the year, three hours and twenty minutes. Philosophical as he was about the loss, it was the second time in successive Asian tournaments that he had lost a match having had multiple match points.

At one stage Djokovic committed the finest racket-trash of the year, mangling his implement into many bits. 'We are humans in the end,' he said.

> We are professional tennis players and we're big rivals, but in the end we're humans. I don't see anything bad in showing your emotions, positive, negative emotions. I think it's understandable. But we are in the middle of the fight, in the middle of an incredible match. Both of us, we want to win. We can't just be flat-faced throughout the whole match.

Djokovic's joy at the victory was soon shattered by the news that his father Srdjan, such an influence, had been taken to hospital in Belgrade with blood complications. His eldest son, who had landed in Paris to compete in the final Masters of the year, then returned to Serbia, made sure his father was in the best care and came back to the French capital. The Serbian media got wind of the extent of Srdjan's illness and blurted it out. When Djokovic came to press at the Palais Omnisports, it was with the proviso that no questions other than tennis ones were asked. 'ATP–KGB' a French colleague whispered. Djokovic, perhaps affected by his father's ill health, opened his campaign with a love set against Querrey but lost in three.

Federer, as he was entitled under ATP rules, chose to miss Paris. He had played his home-town event in Basel, losing in the final to Juan Martin del Potro, and had been involved in an unseemly row with Roger Brennwald, the president of the tournament, who disclosed that Federer and his team wanted an increase in their guarantee to play in the event in the future. Brennwald, it was alleged, was jealous of Federer in that he (Brennwald) had been the star of his home-town event until a kid rolled up on his bike asking to be a ball boy and had become one of the true greats of the game. It was said that Federer received $500,000 to play Basel, tax free, and 'tournament sources' said he wanted to quadruple that amount. The Swiss press reported that Federer wanted between $1 million and $1.5 million. 'Outside of the court, Federer is more earthly than we would like to admit, somewhat imperfect and very human,' wrote the Swiss daily *Tages-Anzeiger*.

Back in Paris, a lightning bolt by the name of Jerzy Janowicz struck the event. The 6ft 8in., 22-year-old Pole had chosen at the last minute not to play in the Geneva Challenger but attempt to qualify for the last big event he could play in the year. He was ranked No. 69, armed with a ferocious serve and did not drop a set in his two qualifying matches and first two in the main draw (against notables Philipp Kohlschreiber and Marin Čilić). He was drawn to face Murray, lost the opening set, was a match point down when Murray served for it, watched a forehand fly long, snatched the tie-break and won in three sets, dissolving into floods of tears at the end. It was the same after the next round, when Janko Tipsarević retired 4–1 down in the third and the same when he defeated Simon in the semi-finals. This was just too good a story to be true. When Janowicz was beaten in the final by David Ferrer – who won his first ever Masters 1,000 event – he had risen to No. 26 in the rankings and would be seeded for the Australian Open in January 2013 and many events beyond with very few points to defend. It was not long before the phone was ringing from prospective agents armed with prospective deals from various clothing manufacturers. Janowicz could be very big business.

If Paris had been traumatic for Djokovic, it was equally so for his fellow Serb Tipsarević. He could still be pipped at the London post though that would need some odd results. Tipsarević had turned professional ten years earlier; he was an original, who had various tattoos on his body, including 'Beauty Will Save The World' in Japanese on his left arm, and a beautiful wife, Biljana on the other. There was no more erudite player on the tour.

I love tennis so much because it is so pure. In singles, you are alone, there is a scoreboard and even though sometimes it is not pretty, you are going to win or you are going to lose, there is no Hollywood deceit presenting you with something that you don't want to see or a team mate you can toss the ball to and get credit and achieve something, it is all you.

You either make it or you don't. The bad thing is you don't have too much time to digest your success, or to feel happy about what you have achieved because in my experience everything I did in my career which is big in my eyes, I never felt happiness the same day.

Our season is completely crazy with its length, it is great in terms of self-recognition, because if you perform badly there is always Monday. Monday comes and it is a great day for us. Monday is normally the worst day ever if I read the news because everyone hates going back to work but for us it is great especially if you feel shitty. You have a guy across the net, to help you feel better about yourself.

What is sport? It is entertainment for people though I'm not on the court to entertain anybody even though I'm delighted that someone is actually paying real money to see my backhand. This is why we are gladiators. We see these people [the opponents] every day of our lives, we play them one time, ten times a year maybe and you are still fighting to beat them for the very first time like you never played them before and never will again.

I have been trying to see things much more simply than usual, to make my life go in a way that 2 + 2 + 2 + 2 = 8 and there are no multiplications and divisions. I don't want to say that I was a failed player but to achieve mentally what Djokovic and Nadal achieved, they were like this when they were ten years old. I'm twenty-seven years old and now I'm trying to use every last bit of what I have.

To be honest with you my loss to Žemlja is hurting me more than to Ferrer in the US Open [he led 4–1, 0–30 in the fifth set]. I'm aware that was 360 points and I would be in London already and being relaxed and not watching this fucking [Kevin] Anderson on the screen. I lost to Andy [Murray] in Miami this year and it was hurting me so much, especially the fact that Rafa retired in the next round. I was playing good and Andy had some problems and I started being arrogant and to try to finish the point fast. And everyone knows that against Andy you need to be patient and wait for your chances. I was so angry and I still am but matches like these are a great experience.

I have a coach, trainer, fitness coach, PR lady, mental coach (for this week). I'm willing to do whatever it takes. I lost to Žemlja, I felt nervous and immediately after the match I talked to Dirk [Hordorff his coach]. I don't want to have this feeling in Paris, I was feeling tight and nervous and I'm in a position unless Gasquet wins Basel that I will be chased. I am always behaving better if I have to chase, rather than someone is chasing me. But you cannot buy experience and it is making us all wiser year after year. If you have this experience and take care of your body well there's no reason why you cannot play better when you are twenty-eight than when you are twenty-two. I know much more about the sport now than when I was twenty-two. Trust me I still kicking my nuts why was I like that when I was younger.

Such is the way of the tennis world that while Tipsarević wanted to be surrounded with more people, Simon was working everything out on his own and a semi-final place in Paris was a decent way to end the year. In October, he had parted with his long-time coach Thierry Tulasne. 'I am sure I am too nervous on the court and in some matches I am talking too much and I don't manage to focus on the game and when I am alone for me it is easier to go with my ideas on the court without any ideas from the outside,' he said.

> Today I feel I have to stay quiet and more focused on what I want to do. When you are on the court you have to find your own solutions and finally every little thing that someone told you before stays in your mind and it is 'why not this?' and 'why not that?' and I felt like I needed to go just with my ideas. I was changing too much, I didn't find my behaviour on the court, the one I need to have every time and that is what I'm looking for.

He is not alone in that search.

Simon's personal journey, like everyone's in tennis, was trapped in the wider context of where the sport was heading and what it was attempting to achieve. Simon had little time for women's tennis – the point he had made elaborately at Wimbledon – and therefore it probably escaped his attention that there was plenty of turmoil behind the scenes as the future of the Fed and Davis Cups were being picked over on a weekly basis.

Indeed, 2012 marked a watershed in the future of both competitions. In Miami in March, those Davis and Fed Cup captains on site were called to a meeting with ITS president Francesco Ricci Bitti and Juan Margets, the executive director, at which they outlined proposals for the future of the events. It was announced that, if players wanted to take part in the Olympic Games in Rio de Janeiro, Brazil in 2016, they were going to have to play four ties in their respective competitions between 2012 and 2016, rather than two as had been the case prior to 2012. The ITF's intransigence caused a firestorm of protest.

The WTA believed the ITF had not acted in good faith and had barely taken the trouble to communicate with its membership beforehand; it decided at its own board meeting that, at the end of 2012, it would cease to honour its 'agreement' with the ITF over calendar dates and called publicly for format changes in the Fed Cup as well as privately raging at the federation's position.

Using the Olympic Games as leverage – the ITF president was prominent within the IOC and further established his position by becoming president of the Association of Summer Olympic International Federations (ASOIF) in May – was anathema to the tours. I was told by several sources that Wimbledon would not have earned the right to stage the 2012 Olympic Games tennis event had the All England Club not agreed that the women would receive equal prize money in the Championships, a decision they ratified in 2007.

Margets wanted to state the federation's case amid the furore. We spoke at the ITF's headquarters in Roehampton after the contentious meetings with the WTA. 'We don't feel we are interfering [with the advent of the rule change] with any calendar or the ability of the tours to run the weeks they run, it is just that we want to give more beef to our current rules,' he said.

> We were prepared to sign an agreement. They [the WTA] should explain why not. It would not just be a disaster for Fed Cup [should they carry this through] but also for any tournament that [the WTA decided] would be held in that week.
>
> Francesco wrote to the CEOs of the tours in December 2011 with our position. What the current draft is saying is a player should play Fed Cup four times during the term and at least once every two years [if a nation was in the world group] and we acknowledge the possibility of injuries. Long term injuries are written into the draft as an element to soften the rule, as is years of service – the idea that a player who has played for his or her country x number of times until now will have a reduction. Does it mean we will agree on the figure? I'm not sure. But we have the right and the duty to protect our event. The ATP has expressed a more moderate or soft disagreement with the rule and when we have spoken about long service they say 'okay' so I don't see this rule creating a major divorce in tennis.

The WTA argued that playing more Fed Cup ties increased the threat to the health and well-being of the players. Margets mocked that suggestion. 'Can someone tell me that moving from two to four commitments poses a question mark over the health of the players? I have to strongly disagree,' he said.

The time had come to address the case for alternatives. Those inside the sport had grown tired of trying to explain to others without such a depth of knowledge how convoluted the Davis Cup set-up was. The draw was usually unfathomable. The ITF's go-to argument was that without its home and away element, the event would simply not be the same. I had long been an advocate of the previous year's champions receiving a bye into the second round of competition the following year. It was ludicrous that a team could win an event in December and be out of next year's competition by February. Margets said it was looked at 'very often' but that the value of that first week of competition was enhanced by the participation of the champions.

How to entice more of the best players to play more of the time was the ITF's perennial conundrum. IMG saw a stark problem forming. Fernando Soler, the head of their tennis division, approached the ITF telling them that the two competitions were increasingly disconnected from the reality of the players, sponsors and media.

> There were people considering the idea of building team events, the players were bitching about the Davis Cup and Fed Cup, and we said if they didn't do something you will have a problem in five years. I said they should conduct some research to discover what the stakeholders were saying so they could move forward,

Soler explained. 'We needed to make the sport friendlier for the players because it was becoming more challenging for them and requiring bigger efforts, physically and mentally.'

As such, IMG operatives were sent out with a questionnaire from which, I assumed, the answers would be acted upon rather than shoved into a bottom drawer and left to yellow. There was nothing particularly rigorous in the questioning: likes/dislikes alongside suggested improvements.

The 'likes' were relatively straightforward, for this was a team competition and that was its most vivid selling point. But when it came to 'dislikes' the bugbears were those which should have made the ITF sit up and take notice, not least the competition's lack of international resonance, the indifference of many leading players towards it and the confusion of the format, with many suggesting a reconditioning of the entire structure.

Something that came through loud and clear, though, was that there were too many Davis Cup dates and they were not arranged in a manner understandable to the watching world. Was three days too many for a tie, should there be doubles on the Saturday (ties were held over Friday/Saturday/Sunday) which was generally the best day for attendance and television interest? The home and away format – stoutly defended by the ITF – was criticised, too. It was surely more important to have a structure that was easily understood than to put all the eggs in the home-and-away basket?

In total, there were enough considerations from well-intentioned, influential people with no axe to grind for the ITF to have to agree to listen to the sport's constituents. Only in this way would there be a viable future for the tournament. Even they could not argue that the questionnaire hadn't come up with damning outcomes and only by carrying the best players could competition be sustained and be meaningful across the globe, not just to the hardy few who understood how the event panned out.

In 2012, the top four in men's tennis played a total of three singles matches in the competition – all by Federer. The final in late November pitted the Czech Republic against Spain in Prague, a wonderful occasion for reminiscences of great teams past. Ivan Lendl, Pavel Složil, Jan Kodeš, and Tomáš Šmid all supported the final in person.

The last match of the 2012 men's tennis year was between

Radek Štěpánek and Nicolás Almagro, a match that would not have drawn a quorum at the US Open. Štěpánek won it in some style, a 33-year-old player of long standing had one of the most satisfying days of his life and the Czechs went home happy. I doubt anyone in America knew it was happening. The result was given a paragraph in *The Times* and Mike Dickson of the *Daily Mail*, who had been invited to attend by the ITF, did not get a word in his own newspaper.

Jim Courier, the United States captain, sent out a tweet in the aftermath of the final which said: 'Davis Cup – best players can't fit it into their schedules and there's nothing special about it.' This, from the skipper of the nation that gave us the competition in the first place, was surely enough to make everyone sit up and take note.

And at the end of the year, Federer announced that he would not compete for Switzerland in 2013, which drew a pointed response from his compatriot, Wawrinka. 'Roger has been saying for years that he wants to play the Davis Cup and it is important but apparently that is not the case. It is a shame how he interprets things to suit his own opinion. Davis Cup is not a priority for him at the moment.'

Nadal's participation in 2013 was likely to be negligible; Murray would play when it suited him. The Cup had had its time and now it was in trouble. We all knew it.

Chapter 13

WTA Championships

ANDREW KRASNY, THE Master of Ceremonies for the TEB BNP Paribas WTA Championships (to give it its mouthful of a title) greeted Petra Kvitová on the stage at the luxurious Ciragan Palace Kempinski Hotel in Istanbul with 'my, what big blue eyes you have'. Kvitová blushed. And the blue eyes went perfectly with her crimson cheeks.

How would Krasny express his admiration for Serena Williams as she sashayed confidently forward to be greeted by the Turkish throng? It would have taken a brave man to say what everyone was thinking for there was no doubt this was a stunning Serena, as well as I had ever seen her look, in a figure-hugging blood-red one-piece that showed off every curve. Everyone in the room reached for their cameras. Patrick Mouratoglou was no exception.

The chatter in the tennis world was that Serena had found more than her tennis game with Mouratoglou, the Frenchman to whose Parisian academy she had retreated after her first round melt against Virginie Razzano at Roland Garros. A week after her US Open triumph – where she had dug deeper than ever before – they were pictured in the French town of Valbonne, near Nice, dining together before looking in the window of an estate agency, with Serena's right hand tucked into the back pocket of Mouratoglou's blue jeans. The accompanying text was of the nudge-nudge-wink-wink variety.

In Istanbul, Serena oozed warmth and an easy self-assurance that had not always been there, even when she was collecting tennis titles by the dozen. Where once I was *laissez-faire* about her conferences because they were so self-absorbed, she was now witty and charming and I felt attendance was compulsory. In the press room, her 'relationship' with Mouratoglou was a prime topic of conversation, made all the more intriguing because he spent an awful lot of time there with us during the week.

Mouratoglou had first come to my attention when he coached Marcos Baghdatis of Cyprus to the Australian Open final in 2006; he was working with the talented Bulgarian Grigor Dimitrov and had also travelled with Laura Robson to Australia in 2010 after she had spent time at his academy. They parted company soon afterwards, but Mouratoglou often reminded me that Robson was a top twenty player of the future.

There was no doubt the Frenchman was settled in his current liaison, for he was the centre of attention and took to the lime-light very easily. Everyone wanted to know what magic dust he had sprinkled on Serena, what turned her from the sad figure who departed the French Open, into a ravenous champion who had lost just once since, in Cincinnati to Angelique Kerber of Germany (a match Serena rather conveniently said she had forgotten).

'I always said that in a career there are two or three key moments when you take a decision or you take one direction or go in another way, I really believe it,' Mouratoglou told me. We were seated on a sofa in the players' room at the Sinan Erdem Stadium, a spot for quiet reflection. Serena was hovering in the vicinity, seeming to want to come over, but left us to chat.

It is the same with life. How many very big decisions do you take that completely change your life, not so many maybe, but if you look back, if you didn't take those decisions, you would be completely somewhere else. I'm not saying it would be better or worse but you would be completely somewhere else.

Serena, I said, radiated happiness; he agreed, and appeared to await a follow-up. I pondered whether I might blow the whole interview if I asked if they were in love. 'She knew what she wanted, maybe she didn't know how to get it, but she knew what she wanted,' he said (the conversation was still about tennis).

> She said straight away when she came to the academy that she wanted to win Wimbledon – that was in her mind and was very clear. In the Razzano match, she didn't understand what happened. Because she lost her tennis completely and lost her way, sometimes a match hurts you a lot.
>
> She knows how to play tennis, to win a grand slam, many, many grand slams, so the main goal is to make her get in contact again with her sensations, her confidence. She has an unbelievable natural confidence but at that time she was not in touch. She lost her game, but it was not very far away. Sometimes you lose your way – not just in tennis – and feel completely lost but you are just one road from the right way and you just don't know it. Being lost is not being ten miles from the destination. Sometimes it is very, very close. It is the same feeling.

Joining Williams's team was not easy; they had become one of the most tight-knit groups in the sport. I was on nodding acquaintance with Oracene, her mother (and shared a courtesy car with her on one trip to the court in Istanbul, finding her exceptionally gracious); I had interviewed Richard, her father, on numerous occasions and, when he was in the mood, he could be riveting copy, but he was not in Istanbul. Richard and Oracene had divorced in 2002 and Richard married Lakeisha Graham in 2011 and had just become a father again at the age of seventy in September. Also in the group was Serena's physical trainer Esther Lee and long-time hitting partner Sascha Bajin, who travelled everywhere with her. We met for the first time on the last night in Turkey, and, though having initially exclaimed 'Oh God no, not a press man', I found Sascha relaxed, open and engaging.

Mouratoglou, if he had been viewed suspiciously at first, was a part of the 'family' now and that was imperative.

The family is very close and that is a big strength because they have been together for so long and there is a lot of trust. You feel surrounded by something really strong. I was welcomed. If the parents feel that Serena trusts a person, they trust them also. It is real love too, you love your kids and you trust them.

He did not want to say whether he talked to Oracene about tactics but that 'it is team work and everyone has a role definitely'.

There was a definite glow about Mouratoglou.

It's true that she [Serena] is special but I feel it is normal because when you have the chance to be with Serena, nothing is incredible. You know that she is capable of doing what no one can do. She did it already so many times in her career. You have to expect the unexpected. I cannot be surprised by her. She always gave the feeling of being a strong personality and incredible competitor. I am with Serena. What is unbelievable is that you feel like you have a role in writing the tennis history. She may break the records of all time and this is the most strong feeling that I have. When I see her winning those titles, the happiness, this I really take emotionally. This is strong too.

Mouratoglou was still officially coach to Grigor Dimitrov, the young Bulgarian who ended the year ranked No. 48, but there were ongoing discussions because he was specialising more and more with Serena. 'For Grigor I don't think he can feel well with a part-time coach so he is working with Jean-François Bachelot [former French player]. We will see how it will work. I have been with only Serena since the US Open.'

Even with Serena, Petra and the rest of an appealing field in town, the WTA (they had officially dropped the word 'Tour' from their title in what appeared little more than another expensive rebranding) had still spent a year in fruitless search for a lead partner. The six-year Sony Ericsson deal, signed in 2005 and worth $88 million at its inception, had been the largest of its

kind in women's professional sport and represented a tremendous coup, but it finished at the end of 2011. Miles Flint, the
British executive who had done more than anyone to draw up
the deal, had left the company in the meantime and said that 'it
wasn't quite the same any more'.

Sony said that their brand had evolved and their business as
well, so tennis had worked its magic for them. They remained
the title sponsor of the Miami tournament, which was the Sony
Ericsson Open in 2012 and would be the plain old Sony Open
in 2013. The deal had obviously been as good for them as it had
been for the women's game. 'They have been a great partner and
we will miss them,' the WTA said at the time. In 2011, five million
people had attended women's events, up half a million from the
2005 figure. Prize money rose in 2012 to a record $96 million. In
2005, it had been $60 million.

In a world economy that was stagnating at best and receding at
worst, the WTA's options for a lead global partner were limited,
so they had to enhance their support brands. BNP Paribas and
the Rolex Group stepped in with new deals and the women's
tour also entered into a four-year deal with digital sports-media
company Perform Group PLC with the aim of doubling the
profile of the women's game.

That may have been true in time but the press attendance
for the fancily titled championships was the lowest I could
remember for such a prestigious event. The only two British
writers present were me and Richard Eaton, a long established,
diligent and knowledgeable freelancer who had agency and radio
work and said he would try to sell his prose to a few UK outlets.
His emails weren't answered.

Why had it come to this? There was a powerful field for the
event. Williams, who missed the finals when they first moved from
Doha to Turkey in 2011, Kvitová and Kerber were in attendance as
were Maria Sharapova, Victoria Azarenka, Agnieszka Radwańska,
Sara Errani and Li Na. Stosur and Marion Bartoli tagged along in
case of a mishap. Unlike the men's event, which showcased eight

doubles teams and included doubles in each session, the women restricted their field to four teams who played a semi-final and final, with a golden tie-break to decide if any match went into a third set. The doubles players were not exactly thrilled with that. As it happened, Lisa Raymond and Liezel Huber, the latter of whom had just adopted an eight-week-old child, came to Istanbul and stayed on the tour's tab for a week for the thrill of one match (the same was true of the Italian Roberta Vinci, whose partner Errani had at least played three singles).

As the speeches droned on at the draw, Williams and Sharapova, who were seated side by side, seemed wonderfully chummy. What did they find so funny? 'It was PG-13,' Sharapova said when asked about their conversation. 'And it was nothing whatsoever to do with tennis.'

The last player onto the stage was Azarenka, world No. 1-in-waiting and looking every inch at home. She wore Alexander McQueen, as befitted a young lady in her position. The year had been rather good to Vika who, if results went her way, would become the eleventh different player to finish a season at No. 1 since the introduction of the computer rankings in 1975.

The morning before the event began, I had an hour-long conversation with her coach Sam Sumyk, a Frenchman who had worked on the tour for many years and had been with Azarenka for almost three years. I had come across many tennis philosophers in my time but Sumyk was one of the most intelligent and thoughtful people out there and was obviously very good at his job. He was also in the middle of one of the more unusual arrangements in the game, for he was married to the former professional player, Meilen Tu, who represented Azarenka on behalf of Lagardère Unlimited.

'To be honest, first it is Vika who has chosen the two people,' Sumyk said.

I was pleased for Vika because she chose her and I guess she was fine for that choice but I did think 'shit, this is going to be complicated to have my wife as the manager' but I was wrong. It is very easy and simple, and the reason is Meilen is an agent and she has to think business of course but it was important to take into consideration that she was a player, and she has not forgotten that. She sees the two aspects. Meilen knows that the main thing is to make sure the player delivers. Basically, you let the racket talk.

Meilen sees more of a mid and long term. She is not 'okay Vika is the No. 1 let's make as much as we can immediately'. She has that quality. I think they get along, they don't tell me everything [he laughs] but that is normal. I don't need to know everything. I don't want to know everything. What interests me is the training and the tennis part, the rest is not my business. I adapt with it, that is the best I can do. I was sceptical at the beginning and I was completely wrong.

The 23-year-old Azarenka's season had been extraordinary. In the first month, she won the title in Sydney, then followed that with her grand slam breakthrough at the Australian Open, which coincided with her rise to the top of the rankings for the first time. She won her first twenty-six matches, taking the titles in Doha and Indian Wells as a consequence. After her crushing defeat in the US Open to Serena in the final, she had won fourteen straight matches, winning the China Open in Beijing and, a week before arriving in Istanbul, the Generali Ladies Linz event in Austria. She had fourteen titles in total, the fourth best among those currently on the tour. She had won gold in the mixed doubles at the Olympic Games and a bronze in the singles.

I took Sumyk back to January. He did not believe she would win the Australian Open, even during the final, and thinks that win is what may have made the difference. At no time did he get ahead of himself.

But I think it is huge what she accomplished. I don't know if people realise but there is a lot at stake because first she is a player who everyone feels has the potential to win one, maybe a couple but she hadn't done it. It is her first final, playing Maria [Sharapova] who is a fantastic champion and there is the No. 1 spot at the end if she wins. And she walked through the match like she was going shopping to the mall. She performed incredibly considering all this and she did it on a big stage in front of the world. The feeling was good, seriously. It still feels good.

I think she is becoming a helluva professional athlete and a helluva young lady and I mean this in a good way. She wants to be the best possible, so as a coach it is a privilege to be beside this type of person and athlete. I am a little part of it every day, I share things every day with this person and this is a cool thing.

We had become used to teenage phenomena in tennis: the likes of Chris Evert, Jennifer Capriati and Martina Hingis had blown us away in their eras but all the current evidence indicated that champions were blossoming later on (Francesca Schiavone of Italy and Li Na had both won the French Open in the past three years at the age of twenty-nine). But at twenty-three, were not the expectations on a young lady in this crazy world still much too much? The press, especially, demands perfect elocution, great manners, incredible resolve, humility and common sense. And if anyone falls short, they are judged harshly. These are sometimes intolerable burdens.

Sumyk often can't believe what he hears and pointed out to me that these are extraordinary, special humans that the rest of the world often struggles to comprehend.

We expect so much out of people who are twenty years old, twenty-one, because I think they are dealing unbelievably with what they have to deal with. The media, nobody is ever happy, [there is] always crap to write and to say because that is [what] human nature is. We go easily to the negative side but rarely to the positive side. And as far as I know there is the same distance, one way or the other, we always see the negative aspect. I have no idea why but that is what it is and they have to deal with that. They have to perform, they have to train, not complaining because it is a privilege, it is a beautiful thing but we forget that. I think we ask too much of young exceptional people. I don't know about you but me at twenty-three, I wasn't as good as they are – tennis-wise guaranteed – but as a person, there is no way I could handle life as well as they are doing. But we are still criticising, trying to find this, this and this and why don't they do that, that and that.

A good example is with the grunting. Okay, a lot of people love to write and talk about it. What would be nice is if all these people could stop wasting their time and talk about how well they are playing, how great are these players, obviously I will name two, Vika and Maria, they would rather talk about than say 'damn, those girls are playing great tennis, they are offering a great show here,' but no that is not good for business. Certain people don't talk about this, they would rather talk about the bullshit.

As social media opportunities increased, so did the level of criticism. 'I think it is very good that every single person has their own opinion and we have to respect everyone's opinion,' Sumyk said.

What is difficult to respect is the people who are insulting and definitely something that is unacceptable is the people who make comments on the internet, that is so easy. Most of the time they use a stupid name to hide their true identity. You cannot let those comments affect you, you put them in the toilet and you flush.

If she pays too much attention to this, she will shoot herself. She has to be strong enough and focus on something else. Her priorities are the same as they were a year or two years ago, to improve and be the best tennis player she can.

Of course not everything runs smoothly, even for the top player. When the WTA declared at Wimbledon that it was working with the grand slam events to 'drive excessive grunting' from the game with a series of educational measures for younger players, it ran its statement past Sharapova but not Azarenka, which upset her deeply. As these two were regarded as the 'excessive grunters' of the modern game, the WTA ought to have consulted both. It was a commonly held belief that there was one rule for Serena and Maria and another for the rest, as manifested by no one other them being allowed to hold a cosmetics contract because of the WTA's deal with Oriflame.

In terms of stepping up her public relations portfolio, Azarenka decided to employ Benito Perez-Barbadillo, whose company BPB1PR was linked almost exclusively to Rafael Nadal. This was seen as a significant development though; as he watched her press performances in Istanbul, Benito marvelled at how confident and erudite Azarenka was for one so young.

Just as Perez-Barbadillo was arriving, so were representatives of the four grand slam tournaments. The women felt that in all the discussions and debate about prize money levels at the majors in 2012, they had been sidelined. There was also the distinct animosity from male players who felt that the women had spent the year tagging along. When Stacey Allaster, the chairman and CEO of the WTA, said that women had done their bit to move the discussions along, it inspired a chorus of derision, most notably from Sergiy Stakhovsky.

Allaster expounded:

This summer, I heard for the first time from my players that it is getting tougher financially and when we did our 2013 prize money distribution, we made a conscious effort to get more prize money down to the early rounds, the first group of players. Through my conversations with Brad [Drewett of the ATP] he is 100 per cent spot on, to have made the main draw of a slam you are one very good player and what we want to be able to do is to attract the best athletes in the world because we are in competition and we need to show these young athletes that tennis is a sport in which you can have a viable career. To be 100 in the world you should be able to make a good living, and that is what we are trying to calibrate. It's there.

It helps the sport overall if players can hire a good coach, take care of their bodies and even put a little bit away because some will need a second career and it is important they have something in the bank so that they can carry on after tennis. And we need these players so that we have a competitive tour.

The competition in Istanbul was fierce, with the exception of Serena Williams who thumped everyone in sight. There were 73,000 ticket holders over six days of women's tennis, the matches were invariably high class and quite often exceedingly long. It was uplifting to see the event so widely supported, especially after the experience of three years in Doha, Qatar where there were always more empty seats than occupied ones. In a sense though, without Doha there would have been no Istanbul. The WTA was using its property to appeal to distinct markets – and those countries with ambitions to stage other major sporting events. Qatar had since won the right to host the 2022 World Cup football competition and Istanbul was one of the cities bidding to stage the 2020 Olympic Games. Before Doha, the WTA made almost nothing from its championships, and it was going to market for those who wanted to stage it after the Istanbul deal expired in 2013, with $15 million as its bottom line. Seeing full stadiums day after day could not hurt the WTA as it sought to step up its search for a new lead sponsorship partner either.

There were some tired girls on parade. Kvitová, the 2011 Wimbledon champion who had struggled to live up to that billing, played one match against Radwańska and was red-eyed as she felt neither her fingers nor legs moving. She announced the next day she was suffering from a virus and would take no further part. There was a Fed Cup final coming up the following week between the Czech Republic and Serbia which further made up her mind. So Stosur would be summoned from the bench and Linda Pearce of *The Age* was exceedingly happy. The matches perked up; those between Azarenka and Kerber in the Red Group (Azarenka won 6–7(11), 7–6, 6–4) and Sharapova and Radwańska in the White Group (Sharapova won 5–7, 7–5, 7–5) were among the best of the entire year and tied the tournament record for the longest matches in terms of games (thirty-six) in a three-set match. They were followed by one that was even better, in which Radwańska defeated Errani 6–7, 7–5, 6–4 in three hours and twenty-nine minutes at gone 10 p.m. at night. She had to come back and play Serena in the semi-finals the next day and she was toast.

The Azarenka victory was vital to protect her chances of ending the year with the top ranking, and she knew that by winning two round robin matches she would succeed, regardless of results elsewhere. The only player who could pip her was Sharapova, though that would need an Azarenka meltdown. And though Serena defeated Azarenka in straight sets and cranked up the pressure, the girl from Belarus held her nerve against Li Na and the acclamation was all hers. Her press conference on the Friday evening went on for longer than any of hers that year. 'When I first started to play tennis as a little girl, becoming No. 1 in the world seemed so far away, and now I'm standing here with that trophy,' she said. She had also become the first woman to surpass $7 million in earnings in a single year and won the WTA Diamond Aces Award presented to the player who consistently 'goes above and beyond' promoting the sport to fans, media, and local communities by performing off-court promotional and charitable activities.

Sumyk was looking forward to a holiday in Hawaii after such an exhausting year but in his mind he was planning ahead, because nothing ever stopped in tennis. 'There is the economic boss and that is Vika because she sponsors everybody, she is the financial boss but the boss of the project, the logistics, the training, that is me, nobody else,' he said.

You are going to tell me the person who holds the cheque book is more powerful than the other one and that is possible but if it is, it will not work. It is not about power, it is about the chemistry. You have to find people who complement each other, and that can be despite age difference, sex difference, whatever.

I don't know why Murray chose Lendl or why Lendl accepted but I'm sure they both thought about it more than twice before doing it. They understand each other but to do that you have to be a good listener and I have to believe they are both good listeners when the other talks. That is the base to have. At the end of the day, if there is a decision to make about the tennis then it is Lendl who should make it.

Sumyk hoped, too, that a greater emphasis would be placed in the year ahead on making sure as many players were as healthy as possible all the time.

It is very contradictory the people who lead tennis saying we are here for the health of the players, yet the rules force you to play even if you are not 100 per cent. That is going against their principles. We want to have ten months of great tennis, the best players fit all the time but basically they are not allowed to get sick or a little bit injured. You can only be healthy or REALLY badly injured.

Radwańska, more staggering than hurt, could not put up much of a fight against Williams in their semi-final and Azarenka lost against Sharapova to no great surprise, though she was taken aback to be told she had to stay at the event for the final just in case neither of the finalists could appear on the Sunday afternoon, and she would have to go out and play an exhibition match. This was laughably indulgent of the WTA, but it had the power to impose a fine on Azarenka so she did as she was told.

As for Serena Williams, the prospect of facing Sharapova for a third time in the year was nothing to be too concerned about. She had only dropped five games in their previous four sets and had won their last eight matches in total. She was incredibly relaxed, as was evident to me as she perched herself on a sofa in the players' lounge with her Yorkshire terrier, Chip, in her lap.

We recalled that moment at the French Open when she had a decision to make, the ramifications of which were not apparent at the time. 'Emotionally I was going through a lot and I guess I couldn't pull myself together,' she said.

I really tried, but I put too much pressure on myself. I had been playing so well and expected to win that tournament. I wanted to do great things and it all went down. Whenever I lose I hate it. I hate losing more than I like winning.

It was an impulse thing. I didn't want to go home. I had a flight and I sent a BBM to Patrick asking are there any courts in Paris I can work on and he said, 'Come to the academy.' But I said, 'It's a bit far, I don't want to go.' He said, 'We will figure something out.' And I just decided to cancel the flight and went and trained there. It's funny how one little thing can change everything. I was packed and I was in that 'I want to go, I don't want to go' dilemma and one little BBM text totally changed my path.

It happens in everyone's life. Did you ever see the movie *Sliding Doors* with Gwyneth Paltrow, where she misses the train and the story unfolds about the differences that would happen in her life if she caught the train and missed it? Her life would have been so different. My life could have been different – maybe better, maybe not. But it would have been completely, completely different. I'm happy and really excited about what the future holds.

The warmth that had been shown towards her in Turkey was, perhaps, a mark of a growing sense that Serena was loved in greater part than before.

I hope so. I can only say I am who I am, and as time goes on you gain fans and you grow older and you learn and you gain respect. I understand that not everyone is going to like me. I like some singers more than other singers and actors more than others – it's the same. I don't take anything personally, but the rewards I'm getting [in fan support] are awesome.

But she accepted she had polarised opinion in the past: 'Oh yes, I know there have been [those who didn't like her at all].'

There was no debate that, as Serena had raised her playing standards – a style of play based around indefatigable will and a serve that would dent rock – so the rest of women's tennis had to step it up. As they had improved, so she had to get better. It was a virtuous cycle and one that she marked with a scorching victory in the final over Sharapova and the WTA Player of the Year award, proving that whatever the computer might say, she is the No. 1 athlete of this age and quite a few others.

Chapter 14

The Season Comes to a Close

THE ROYAL COURTS of Justice on The Strand were as iconic a setting as the ATP could have nominated for its launch of the last great tour event of the year. In previous years the finalists had been guests of the Prime Minister at No. 10 and also been to Battersea Power Station, whose cavernous insides were turned into a giant party-piece for the evening.

Onto the stage the superstars came to raise funds for Great Ormond Street Hospital and the night ended with a cheque for more than £400,000 donated to this most worthy of causes. Andy Murray thanked Roger Federer for being the man who transformed his life following his teary defeat in the Wimbledon final. Fourteen-year-old Sam Cheetham, a GOSH patient, talked emotionally about how the hospital had been pivotal in his life and the entire audience welled up.

Only David Ferrer – appearing in the Paris final – was missing from the gang of the eight singles players that made up the Barclays ATP World Tour Finals, the fourth time it would be held at the O2 arena on the river Thames and to where, with little pomp and circumstance, it was confirmed that the contract was to be extended until 2015. British tennis had more reason to rejoice.

The event and the location had become a perfect fit. Almost every session was a sell-out (even the doubles), and the decision to ask Chris Kermode to take over the planning and execution of the event in 2009 had proved an inspired one. He said the ultimate obligation of any tournament director was to fill his venue and, by tagging a singles match on to a doubles once in the afternoon and once in the evening, he fulfilled that obligation. Kermode attended pop concerts at the O2 to get a feel for what would suit an event about as diametrically opposed to Queen's (where he was tournament director) as you could imagine. The court at the O2 was raised and the lighting picked it out superbly. What was almost as important was that the public got the best seats and filled them, so the sponsors had to swallow the compromise of seats a little further away from the action. It was the right thing to do. Too many tennis tournaments – and prize ones at that – are spoiled as television spectacles because the front six rows are empty. Kermode's 'trick' had been a decisive success. The players loved the intimate feel and the fact they played to full houses. By the close of 2012, a million people had passed through the turnstiles to watch tennis in November, an amazing number and a terrific tribute to Kermode's foresight and planning.

This was the ATP's big sell of the year and what they were selling was well worth purchasing. They had to make hay while the Fab Four (Nadal would be back one hoped but for how long?) kept going. The final was on a Monday for the first time because the Paris event had been played the week before rather than with a week in between, a decision taken in 2010 in order to lengthen the off-season. The squeeze meant that pre-publicity time for the finals was at a premium.

This was Federer's eleventh consecutive appearance in the finals, a record of consistent excellence that might not be surpassed. I had been to them all, from his inauguration in 2002 when the event was first held in a makeshift centre in Shanghai and he lost in the semi-finals to Lleyton Hewitt, to this celebration on the banks of the Thames. It was not until 2005 that Tony Godsick began representing Federer on the recommendation of one of his clients at the time, Monica Seles. It turned out to be the second best decision of his life (after marrying Mary Joe Fernández).

The split from IMG in May that led to the forging of their

own association had been an immense and emotional wrench. 'After nineteen amazing years, I decided I needed a new challenge,' Godsick said.

So when my contract ended, I decided not to renew and leave to start my own company. I will continue to represent Roger in the same way but will be able to do different things I might not have been able to do for him at IMG, just based on the size of the company. IMG was a great place to get my career started and I was fortunate to learn a lot from some incredibly bright and creative people. Mark McCormack [IMG's late founder] was a genius and all his lieutenants were incredibly smart and driven so the opportunities afforded me during my tenure at the company were awesome. Many times when people leave a company after so long, there are negatives. But in this case, it was a friendly split. I will always root for IMG to do well. In terms of large firms, they are miles ahead of their competition. I will always have their DNA in my blood. I will never lose this.

Today, I handle all Roger's business affairs on a global basis, which include endorsements, licensing, exhibitions, appearances and social media initiatives. Roger works with a bunch of global brands and part of the reason he has become well known around the world is he has associated himself with brands that are strong, powerful, global and well liked. Many of these partners market and advertise Roger in parts of the world where he might not actually play and this really has helped grow his brand around the world. He is amazing to work with. What is so nice and special for me is he takes an active role in his business. Many other athletes rely on their agent to just bring deals and really don't like to participate in the process and he is exactly the opposite. He likes to be involved with the entire process from A to Z. The fact that his participation and the energy he puts into his business relationships is authentic is felt by all his partners. Roger has an amazing perspective on the world and he enjoys this aspect of his career. We spend a lot of time brainstorming and talking about how we can enhance his partnerships not only because he feels his partners deserve it but because he really does enjoy this part of his business.

I never take for granted the fact that for the last seven years I have had a front row seat to watch history unfold. Sometimes I am able to take a step back from the business relationship and really just enjoy him playing as a regular fan. I always try to get into the stadiums before they introduce him as I not only like to hear and see the crowd's reaction when he walks on court but to hear it when the announcer introduces Roger and lists his credentials. I never get sick of hearing what he has accomplished because it really is so incredible.

There had been new announcements this year, however, as the four grand slam finals had been won by the No. 1 (Djokovic) winning the first, the No. 2 (Nadal) taking the second, the No. 3 (Federer) securing the third and the No. 4 (Murray) claiming the fourth. Now Djokovic was assured of the No. 1 position again but his mind was cluttered, with his father Srdjan's illness uppermost in his thoughts. Here was a chance, perhaps for someone else to strike. Djokovic may have had the top ranking assured but the thought-provoking Jon Wertheim of *Sports Illustrated* indicated that he felt Murray had been the player of the year. His had certainly been the most compelling storyline.

These two were worth every penny they made and it was a decent time to be a good earner for, in 2012, the French Open had increased pay by 7 per cent, Wimbledon 10 per cent, the US Open 11 per cent and Australia would initiate a 15 per cent increase for 2013. In the light of systematic criticism that the men had led the way on prize money reform, Craig Tiley turned his mind to whether there might be more than one way to determine a player's worth.

The Australian Open tournament director said that tournaments needed to be 'creative and innovative' at looking at their payment structures for the future. 'Every player has value equity but how to calculate that value?' he said.

The sweat equity is easy: you win a round, you earn. Perhaps we should look at what they generate in ticket sales, their social media activity, broadcast value, their consumer awareness and likeability in the public's mind. You could come up with a formula where you gave a player a score. All these things are worthy of consideration. The time has come to welcome the prize money discussion because it is driving a change and change is healthy. We are good in tennis at talking among ourselves and we don't ask enough of what the consumer really wants or believes in.

The really strong sports move fast and innovate quickly. They are not tied down with heaps of bureaucracy, they have governance structures that are modern, leadership that is independent. We must not put our heads in the sand and think it is all going great just to protect our positions.

The grand slams had long been looking at how they might determine a better way forward. There had been talk of incorporating a fifth slam. Some were in favour, others not, but how long would it be possible to fend off the wealth of the Chinese who were increasingly certain in their own minds that they should be a part of the grand show? Much was happening to the profile of the sport in South America, which did not have a single 500 series event on the ATP Tour (unless you count Acapulco).

Perhaps the grand slams could come up with a better overall concept for the future of the sport. Bill Babcock had long been working on such a plan and at their various 'retreats' during the year, the subject came up for discussion. Was the prospect of the grand slams determining the calendar (Wimbledon had shown that they had the muscle and determination to move) and taking over the governance and the finance of the sport, a possibility? I felt it was and, what is more, so did they. There was a sense as long ago as 2003 that the rest of the sport did not have the wherewithal to construct a coherent and coordinated professional tennis calendar and, as a result, players at all levels were denied a clear understanding of where and when to play (and when to rest). There was much talk of a confused public and an uncertain market that did not know where it should invest beyond the recognised assets. How much farther forward had we come in almost a decade? Not far.

The grand slams appreciated the risk they were taking in throwing their weight around, but felt it was better than staying 'outside the fray' and continuing non-beneficial contractual relationships with the tours. It was, I believed, a subject to which they would return, better prepared and more robust, in the months to come.

⟋⟍

The prize money in London was hugely significant; a singles title winner who did not lose a match would take home $1.75 million. 'You can feel the importance of this among the players,' Federer, the defending champion, said. Last year, when he had won the title, the Swiss had angered Barclays, the main sponsor, by stuffing the ribbons on the handles of the trophy into the top of the cup where they could not be seen. The fact that he was sponsored by Credit Suisse was seen as justification. Quite who Barclays wanted to win this time around they were not saying.

Murray started proceedings with a come-from-behind victory over Tomáš Berdych about which Simon Barnes, writing in *The Times*, said:

> Murray still goes in for, as it were, self-abuse, but it's no longer self-destructive. He knows that he has one of those big titles in the bank now: that makes all the difference – a bit like talking to girls before and after losing your virginity. It's not that you're going to have your own way every single time, but you know that having done it once, there's every possibility you will do it again. Life is never quite the same after that.

As matches came and went, some fascinating, others a little more predictable, we ended up with the usual arithmetical conundrums.

To qualify from Group A from the last series of round-robin matches, Djokovic and Murray had to win against Berdych and Jo-Wilfried Tsonga respectively; similarly if Berdych and Tsonga won, the Czech would top the group and Djokovic would be the runner-up. Beyond that, all sorts of outcomes were feasible, involving sets, games and percentages. In Group B, Federer guaranteed his place in the semis thanks to a straight-set win over Ferrer, but a subsequent loss to del Potro [the second time in successive events he had beaten Federer indoors] meant that the Argentine had gathered enough sets to deny Ferrer a place in the final, even though the Spaniard had defeated him in the round-robin.

The Sunday semi-finals were out of the top drawer. Initially del Potro was swinging free against Djokovic; there seemed no stopping the big man, who led by a set and a break at 2–1 in the second. Djokovic knew he must respond here and his immediate recovery of the break seemed to sap all the strength from del Potro, who had been taken to three sets by both Federer and Ferrer in the qualifying process. Djokovic won 4–6, 6–3, 6–2, charging through the last set and a half.

The reception that greeted Federer when he walked out to play Murray was astounding; that for Murray more muted, which was odd for a home audience. During the match, it became clearer still that the stadium was divided, indeed a fraction more were in the Swiss corner, or were the Swiss simply making more noise than the locals? I was shocked, in all honesty. Of course, Federer is a much-adored iconic figure, but Murray was a grand slam champion, an Olympic gold medallist. Where was the love this time? Murray was heckled in mid-serve as he attempted to fight back in the first set and double-faulted. Towards the end of an enthralling tie-break, Murray changed rackets and a tiny section of the crowd booed him – which was completely unnecessary. At other moments, minor errors were jeered and his better efforts received with what one might describe as a ripple of applause.

Federer won the match 7–6, 6–2; no one denied him his

success but the reaction from the crowd prompted me to write a commentary in *The Times* the following day that received the most responses to any piece I had written since the paper's content was placed behind a pay-wall. The headline said HOME IS WHERE THE HURT IS.

> Yes, Murray has been a bit of a boor; he still chides himself probably more than any other player at the highest level, openly, outwardly, aggressively, often shockingly. He wants to win so badly. He utters loud swear words [I have heard Federer berate himself but he disguises it as beautifully as he moves]. My goodness, sometimes Murray's hair is a mess and he has a bit of stubble whereas Federer is so wonderfully neat and he has a $1 million Gillette contract. Now what else can we have a go at Murray about? Ah yes, he's from Scotland. Can't ever let him forget that.

Many of my relations are American and they acknowledge that they may not be able to pinpoint immediately and exactly where Scotland is on the globe. Thus, when Murray won the US Open in September, it was because of his heroics, because they knew he had striven so hard, because it had been such an exhilarating match, because he had tried and tried and finally made it, that they went mad for him. I am actually rather glad he won there first. Americans 'get' Murray. We don't. Even Federer was a little taken aback. 'Well, we have played here twice before, and twice the crowds were amazing, electric, and sometimes even in my favour,' he said. 'So today was somewhat similar again.' It was a particularly anti-climactic backdrop to Murray's final match of the year.

The final lived up to expectations in that it proved, once again, that Djokovic refuses to take 'No' for an answer. 'No' when he was 3–0 down in the first set, 'no' to being denied when serving for the first set at 5–4, 'no' when he led the second set but fluffed a couple of forehands and Federer broke back, and 'no', a great big final 'No', when Federer felt sure he had seen off a match point at 6–5 only for the Serbian to launch himself horizontally at a backhand and send it spearing down the line for an outright, title-clinching, majestic winner. Djokovic had won the first major title of the year and its last. The Barclays ribbons were safe in his hands.

During the week I spoke to the man about his year and its consequences. His father was recuperating, his team was invigorating, his life intoxicating, his talent stupefying. 'Losing my grandfather, who I was very close to, was a big blow for me mentally and having my father critically ill in the last few days has been very difficult,' he said as his car made its way through the capital's throng.

These are the things that make you wonder who you are. I was fighting this week on many fronts. It's not just thinking about tennis because all of these circumstances mean your thoughts are all over the place and that is something normal to expect. You are human, you have your feelings and it is natural to be thinking of the health of people but generally, we are professional athletes and this is what we have to do, we have to fight our way through. It is a responsibility but also it is a privilege and a pleasure.

I am aware that the tennis career is not very long, you cannot predict to what age you will play because it has become so demanding physically and I think people underestimate how difficult it is for the body and the mentality, going week after week in different time zones on different surfaces and conditions. All these things can affect you.

Knowing you have done really everything to be where you are, that is an even greater success and has more value. When I came onto the tour, the majority of the players didn't care what they ate or what they drank and now everyone takes care of their diets and that makes our sport even more competitive. That is why it is important to remain so professional and committed. My ambition has not dimmed. Remaining No. 1 in the world is definitely one of the goals and so is trying to win every grand slam I play. I really have nothing to fear and nothing to doubt.

The doubles title would be won by Marc Lopez and Marcel Granollers of Spain, the weekend before they represented their nation in the Davis Cup final. This tall and thin, short and squat pair had brought an end to the romanticism of a victory for Jonny Marray and Freddie Nielsen in the semi-final, which showed once more that what the pair achieved at Wimbledon was no trick of the light.

In the O2 final Granollers and Lopez defeated Mahesh Bhupathi and Rohan Bopanna of India who, by a quirk of fate, defeated Radek Štěpánek and Leander Paes in the semis. The post-match exchanges between Bopanna and Bhupathi with Paes were of the cursory kind. It was the 1,000th match of Bhupathi's career and one of his most satisfying victories, especially as it was his final match with Bopanna.

'I'm playing with [Daniel] Nestor next year and then I am retiring,' Bhupathi said. 'There is a lot of juggling in the doubles. Rohan wanted to get back on the "ad" court. I understand that. A lot of people are changing partners. This was my fifth world tour final with five different partners. Six would be nice.'

It was a special moment too for Lars Graff, who took control of his final match in the chair when he umpired the singles final. Initially the ATP was cool about allowing me to interview the Swede [the paranoia about officials speaking to the media prevails] but eventually we were allowed to talk, so long as Gayle Bradshaw, the tour's head of rules and regulations, could eavesdrop our conversation.

It was a mark of the esteem in which the 52-year-old former marine from Bastad – who is remaining in the men's game in his capacity as a supervisor and an instructor of young umpires – was held that Federer mentioned Graff in his departing speech. It did not get much better than that in terms of respect for an official. But he knew the time was right to leave the chair. 'It is like being invited to a party – it is better to leave it when people still want you to be there rather than when they are turning out the lights and saying, "Can't you go home now, it's three in the morning",' he said.

This was the first time that the official tennis tours had ended so soon. The women had already packed their bags in late October and by the second week of November the men had joined them too. Caroline Wozniacki took the time to go and watch Rory McIlroy play a bit of golf in the Middle East, in Asia and in the United States. They travelled to Brazil together where Wozniacki played in a couple of exhibition matches with Maria Sharapova, Serena Williams and Victoria Azarenka. McIlroy was full of praise for his girlfriend. 'Seeing how hard she works, and how hard she practises and how dedicated she is, definitely flipped a switch with me that I could be more like that,' he said. In 2012, McIlroy earned $14,359,035 (£8,956,305) on both PGA and European Tours, which equates to $1,982 (£1,236) for every shot he hit.

> I feel like my personality away from the golf course hasn't changed, but definitely when I get to the golf course I'm a little more professional, a little more business-like. I guess that's just the way you have to be to be successful and to try and win as many tournaments as you can. It's helped me to win more tournaments.

At the same time, Wozniacki had won only two titles, slipped to No. 10 in the rankings and earned a trifling $1,408,240 in annual prize money. Together, though, they purchased a $10 million home on the Bears Club in Jupiter, Florida where Jack Nicklaus, Michael Jordan, Michelle Wie and Ernie Els all have properties.

As I was in Florida for four days in December, I tried as best I could for the last time in a year to arrange an interview with them but was told that, as of now, they did not want to speak as a pair. You could not fault me for perseverance but, equally, the depths of my frustration were immense.

Laura Robson was also in Miami, working through the most serious training block of her life with Željko Krajan, her coach, and fitness trainer, Dejan Vojnović. Hers had been an impressive season but there was also a fierce resolve to do better, not to rest, to push on. It was what, we hoped, drove all players. I sensed that Laura had really grown up in the past year, taken big decisions, made bold on-court statements and was ready for the biggest career push. From the innocence of fourteen – when she 'won junior Wimbledon and people expected [her] to go out and beat Serena Williams the next day' – to the sparky resilience of a nineteen-year-old on the threshold of the top fifty, Robson was making important strides. She had heard the whispers that she was not the most athletic of players and how it might hold her back the further she wanted to climb the rankings ladder.

I know I'm not exactly the most athletic person but it is something that can be worked on. I've worked really hard in the last six months and I'm moving better now than I was at Wimbledon so it is just something I have to do. Even the Andys of the world, some of the best movers, have to do it because you must never stop improving at your movement and speed work. I move well enough to get to the majority of balls and though obviously you have players like Serena where almost anyone will struggle to get her shots back, I don't think it [lack of movement] is something that will hold me back at all.

I've still got a lot to work on but I'm going in the right direction. I never mind talking about tennis but you go into press sometimes after a tough loss and you are asked questions by people who don't necessarily cover sport, that's tough when you are fifteen and you've lost your first match at Wimbledon. I think I'm dealing with it better than before.

The choice of Krajan had been bold and decisive, given his reputation for not beating around the bush when it came to work and criticism. 'If you are in this sport for a long time you will always upset a few people but I knew I needed a tough coach with a lot of experience because that was what I was missing,' Laura said.

There were a few options but I had seen him around a lot before, and I was impressed with the work he was doing. [Dinara] Safina was No. 1 in the world and that broke up, but the dynamic we have is very different to that he would have had with other players, I think, because I'm a bit more relaxed.

I've had some coaches in the past where it was very easy to do the same thing every day and you get into a rhythm where you aren't pushing yourself to your limits and that was something I needed to do. It's a natural decision to make if you feel you're becoming repetitive and are going to tournaments and losing to the same ranked girls every week. If you are losing, you want to be losing to the top girls so you have to train like a top player and that's want I think I'm doing now.

There have been a lot of sacrifices my family has had to make and there have been some tough days but it is starting to pay off now. My brother couldn't go to places because I had to go to a tennis tournament and my Mum was away with me a lot. Everyone was very happy to do those things but you have to work hard to make your family proud.

It's tough not to be competitive in our family and this is a tough sport because there are no team mates and you are relying on yourself but I've always been super competitive and I take that into everything I do. I have had my moments on court but I still want my grandparents to watch on TV and think that I come across as a nice person. I wouldn't want to be someone they couldn't be proud of.

♪

Pride in Murray from a British perspective had grown beyond all recognition in 2012. He had said many times that he wanted the press to see how he trained and so, in mid-December, five of us took up the challenge. I knew how hard he drilled on the court and the balance between what he did there and how he prepared away from the lines was every bit as crucial. And so, we gathered on the beach at Crandon Park, opposite the site of the Sony Open with Jez Green, his fitness coach, who set us a few simple tasks.

We ran a mile and back, then sprinted (as best we could) 400 yards and discovered he did that ten times straight with a minute to gather his breath and thoughts in between. We followed a Bikram yoga routine (Murray was more into pilates by then) and joined in a selection of his gym routines, one of which on a killer machine called the 'Versa-Climber' that has helped define a body as strong as anyone's in the game.

He sat with us for an hour, chatting openly and honestly. It was the week of the BBC's Sports Personality of the Year award and his tendency to eschew such events was rooted in 2004 when he was in the nominees for the Young Sports Personality award (he had won the US Open juniors that year) but had inadvertently locked himself in a toilet and had to be freed by someone with a knife. Murray finished third in the public voting behind Bradley Wiggins, the first British man to win the Tour de France, and Jessica Ennis, who won gold in the Olympic heptathlon; it was quite a performance, considering he denied Mo Farah, the 5,000 and 10,000 metres gold medallist, Sir Chris Hoy, the cycling golden boy, and Ben Ainslie, four times an Olympic gold medal-winning sailor, a place in the top three.

Murray talked a little about Dunblane and what happened there in 1996, something he had rarely discussed before. He was inspired on his return there in September by many people saying what a positive uplift his performance in New York had given a town whose name evoked so many unhappy memories. (The very next day a gunman killed twenty children and six teachers at an elementary school in Sandy Hook. Andy wrote on his Facebook page: 'My heart goes out to all those poor children, their families and the community in Newtown in Connecticut, so, so sad'.)

A content Murray had earned time to rest but there was little downtime involved. He was walking tall. And he was talking in the manner of a grand slam champion, with a sure touch, clarity and confidence. He said it had got to the stage where he was embarrassed to be seen in the street, which was quite something to reveal.

I've felt more confident, maybe, as a person, like to just go and walk with my head up, and just walk down the street, whereas before I was always sort of head down, I never wanted anyone to say anything to me. The Olympics final was unbelievable to have that much support behind you. After that match, I just felt much more comfortable, a bit more accepted.

To be honest, I don't really like getting pointed at. I still feel a bit uncomfortable with that stuff... But, you know, it's something you learn to deal with. I just feel a bit better about myself. Maybe I also felt like having lost in a lot of finals or in a lot of tough matches, whatever, I was letting whoever it was down. I know I'd been reminded every day for the last five years, six years, since someone has won a grand slam, and I knew about that, so there was a part of me that probably felt a little bit of responsibility. So it's nice, finally, not to have to worry about that stuff any more. I can just play and see what else I can achieve.

There's going to be downs and I'll definitely lose close matches and I hope I'll be in a position to play for grand slams in the future. You know, I may lose one. I may lose a couple. But I know I can do it now and I've got the right team of people around me. It works well for me, for my work ethic. I have a chance to win more and that's where the US Open was a huge motivation for me, because I realised after that match that all of the stuff that we do here, that it was all worth it in the end, because there are times when you question it a little bit, when you've lost a lot of big matches. But now I know that it's worth it, and it's made me want to work harder, to give myself another chance.

Lendl was in attendance, working his pupil hard, in accord with Green and physiotherapist Andy Ireland. The team-work was exemplary, Lendl having time to school Murray on the latest technical advances he wanted in his game, after Green and Ireland had got the player into the finest physical shape I had seen him. Reflecting on their first year together, Lendl said:

Once again, I have got a lot of credit for Andy's play this year and I'm not sure it is justified. I tried to help him the best I can, I am there for him if he wants to ask questions, I point things out and try to make practices the best they can be for him. However he's the one who plays and if I wasn't around, he could have had the same year. The timing could be just luck. We will never know.

He learned a lot from his former coaches, there is no doubt about that. Many times, I would have a golf lesson and I'd be driving home wondering what the hell the pro was talking about and three months later I'm on the driving range and something starts happening and it is in there somewhere and it is 'ah, that is how it is supposed to feel'. Brad [Gilbert] texted me straight after the Olympics and said, 'congratulations you have done a great job' and I said 'Brad, he has learned a lot from you as well'. I meant it because Andy would not be where he is without his mother, without Leon [Smith], without Brad and Miles [Maclagan] and Mark [Petchey]. I often think with my daughters and their golf, I will hear one coach say one thing and then six months later another coach says the same thing and it works and they understand and they do it. I'm not trained in psychology, so that people understand what I say. Maybe we just clicked, and he understood something from me and one or two words in a sentence and he got it. There are people who can explain this crap but I can't.

Lendl did think that the time Murray had spent with psychologist Alexis Castorri in Florida had been a boon. 'She is brilliant,' the coach said.

I wouldn't have worked with her and I would not have suggested it to Andy if I didn't think she was. It was one of the questions I posed to him at the start, would he be open to that. It was very important. I don't even know what they talk about. There is something to it because Jack Nicklaus never hit a bad shot that was his fault, either the wind came up or 'caddie gave me the wrong yardage' or the club wasn't right and it served him pretty well. He didn't get angry, but he didn't get even either. It's not a bad thing to say about Jack, but it is showing how strong your mind could be. There is something to it and Alexis knows how it works. It worked with my kids and it worked with me.

It is not just one thing, it takes a while and perhaps some things don't get triggered until something else is said. I don't think anyone truly understands it all but for me, the human brain is the biggest area left for improvement in sports, we don't know enough about how the mind works. When I was playing I was throwing my sentences out there in the hope that someone would contact me who understood what I was trying to get at. A lot of it can be luck, you can say something at a certain time that is looked upon as a negative and suddenly it is a positive. Part of it is feel. I have seen Andy saying about me that I have had a feel for the situation [losing grand slam finals] which I believe is one of my strengths.

At practice this week, I am standing behind Andy at the back of the court most of the time because I am watching angles. I am a player on the court again and if he hits it somewhere where I don't think he should have hit it in a standard situation, I will go and ask or offer a reminder. Only a former player can do that. One of the greatest things Tony Roche [Lendl's former coach] had was that he had been on the stadium court on each of the grand slams for the finals in the singles, which is an experience you cannot buy. I don't mean to be down on anyone, in fact I recommended Bob Brett to Andy in one of our initial conversations about who should coach him. [Brett, an Australian disciple of Harry Hopman, had coached for years on the tour but never played to an exceptional level.] I wanted Tony to coach Andy as well but it didn't happen.

Murray then learned that if he was to retain his Open title, it would require another Monday evening finish, as the USTA decided to extend their championship by an extra day in 2013, binning the 'Super Saturday' concept and incorporating a Monday climax and a day of rest in between the semi-final and the final. This would be an initial one-year test with more negotiations to come which, if the ATP had anything to do about it, promised to be very testing.

The opening round of the Open would still be played across three days, a scheduling idiocy that strained credulity, except that it kept as many of the better players in the event as long as possible. And the men's tour was not fully appreciative of a $4 million increase in prize money either, even though it raised the total remuneration for the event to $29.4 million. How the USTA intended to allocate the funds – what would go to first round, second round, champion etc – was deferred until later in the year when they had seen how their grand slam colleagues had decided to act. 'The disproportionate amount of prize money relative to tournament revenue and the extra day demonstrate a tremendous disconnect from where the players felt the conversations were heading,' ATP Board member Justin Gimelstob said.

That disconnect was evident as the USTA officials landed in Melbourne for the 2013 Australian Open and ran headlong into a stream of players voicing dissent at their proposals. Federer had believed that a Monday finish was the last resort, not a set-in-stone undertaking. He thought it would be for one year and then discovered it was two. Chastened by the attitude of the male players, the USTA shuffled back to New York, redid their sums, counted their bruises and came up with a doubling of their initial proposed increase, so that an additional $8.1 million would be paid in 2013, taking the total to $33.6 million. By 2017, the pot would be an extraordinary $50 million. These purses were taking tennis into realms it could not have imagined a decade earlier.

Recognition for the contribution the leading players were making was arriving in many guises.

Djokovic arrived in London to receive the Centrepoint Great Britain Youth Inspiration Award from HRH the Duke of Cambridge at the Royal Albert Hall for his work with a foundation that had raised $1.4 million for early childhood education in Serbia. From there he took a few days' break in the sunshine on

Necker Island, owned by tennis lover Sir Richard Branson, before announcing that he had joined IMG Worldwide 'for exclusive worldwide management and representation', a poorly-kept secret since the US Open.

Under the terms of the exclusive multi-year agreement, IMG would represent him in developing 'a brand-building strategy through marketing, endorsements, appearances and licensing along with select global business initiatives'. IMG chairman and CEO Mike Dolan, welcoming him at a momentous time in his career, said:

> Novak is a superb tennis player, and world-class competitor who demonstrates a very strong character through his passion and commitment to his game. I believe he has the ability to translate those qualities into achieving great success working with global brands in the marketplace.

Djokovic was equally delighted:

> I'm very happy with how my career has been advancing these past few years. Working with IMG will continue to build off of that momentum. IMG's expansive global footprint will offer me a truly unique set of resources to explore business opportunities that simply do not exist anywhere else in the industry.

Federer – six months into his lone venture with Godsick, having parted with IMG – was on a trip to South America, his first as a professional, taking in Brazil, Argentina and Colombia. In Buenos Aires, 5,000 people greeted him at the airport, similar to The Beatles when they first arrived in New York. He was surrounded by security, a measure of the depth of love for him that this particular continent had not been able to show before. The whole experience was stunning in its colour and expanse. Chris Clarey of the *International Herald Tribune* accompanied Federer on the tri-nation excursion and relayed the contrast in vibrance and passion with Wimbledon that Federer experienced on the continent.

> I've had more fans break down here in South America than anywhere else in the world. They cry, and they shake, and they are just so, like, not in awe but so happy to meet you. It's disbelief for them that they can meet me, and that is something that has happened a few times before, but it's very rare. Here I must have had at least twenty people probably hugging me and kissing me and so happy, you know, just to get a chance to touch me, even. And they've actually been very, very respectful when they realised I couldn't sign more autographs because it was a safety issue or whatever the circumstances might have been.
>
> It is totally an out-of-body experience, almost disbelief that it's really happening,

One notices that the great Swiss feels very fortunate to experience such adulation and affection and it is reasonable to think that it is something that keeps him from retiring. After all, it is a phenomenon that might not be so prominent when he calls time on the most stellar of careers.

It was hardly a non-profit mission. According to local reports, Federer received $2 million for each of his six matches, which had to have made this the most lucrative exhibition tour on a 'per-night' basis in the sport's history. It also earned Federer significantly more in thirteen days than the official $8,584,842 he received from the entire 2012 season; a year in which he returned to the No. 1 ranking for several months and won six titles including a seventh Wimbledon. No one decried him a single red cent.

In Majorca, Rafael Nadal was still working towards a return, with the Abu Dhabi exhibition pencilled in. I travelled to Porto Cristo for an interview with him the week before Christmas to see how he was. He greeted me as always with unprepossessing warmth but his manner was more restrained than usual, a little troubled. His knees were still not as good as he wanted them to be. He said he needed to be careful, that the images the doctors were viewing of his knee were good enough that it left him in a state of calm, but that he still felt something was not entirely right. He would take no risks with his future, however long that might be.

I wondered if he had considered modifying his style, to try to play tennis in a more subtle, less aggressive manner. Might that help? 'I would love to be that good to change but I am not that good,' he said.

I am good because I play this way. If I play like Federer I'm not good, that's the real thing. Everybody plays with everything they have, so Federer understands the sport one way, Djokovic another way, Andy another way, Ferrer another way and I understand it my way. Every way is correct but I didn't start playing tennis a few months ago, I started playing tennis at three. My style has been always similar that's true, but my position on the court has improved, my serve has improved, my game has improved but the general game you cannot change, the mind you cannot change. I think my way worked well, I don't have a lot of options. My way is to play when I am ready to play my way. When I have played like this I've had the right results, I've been competing for everything and feeling I can beat everybody, I am twenty-six years old, it is not the time to change a lot of things, it is time to recover well, to improve a few things that can help you, to run a little bit less but the essence of the game will be the same.

Spain, the nation, was hurting. The economy was in a bad way, the talk was of a separation of the Catalan region, a nation fragmenting, looking for something to cling to, for a glimmer of something to smile about. They were waiting for the return of the man who had become a beacon of light in their sporting firmament.

The situation in Spain is negative, a lot of people are suffering. I cannot say being me is difficult [in these circumstances]. What is difficult [is] the people who are trying to find work every week and to survive with very few things. That is difficult. Not being Rafa Nadal. It is a dream for me and I am lucky and I say thanks for the life and for what is happening to me.

I really did in all my life what I felt. I didn't create an image. I don't do things for what others will think of me. I do it my way. I try to do what for me is correct, what the close people to me and family taught me and that is what I did all my life. Then, for me it is not difficult. I feel very lucky to be who I am. I say thanks for the life, the sponsors who have confidence in me even more than ever in these moments.

You miss the feeling to compete, when you go on court, when you go inside the court competing for something that brings you something very special. This is not because you play a tennis match but you are going to play in front of a lot of people who are cheering for you, who you know that are behind you, supporting the sport and that is something I missed but I have to accept and await the right moment to be back.

It takes time. The people have to know when you are outside of the competition and didn't play for a long time, you will have problems to come back to your best, but that is the beautiful thing of sport, of life, that it gives you challenges and this is another one. I think I passed a few before with a very positive feeling and I hope that is going to happen again.

Within three days of our interview, Nadal had withdrawn from Abu Dhabi, Doha and Australia, so 2013 may not start for him until February at the earliest. There could hardly have been a more contrasting emotion as, on the last weekend of the year, it was announced that Murray had been made an OBE (Order of the British Empire) in the Queen's New Year's Honours List. His pride was inestimable.

Epilogue

Doping

In the febrile aftermath of the Lance Armstrong doping revelations of late summer 2012 that sent the world of cycling into a contorted tailspin, it was inevitable – if terribly sad – that doubting the trustworthiness of athletes became, if you will pardon the expression, a blood sport. Tennis was not immune to this rash of judgemental articles which were largely, but not unconditionally, confined to the internet.

Josh Goodall, the British professional, purged his soul.

I swear on my mother's life if someone said 'Josh, take this drug and you'll be in the top five in the world in tennis, a multi-millionaire and there's only a five per cent chance of getting caught' I'm telling them to jog on.

I'd like not to be remembered as a drugs cheat. It's a simple decision. For those who have a conscience. I might be stacking shelves at ASDA but I'd sleep well at night. Armstrong should go to jail for a long time. Cheating scum fraudster. Live strong? Live strong, my arse. How can you get a sense of satisfaction from winning when you are cheating? Maybe it comes with having £10 million sat in the bank account because of it. If he was in my lounge now I'd swing at him with my Babolat.

Though a trifle curt, Goodall's response was what we should expect from anyone who earns a living from sport. Cheating is an abomination. But when Armstrong, seven times a winner of the Tour de France, is 'outed' as one of the most blatant connivers we had ever seen – banned for life, shorn of his immense reputation and with a myriad of legal proceedings in the offing – the levels of curiosity in other sports multiply. Goodall certainly accepted that.

No one wants to believe there are doping cheats and corrupt minds in tennis but as Richard Ings, once a professional umpire, executive vice-president of rules and competition at the ATP World Tour and formerly chief executive of the Australian Sports Anti-Doping Authority, said:

> Performance-enhancing drugs [PEDs] provide athletes in any sport with an advantage. Any sport that requires fitness, speed, strength, longevity, or fast recovery, there is a PED to give those athletes a big advantage over their peers not taking any. Tennis is clearly a sport where all those elements are to a player's advantage.

Did tennis have a doping problem? How deep and dangerous were the evils of match-fixing? There were websites springing up that powerfully articulated a belief that tennis was hiding something, indeed they appeared not to want to rest until someone at the top of the game was discovered to have been a doper. These websites targeted journalists – me included – who they felt were not asking enough tough questions of the people in power. I was accused of 'wilful blindness' to the extent of the doping problem.

Newspaper journalists cannot, on the basis of hearsay and limited probability, cast aspersions on tennis players and yet that is what those writing mostly under the cloak of anonymity on the World Wide Web did with impunity. They did not fight shy of naming names without, so far as I knew, a shred of evidence to the contrary. This is a dangerous game.

The fact of the matter is, I wrote a piece on anti-doping in *The Times* arguing it was time that Djokovic, Federer, Nadal and Murray took a decisive lead and demanded action. They should have told the ITF that its duty was to put in place the finest system money could buy and perform the tests to catch offenders. The anti-doping budget in 2012 was $1.8 million and yet there was a $300,000 under-spend. How can this happen? That would pay for 500 decent blood-doping tests and then the sport would really know where it stood.

The incredible sensitivity of the subject did not mean it was off limits. I may not have asked the question every day, but I asked it often enough. The ITF is responsible, as the international governing body, for running the Anti-Doping Programme in tennis and it does so with all the means at its disposal with the resources, both financial and manpower, it can muster. It is too simplistic to say that because funds are not as ample as they could – and should – be that the ITF is not doing a thoroughly professional job.

The information is there for all to read: the players have a wallet card updated each year that is available to download from the ITF's website. It details the 'substances and methods' prohibited at all times (in and out of competition) and additional substances prohibited 'in-competition only' that include stimulants, narcotics, cannabinoids and glucocorticosteroids. There are Theraputic Use Exemptions (TUEs) by which if a player has an illness or condition that requires use of a medication containing a substance on the Prohibited List, a Therapeutic Use Exemption (TUE) *may* be granted that enables them to take the medication without committing an Anti-Doping Rule Violation. However, it is better to be safe than sorry.

In 2012, only three anti-doping cases were prosecuted by the ITF. The US wheelchair player Kaitlyn Verfuerth, twenty-six, provided a sample at the 2011 British Open that was found to contain a prohibited stimulant. Verfuerth asserted that the substance had entered her system through her ingestion of a prescription medication; however it is a player's strict personal duty to ensure that no such substance enters their body and she did not hold a valid TUE. She was suspended for six months in addition to the disqualification of her results from the British Open, with a resulting forfeiture of ranking points and prize money won there. She was eligible to return to competition from 1 March 2012.

Dimitar Kutrovsky of Bulgaria, twenty-four, provided a sample at the SAP Open in San Jose in February which was found to contain methlyhexaneamine, a prohibited stimulant. Kutrovsky accepted the stimulant had got into his system through his ingestion of a supplement Jack3d, denying that he had taken the supplement to enhance performance.

He had, however, committed an offence and the decision was a two-year suspension, backdated to 14 February and thus ending on midnight of 13 February 2014. Kutrovsky appealed to CAS (the Court of Arbitration for Sport) which is permitted to reduce such a sentence by up to half of its original term based on what it regarded as the player's degree of fault. CAS determined the appropriate length of ineligibility should be fifteen months. Kutrovsky could be back playing in May 2013.

The third case was the most intriguing. A Spanish doctor, Luis Garcia del Moral, had been given a lifetime suspension from participating in any sport by the United States Anti-Doping Agency (USADA) for various Anti-Doping rule violations that came to light as part of his involvement as one of the members of the medical staff working for the US Postal Service, the team of which Lance Armstrong was a member. Del Moral practised sports medicine in Valencia, Spain and the ITF announcement said: 'in that capacity [Moral] has worked with various tennis players.' This was a horrible prospect.

The violations for which del Moral was cited included:

possession of prohibited substances and/or methods including EPO, blood transfusions and related equipment, HGH [Human Growth Hormones], corticosteroids and masking agents; trafficking of EPO[†], blood transfusions, testosterone and HGH; the administration

---

† EPO is short for Erythropoietin, a naturally occurring hormone, secreted by the kidneys, whose function is to regulate red blood cell production. The use of EPO in athletes started in the 1980s as a quicker, cleaner alternative to blood doping.

and/or attempted administration of EPO, blood transfusions and
HGH; assisting, encouraging, aiding, abetting, covering up and
other complicity involving one or more anti-doping rule violations
and/or attempted anti-doping rule violations.

Here, it appears, is a signature violator. As a signatory to the
WADA (World Anti-Doping Agency) code, the ITF is obliged to
recognise and respect decisions of the other code signatories that
are consistent with the Code and within that signatory's authority.

The del Moral case sent considerable shockwaves through
tennis. It was said that David Ferrer, the Spaniard who played
ninety-one matches and won seven titles in a meritorious year,
and Italian Sara Errani, the French Open finalist and multiple
singles and doubles winner in 2012, were acquainted with del
Moral, with all the concomitant sinister implications. Errani
admitted contact with him but, though the ITF did not preclude
her from seeing him again, added: 'Of course I'm not interested
in keeping working with a person that is involved in these things.'

Ferrer insisted he neither knew nor had met Dr del Moral. When
he came into a press conference at the BNP Paribas Masters in
Paris-Bercy in November, expecting a gentle interrogation about
his 6–1, 6–3 victory over Marcel Granollers, he was taken aback
at the relentless line of questioning about doping. Ferrer's English
is not anywhere near as reliable as Nadal's and so he struggled to
make his points.

This is the official record of the interview:

First question: I have a question about your relationship, if you
had any, with Dr. Luis Garcia del Moral. Have you ever met him?
How did you work with him? Do you still work with him?
Ferrer: I don't have relation. I don't have relation about this guy.
I never seen. I don't know who is. I know he working in Valencia
with some players, but I never talk with him.
Q. On the same matter, is it annoying to you, frustrating for you,
to have those questions about Dr. Luis Garcia del Moral given

what we know about Lance Armstrong and everything? What do you feel about the way tennis is related to the question?

Ferrer: I think it's not relation about tennis. I think this guy, he works about cycling. But I don't know because I don't know him, so I can't to say something about this guy.

Q. Just on the same subject, you said you know he has worked with some players. Is that with some other tennis players?

Ferrer: I don't know. I don't know him. I never talk with him. I don't know him. He goes there, I don't know who is because I never work with this doctor.

Q. But do the Spanish players talk about the subject?

Ferrer: No, no. In tennis, I don't think so. But no. He's the doctor of Armstrong, no?

Q. We have spoken to lots of players about the subject of drugs in tennis. What do you think about it? Do you think there are some tennis players who may take drugs or is it a big problem for tennis?

Ferrer: No, I don't think so. I think that tennis a very, very sport clean. I play tennis when I was young. I know the other players, and I think the tennis is one of the sport about is very clean. I can't talk about other sports because I don't know. But in tennis, I'm sure not.

We are reaching a stage where the top players are questioned all the time and are begging for more testing. The information to hand indicates there is nowhere near enough smart testing, so what is the impediment between players demanding and it being done? It's not about more money. With that $1.8 million, used wisely, tennis can have a fantastic programme, testing the top 50/100 with a 'tight' programme that ought to do all that needs to be done. The $300,000 underspend is more than AUSADA (the Australian Anti-Doping Agency) spent on its entire programme for all of Australian sport in 2012. This is ludicrous. That amount of money can fund 600 blood tests. Then the players can stand up at their press conference and talk about these numbers and have something to back them up.

Tennis writers were asking the questions, against the backdrop of the sense that the sport, once more, was resting on its laurels. The ATP and the ITF insisted that the testing regimes were rigorous and that no one had been caught but it was not good enough to preach 'tennis players don't dope', especially when the governing bodies could accomplish only a fraction of what could be done if the government stepped in and took the process under its wing.

Governments would have greater power, of law enforcement, of information sharing, of punitive fines, of jail sentences. According to one leading anti-doping expert, del Moral had his programme 'down to a fine art'. Could tennis compel Dr Del Moral to cooperate with any inquiry? No, it could not. The ITF should have been lobbying for government intervention, to get to the very heart of this debasing practice, to be able to properly punish wrongdoing, otherwise we are left with a sense that not all that should be done, has been done.

Horror of horrors, at the start of 2013, 'Operation Puerto' was on the tennis radar, as Spaniard Eufemiano Fuentes, the team doctor for the former Spanish cycling team Kelme and who had been involved in an eight-year police investigation, was brought to trial in Madrid. When police raided his offices, they found more than 200 blood bags and Fuentes admitted that he had worked with athletes from several sports, including tennis players. 'I could identify all the samples [of blood]. If you give me a list I could tell you who corresponds to each code on the [blood] packs,' he said. Tennis awaited further testimony with fear and apprehension but also, as far as one could tell, a clear conscience.

We were rightly revved up, not least because Andy Murray – initially hostile to the intrusive nature of the 'whereabouts' rule which meant the tennis authorities had to know where a player was 365 days a year – indicated that he felt more blood tests should be taken and he was not averse to a stepping up of the Out Of Competition (OOC) tests. His attitude was a welcome one. Tennis had a reputation to protect and having its name linked with Dr del Moral, however tenuously, was not good for credibility.

It was beholden on the ITF to bring del Moral to task, if that was what was required. Stuart Miller, the ITF's Anti-Doping manager, said under the Anti-Doping Programme, the federation had the power of investigation and had been exercising that power.

'There is no allegation that I'm aware of that he has been concerned with doping in tennis, nonetheless that doesn't mean you sweep it under the carpet,' he said.

> There is clearly an issue to be considered at the very least and – I need to be careful how far I go on this – there are a number of players who have been linked with the doctor and we have conducted an investigation. It's no secret that we have talked to players and interviewed players in regard to their links with this particular person and we have corresponded with the doctor himself and his lawyer and at this stage there is no evidence on which to take the matter any further.

Miller was in an unenviable position. He was charged with driving the Anti-Doping Programme forward and without doubt the funding that went into anti-doping in tennis required a massive boost if it was to meet current needs. Complacency was simply not an option. It was suggested that a mere $1.5 million was spent on the programme in 2012, which was a spit in the ocean compared to the profits made by the four grand slam tournaments. It did leave me to wonder if there was enough consideration given to the perils of doping. Were the authorities, as was often suggested, 'in denial'?

The funding was clearly negligible and there were accusations – vigorously denied – that administrators were more concerned with perception than tackling the problem, and those of us who wrote about the sport were more like fans who will 'believe the most improbable things and reject the obvious if their personal heroes are implicated'.

There was no doubt that the physicality of the sport had grown to a proportion that did, on occasion, defy belief. Matches were going on longer and longer and the standards maintained were quite extraordinary. Even those in charge of the physical conditioning of the leading players openly marvelled at their abilities.

Tennis is more dynamic than it has ever been, enhancing strength and conditioning are vital components and people are simply getting bigger and stronger. The average height of the leading players has grown by two inches in the past 20 years. Tennis is pre-disposed in some ways to favour taller people, if you serve from a higher point and have more options, which means there is a greater margin for error so you can hit the ball harder. Miller said:

> The present equipment pre-disposes tennis to become faster, rackets stiffer, bigger, players have learned how to generate more spin and therefore to hit the ball harder. But also there are better training methods, the science of sport has come to tennis in a way that it hadn't twenty years ago and so there are reasons, perfectly legitimate reasons why players can play these long matches. 'Are we satisfied we are doing all that we can?' I think it would be a naive person who would say we are catching everybody. History tells us that that doesn't happen, so it would be stupid if you said you were catching everyone who was doping either inadvertently or deliberately. What follows out of that is to what extent is there an inherent risk of doping in tennis. There is no doubt a sport with physiological demands, you play regularly for long periods of time, expending a lot of energy and play on alternate days – lots of reasons why there could be a risk of doping in tennis.

Miller accepted that there were constraints on the programme, not least its funding. He said he had to apportion the money the best way he could given the finite amount available to him. 'You do the best you can to prevent, deter and educate and those are separate strands we have to deal with,' he said.

If we could, we would test every player every day but we've thousands of players who are part of the programme so that is an impossible task. Within the scope and the constraints that we have, I think we make a reasonably good fist of achieving the goals we have to minimise the doping in the game.

The 'tennis has a steroid problem' websites had Miller consistently in their sights. 'All I care about is can I look at myself in the mirror and say, "Am I doing the job to the best of my ability without compromising any of my principles?" and I say "Yes."'

If there are people who want to question that and say I'm an idiot, I can live with that. It is free speech. There are some things I can't talk about because they are confidential in nature but in general terms I'm happy to talk [about] what happens under the programme.

Tennis operates under the WADA code and thus its programme has 100 per cent legitimacy. It did not make its own rules. There are two means of collecting a sample, either from a player's urine or their blood. A prominent school of thought suggested that the number of blood tests had dropped in recent months. Miller was adamant to the contrary. 'The answer is no, we are actually doing more blood testing,' he said.

What we used to do was what are called 'blood screenings' which were samples we collected and sent to a local laboratory or a haematology lab that were screened for evidence, a non-sanctioned analysis which would give us an indication of whether players were likely to be using EPO or an oxygen enhancing agent.

If these [screenings] indicated these possible uses, we would go back to the corresponding urine sample and analyse that in a different way. But those samples in and of themselves had no intrinsic value; you couldn't use that sample and analysis as the basis for a violation. Even though they were relatively cheap, we weren't getting value for money.

When Wayne Odesnik of the United States appeared in the main draw at Wimbledon as a 'lucky loser' – someone who had lost in the final round of qualifying but replaced an injured player – a sense of unease filled the men's locker room. In March 2010, Odesnik had been caught by customs officials at Brisbane airport in Australia with eight vials of HGH in his baggage. He was banned for two years from the sport, a sentence reduced by half on account of his 'substantial assistance' to the Anti-Doping Programme.

This left a lot of his fellow players feeling very uneasy. Murray called him a snitch. 'You want to make sure that people who are fined or suspended aren't let off because they are telling on other players', Murray said. Justin Gimelstob of the ATP Board was equally troubled: 'This is an isolating sport at any time but when you are confronted with something like this, you can multiply that a thousand times. There is a chill when he [Odesnik] walks into the locker room, that you can easily discern.'

Odesnik, who lost his first round match to Germany's Björn Phau, was bitter at the coverage surrounding his appearance in The Championships, which largely consisted of an article of mine in *The Times*. 'I heard today that there was a pretty harsh article and I think it's a little bit unfair for the media to write something that is completely and utterly 100 per cent false,' he said, adding that he had been able to demonstrate through his medical records the reasons why the medication had been recommended to him by doctors. 'I would 100 per cent never say anything about a player or do something that suggested I was a spy or something of that sort.'

That is utterly 100 per cent false. I provided to them [the ITF] medical information of why I had it. I was completely honest with them, and, therefore, they understood the reasoning and reduced my sentence.

The suspending of half of Odesnik's sentence on the basis of his providing 'substantial assistance' left many feeling distinctly uneasy. What did it mean? In effect, he had provided the authorities with help and would continue to assist them in their inquiries as 'an on-going obligation'. If the ITF discovered at some time in the future that whatever he had helped them with did not stack up, they had the power to reintroduce the suspended part of his sentence.

Miller said:

> We are trying to minimise, eliminate doping in sport and if some-one can say 'you've got me, fair cop but I can provide you with lots of information that you wouldn't otherwise have', what do we do about that? Should there be some kind of incentive or plea bargain which exists in other forms of law to say I will exchange that in consideration for a suspension of part of my sentence? The people who set the Code decided that was an appropriate means of satisfying the wider interests of the sport. You can look at it from one side and say it is snitching, but I would like to think the player who said that might one day say 'isn't it great, they have found out more about doping practices in sport'.

I asked Miller if he was able to say that in the light of Odesnik's testimony, the fight against doping had taken a step forward. The answer was an unequivocal 'Yes.' He added:

> If you are looking from the perspective of the wider interests, it is a positive move. I am not oblivious to the counter argument and I would never ignore that side of things because there is a different perspective, however, under the rules it was a provision that was available and he took advantage of [it] knowing the risks associ-ated with it.

What we did know however was that HGH, which Odesnik had carried into Australia, aided in fat-loss and recovery (from train-ing and injuries) and was on the banned substance list.

When Odesnik was apprehended in Brisbane, the customs officials there called Ings, the former head of AUSADA, who had developed a vital working relationship with the authorities. He would 'flag' customs when sporting events were taking place – most especially the cycling 'Tour Down Under' – when forensic searching of competitors' bags was stepped up and, yes, when the Australian Open and its feeder tournaments were on the horizon.

When anyone arrives in Australia there is a customs form to fill in and you are liable to declare if you are carrying steroids or other performance enhancing drugs. Odesnik had ticked the 'No' box, but customs, alerted by AUSADA to beaver through athletes' bags, found the damning evidence. 'They [customs] called me and said we have a bust,' Ings recalled.

> It was a slam dunk case. I called Francesco Ricci Bitti [the ITF president] and said that customs had busted a main draw player and he needed to know about this. I told him 'you've got to think about whether you should suspend him' but there was no mandatory requirement to suspend an athlete in the rule that would allow a non-positive case (we found it in your bag but there was no proof he had taken the substance). In my mind, possession is equally as serious as use, he had eight vials in his bag, he could have been passing it on to other athletes.
>
> I said to Francesco that the case was to be heard in a public court just as Odesnik would be walking on court at the Australian Open and you've a disaster on your hands. He wasn't convinced.

So Ings called the ATP to tell them of the serious nature of the implications for tennis and what a shocking affront it would be to the sport if Odesnik played in the Open. He pulled out.

Then came the reduction in the ITF's initial two year ban for the player's 'substantial assistance' which led to inevitable and deep-rooted concern among his fellow players as to what Odesnik had stated for the ITF to let him off half of his sentence. Ings takes up the story. 'There's obviously a conspiracy theory and he got let off, this is another problem, you should always release the basis for your decision,' he said.

> You can redact parts of it, if there's a name you can't make public or a particular fact you can't make public, but the reason why it's a one or two year ban, you should make it public.

Ings understood why his fellow players would want nothing to do with Odesnik, in the sense that he had betrayed a trust, but that:

> What they should have been saying is 'shit we're disappointed, he's a cheat, he needs to come forward and say what he knows, and we support that, we want a clean sport.' When I was at the ATP there was wall of silence, no one wanted to snitch on anyone else. I talked to a lot of players and they knew what was going on, they'd seen players making bets and when I asked them for details, they didn't want to be the rat in the locker room.
>
> WADA are all over this [the Odesnik case]. They are watching and they have appeal rights if they don't think the decision the ITF have announced is right. Substantial assistance has to lead to the conviction of someone for a doping offence. There are a lot of things to do to tick off the box to get that reduction in the penalty.

Odesnik just wanted to be able to play tennis again, as free as possible from the taint of suspicion: 'They [the ITF] saw fit to let me play. So what do you want from me? I'm here, I'm doing the best that I can, I'm playing, I'm proving that I belong here. I'm trying to keep to myself the best that I can, be friendly with people if they're friendly with me. That's it.'

Odesnik's contemporaries all had case studies to impart. Janko Tipsarević was in Kenya this year, in a house three hours by car from the nearest airport, when there was a knock on the door at 6 a.m. 'I'm telling you, it wasn't pretty,' he said.

I was very rude to the people but it was not their fault I was so pissed off. Dirk [his manager Dirk Hordorff] woke me up and said, 'come on Janko, doping' and I said 'Yes, go away.' You know how you wake up and don't know where you are? Then I realised I am in Kenya and Dirk is saying 'no get up they are here' and I said 'yeah sure'. And there they were. Trust me we get tested *a lot*. I am sure that in my circle I am surrounded by clean people. The Serbs I know are clean because I know a lot about their lives.

Murray recalled, among the many tests he underwent, one a couple of days before the Olympic Games when he visited the athletes' village. There was a tester outside the food hall waiting for him. 'At the French Open I was tested, at Wimbledon, twice before the Olympics and once afterward, after Toronto, and then after the US Open,' he said. 'I believe it is seven times since the French. I imagine I get tested twenty to twenty-five times a year. Tennis need to meet their quota, so I tend to get tested quite a lot.'

Miller's office in a corner of one floor at the ITF offices in Roehampton does not exactly offer the impression of a throbbing detective agency at work. It was clean, orderly but small. It seemed very remote from the world in which he and his team were expected to operate. It was from here that Miller had spoken about the idea that a 'cultural omertà' may operate among tennis players, that they kept what may be happening in the sport strictly between themselves.

We do our job to some extent a long way from tournaments and events and the testing which is done on our behalf, and to that extent we are isolated from the players. I imagine that they know as much if not more about doping in tennis than I do. You only need to read the book by Tyler Hamilton. [*The Secret Race*, which won the William Hill Sports Book of the Year, was the cyclist's story of the widespread doping in the Tour de France.] I would imagine there are players who have seen or heard things in relation to doping that haven't been reported and to that extent there has to be a culture of silence. I'm not saying it is endemic or there is a systematic problem that everyone is aware of or keeping a lid on but I'm saying I would imagine that somewhere there are things that players could report that haven't been.

I asked if more light could be shed on the subject of anti-doping measures but Miller said it was tricky.

By necessity there has to be a strong confidential element and a balance struck between providing information about the way in which the programme operates and trying to give people confidence that the programme is robust and fit for purpose. And you cannot allow people to know too much about how the programme operates to give them an opportunity, perhaps, to circumvent it. It is a difficult and uncomfortable balance.

Ings had been one of the first professional umpires on the tour, recruited at the age of twenty when he was thrown to the wolves (John McEnroe and Jimmy Connors) and equipped himself superbly in extreme conditions. When the ATP Tour was looking for someone to rewrite their rules on rules and discipline, he was just the man. He said:

When I rejoined the ATP the main focus was on supervisors and umpires and the code of conduct and they had this little thing called the Anti-Doping Programme and I wanted to make it better and close more loopholes. One of the things about testing is that it will only catch a fraction of those involved. It does not take a lot of technical sophistication to dope systematically for years and to be tested hundreds of times and be tested clean every time. We either have caught the arrogant or the ignorant. Testing is a great and powerful tool but it is only catching a fraction, which is why you need other methods.

Ings left the ATP two years later to become CEO and chairman of Australia's Sports and Anti-doping Agency and immediately felt a lot more powerful – for it is a government agency with government funding which was able, in the case of Odesnik, to call its brother agency in the United States to share the information, rather than anyone in tennis.

'Agencies cannot share confidential information with them [the ITF],' Ings said.

> Money will help to allow you to do more testing, but it won't solve the issue, you need other tools. The partnerships with law enforcement is one and you need to build a culture within a sport where when you see something as an athlete or player you go to the authorities and you let them know and you have the confidence they will listen and believe you and protect your confidentiality and view you as part of the solution and not part of the problem.

The other speciality in Ings' portfolio was anti-corruption, the second element of the sport that had grown wings in the last ten years, with so much betting on so many matches at so many levels. He said that 'if you were going to invent a sport where corruption could thrive, it was tennis because the opponent doesn't need to know a player has decided to miss the baseline by a couple of inches, they can do it themselves without consulting anybody'.

When Ings joined the ATP, the rule book had three sentences dealing with corruption. He developed an anti-corruption programme, saying that the 'flagging' of potential crime had to come in working with bookmakers. 'That is integral,' he said. 'I established relationships with major bookmakers who would give me a heads-up in a shift in the betting patterns and I could get word to the on-site supervisor to be in the locker room and to watch or videotape the match. It gave me a whole new cycle of information.'

> Before the anti-corruption programme there was open opportunity, the rules were very poor, there wasn't a belief that corruption

could happen and yet there was a massive amount gambled on the sport and I have no doubt then, as now, that there are players involved in fixing and tanking matches. We are talking of thousands of players from all countries at all levels but now there is a really solid programme and there are people being caught and that's good.

One of the staggering things I found is that there were [ATP] Futures tournaments where the amount being bet on a particular match would dwarf the prize money for the entire tournament – players could earn $100,000. But online betting companies have account numbers, what computers the gamblers use, what country they are in and it gives you a visibility you would never have in the past and is a very positive step in addressing the issue. There is a Tennis Integrity Unit (TIU) with ex-Scotland Yard detectives who quietly work with the law enforcement agencies and to a much greater level of sophistication.

There was to be a new hand on the anti-corruption tiller from 2013. The retirement of Jeff Rees, the first Tennis Integrity Unit Director, would mean a promotion to the position for Nigel Willerton, a former senior police officer with thirty years' experience in the Metropolitan Police dealing with complex criminal cases. I had dined with Willerton earlier in the year. You did not have to speak to him for long to realise there would be no hiding place from him.

Funding and Coaching

At the close of 2012, a year without parallel in the British tennis realm, the No. 1 tennis players in the world were Novak Djokovic and Victoria Azarenka. They were fiercely proud of representing Serbia and Belarus, neither of which had sovereign nation status the year Andy Murray was born. Together, their federations would not turn over in a year the amount of money the LTA listed in its balance sheet for the year as 'intangible assets'.

If anything was designed to heap pressure on the grand slam nations to step up their programme of player development it was that these 'new' countries were able to celebrate champions of such quality. On 31 December Serbia had three men, Djokovic, Janko Tipsarević and Viktor Troicki, inside the world's top forty and Novak's youngest brother Djordje was looking like he might become a bit of a star; Azarenka and Max Mirnyi had won the mixed doubles gold for Belarus at the London Olympic Games.

Millions of pounds are spent on 'development' in its many forms – most notably the lavishly backed but highly controversial Talent Identification system that was seen, by the Lawn Tennis Association hierarchy in Britain, as a panacea and upon which the reputation of many coaches and administrators hinged. Yet, behind the façade, its credibility as a programme was being called into question – tagging eight-year-olds as worthy of progress or not was a very dangerous game. The LTA was setting itself up as judge and jury.

There are so many parts of the system too fallible for judgements to be made. A major issue for coaches in the sticks is the credibility and experience of those who decide who is 'talented' on the testing days. The whole environment is perceived to be negative – 'coaches with arms folded and holding clipboards'. How could a child be graded after three minutes on a small court when club coaches are geared to long-term development, together with age-appropriate fitness work? How is it possible to determine if an eight-year-old has talent on one day of testing? Tell them they do not and they are almost certainly lost to the game. They might give up, deflated and demoralised. The whole system is uniquely flawed.

But the national federations will do anything, try anything and endorse anything that might uncover a star. They need to be able to shout 'WE DID THIS!' The grand slam tournament nations, those who enjoy staggering profits from the success of their championships, have most to gain and, similarly, to lose from the desire to produce a champion. The sport had become increasingly global and the more the countries that host the 'majors' spend trying to find the player who might save their collective reputation, the more the rest of the tennis world argue that profits from these failures ought to be more evenly spread. In the past ten years, the LTA has benefited to the tune of over a quarter of a billion pounds from the surplus from the Wimbledon championships and at the end of 2012 – a year in which they invested £73.2 million to 'grow and sustain' the sport – Britain had one male player in the world's top 200. It is a national scandal.

One can only marvel at the architectural breadth of the £40 million National Tennis Centre (NTC) in Roehampton in south-west London with its state-of-the-art sports science and medical facilities, splendid indoor courts, a restaurant with the finest cuisine, people staring earnestly into computers, but a distinct lack of trophies in the cabinet. Heck, even David Beckham uses the gym there when in town. The LTA has a plan though (who didn't) and wants time to see it to its fruition, though this has shifted from five years to ten and then, mercy save us, to fifteen.

But the more I understand the politics of the organisation, the more it is clear that the various departments inside the NTC are keener to protect their own positions than work for the greater good. There is a distinct lack of collaboration across the strands. 'There is no joined-up thinking in here,' one prominent employee told me. 'It's no wonder the "system" doesn't work.'

The No. 1 task for a writer in their designated sport is to form workable relations with the governing body, which ought to be firmly established and enriched as the years go by. In my case, this means trying to get along with the LTA. Throughout 2012 – and a long time prior to that – it was evident our relationship was viewed through a prism of doubt and suspicion. Why would I expend energy attempting to build a consensual understanding with an organisation when many of those appointed to 'leadership' roles since the present regime took over in 2006 had been warned 'not to have anything to do with Neil Harman'? Lunch appointments that were made in good faith were dropped because those wishing to dine had been warned they shouldn't be seen with me.

In a strongly worded three-page letter to Tim Hallissey, the sports editor of *The Times*, in May 2012 in which he could not bring himself to mention me by name, the LTA president Peter Bretherton wrote that the governing body 'is so often the focus of your correspondent's coverage' as if he supposed I would learn more about British tennis in the company of the Football Association or the England and Wales Cricket Board.

I subsequently learned that Bretherton would not have written it had it not been for the prompting of Richard Baker, one of two non-executive directors on the LTA board, a man who had been the chief executive of Boots, the pharmaceutical chain, and was now chairman of Virgin Active, which purchased the Esporta chain of tennis and health clubs for £75 million in 2012, of Nectar and of DFS, the furniture giant.

Baker had been spooked by a speech in the House of Lords by Baroness Angela Billingham, the Opposition spokesman on Culture, Media and Sport. She described the LTA as a 'total shambles'. I had seen excerpts from the speech and duly reported what she was going to say (journalists are often given advance notice of political speeches). Two years earlier, the Baroness – who occasionally partnered Prime Minister David Cameron in Lords and Commons tennis matches – had been asked by Gerry Sutcliffe, at the time Labour's Minister for Sport, to review the LTA and co-opted nine members to form a panel. 'We had a very short time, only three weeks before the General Election; we held hearings and wrote a highly critical report,' the Baroness told her fellow peers. 'We were shocked at the performance of the LTA, given its resources and freedom of action.'

> At last, Sport England, which distributes funds from Government and Lottery sources, found its voice. In April it announced that it would cut £530,000 from tennis because of a fall in participation figures. The drop of almost 30 per cent in two years was dire and the funding cut fully deserved.

Baroness Billingham had nothing to gain or lose by her account but the LTA was livid, not just at her contribution to a debate on the Queen's Speech (where peers could talk on any subject they wanted), but the tone of my article the next morning. Baker told Bretherton he should not take this opprobrium lying down. A letter duly arrived at *The Times* office, copied to me. It was highly critical of what the LTA regarded as my unfair and unbalanced reporting style and demanded a right of reply. Hallissey's response was succinct and supportive. I was grateful for his defence. A two paragraph précis of Bretherton's missive appeared on *The Times*'s letters page. I asked if the original letter could be reproduced in its entirety for this book but the request was denied.

During Wimbledon, I was introduced to Baker by the LTA's director of communications, James Munro, who had been brought in from the BBC and Sky to improve public relations, and yet was remarkably ill-at-ease in the company of the media. The venue was the partisan ground of the press restaurant. Munro scribbled furiously as we spoke. Baker acknowledged weaknesses in the set-up, but said he did not accept the premise of Baroness Billingham's speech and that the implication of my reporting of what I saw as LTA incompetence had tarred him with the same brush – 'we have had a four-fold increase in commercial revenues during the longest ever recession – is that a shambles organisation?' he said.

On the face of it, the LTA had made wise choices in Baker and

Val Gooding CBE, the former chief executive of BUPA, as its two non-executive directors. Their CVs were sparkling but how far did their 'independence' stretch? Baker and I met for the second time for breakfast at the RAC Club on Pall Mall. It was the morning after Heather Watson had won her debut title on the Women's Tennis Association Tour, in Osaka, Japan, an occasion *The Times* trumpeted across four pages. Before we had begun our conversation, Baker wondered why there had been no mention in any of my three articles on Watson's triumph of the funding the LTA had given to her. I said I did not consider it relevant. He firmly disagreed. (In fact Watson was first funded by the LTA to the tune of £5,000 by David Felgate, the former performance director, when the two options discussed were to attend the High Performance Centre in Loughborough or travel to the Nick Bollettieri academy in Florida. The family chose Florida.)

The poached haddock had arrived when I asked what Baker believed was the role of the governing body over which he could exert a considerable degree of influence. 'There are three elements that drive the success of British tennis,' he said.

> The first is the performance of elite players which is not an end in itself, we are not here to line Andy Murray's or Laura Robson's pockets on a personal level, they are professional adults making their own way, but there's no doubt that probably the single biggest driver of the game is success at the elite level.
>
> The consequence of having good players doing well means that tennis is in the spotlight for over forty weeks a year rather than just two weeks at Wimbledon. We spend more than we have ever spent – because we have more money than we have ever had – supporting elite players because success on the global tour has a big promotional effect. We are there to support and identify talented juniors, so I regard what has happened in the last three months (we were speaking after the US Open) as quite an endorsement of that leg of what the LTA does.
>
> The second leg of our role is to run major events. We are

involved in the ATP World Tour Finals, we are members of the committee of management of The Championships, which drives a big part of our income [£37.7m in 2012 alone] and we work with the All England Club to create a grass court season where Britain becomes the centre of the tennis world. On the back of that we generate another strand of income, through the sponsorship of those events, where we control the rights, with the likes of AEGON and Highland Spring. These events create occasions for fans to go and watch the best in the world playing in Britain and from that we drive revenue so that we can do the third tranche of the LTA's job, which is to encourage grass roots tennis and drive participation.

Baker agreed that participation was 'the great undone in British tennis' and 'we need to make a lot more progress at it'. In the LTA's annual report produced in December, it was suggested that £5.1 million had been invested in a year in facilities across eighty-seven projects, creating thirty-four new indoor courts, 113 new floodlit courts and 238,325 additional playing hours. And yet the numbers playing tennis, certainly in adult terms, had dropped. This, surely, went to the heart of the lack of dynamic leadership at head office.

In lieu of that, Baker was looking to cut costs and streamline at the NTC, which is exactly what Roger Draper, the CEO, had said he would do when he came into the organisation in 2006 – since when it had become bloated beyond all necessity. 'I think our central costs are a bit too high and there is an efficiency measure now sitting in the accounts of the LTA which wasn't there when I arrived and every year our central costs as a percentage of the revenue raised have been coming down,' Baker said.

I'm a fan of not jerking about strategically but having a simple plan and sticking to it. Learn as we go, be self-critical and the bits that aren't quite right, let's make them better next year. We know our broad direction so let's not put a different head on the horse every five minutes because you will not get delivery of something that takes a very long time to fix.

I liked Baker because he was straight and clear and even if I felt he knew little about the true extent of the incompetence of the operation and how it was viewed both at home and abroad, at least he did not go in for obfuscation. He had clearly never been to an LTA press occasion. At recent Davis Cup ties, we would be invited for drinks on the eve of the opening day but the atmosphere was uncomfortable and forced. We sat around and chatted, then parted, glad it was all over.

Briefings had become a strain for both parties, full of statistical mumbo-jumbo where one train of thought disappeared before another one, even less understandable, had been formed. Draper answered every question with a trail of statistics that were generally impossible to follow. In Glasgow, in April, we were summoned to discuss Sport England's funding cut, where Bretherton came out with an immortal line: 'The board has a strategy and we know what the strategy is, the putting into practice of that strategy is part of the strategy and the board is satisfied with the strategy and the way it's being put into effect. Until the board decides otherwise that's where we are.' Perhaps I would have learned more from the Football Association.

When Draper took over, the sport's leaders said it was a watershed moment for delivery. I called it the 'Night of the Sharp Suits'. There was something that didn't feel right – call it a veteran journalist's intuition. John Crowther, whom Draper had replaced, was a steady hand on the tiller, nothing spectacular, nothing dramatic, but nothing smooth either. Somehow, when the Draper team came on board, there were too many self-satisfied people around, all of whom seemed to know a lot more about what was needed in British tennis than people who knew it a lot better than they did. It seemed more MTV than LTA.

During the Rome Masters in 2012, I returned to the pizzeria a stone's throw from the Foro Italico where the British press were wined and dined by the takeover team of president Stuart Smith, Draper and his right-hand man, Bruce Philipps, a month after they had moved in. (They planned to hold the event at a grander establishment in the centre of the city but were apparently unaware that Tim Henman was playing that night and that the press might have something more important to do. The meal was hastily rearranged at a local restaurant at which we arrived in dribs and drabs.) Philipps has since left the LTA and Smith, who had served his presidential term, is now ascending the ITF hierarchy's greasy pole.

The LTA's mantra was growing the game, but not in the way Draper saw it. The new boss immediately tried to sign every coach who could move, apparently regardless of the cost or nationality. The most eye-watering was the hiring of American Brad Gilbert in 2006 for an alleged £700,000-a-year to coach Murray, a move designed to take the pressure off the governing body by providing the instant gratification of grand slam results. Gilbert was a really good coach with a fabulous pedigree but the sums involved succeeded only in upsetting every other governing body in the world, whose players started to demand that they were similarly funded.

John Lloyd, an old friend of mine, was appointed Davis Cup captain, Paul Annacone became coach and after spells coaching Pete Sampras and Henman and working for the United States Tennis Assocation in player development, he did not come cheap. Peter Lundgren, the Swede, was also brought in but did not stay long. As respective heads of men's and women's tennis, Draper appointed the former Davis Cup captain Paul Hutchins and Carl Maes, the Belgian. On the day of his appointment, Hutchins said to me: 'If we don't get it right this time, we never will.'

Greg Rusedski, the former British No. 1 and US Open finalist, had been sounded out for the captaincy when Lloyd departed in 2009 after defeat in Lithuania, when the LTA announced that a detailed investigation into the captaincy and coaching of the Davis Cup team would be held. There was much back and forth between Lloyd, his agent, and the LTA and their lawyers before a compromise was reached. It was exceedingly messy. Lloyd said that one day he would tell the world what really happened. It would be worth waiting for.

Rusedski was prominent in the frame but he was dropped from consideration when it became clear to the LTA that he was not Murray's cup of tea. Instead, he was brought in at considerable cost to become spokesman for the Talent ID programme and was made captain of the junior Davis Cup team which afforded him vital input into the programmes of the intakes at the NTC. Leon Smith, formerly Murray's junior coach, was appointed head of men's and women's tennis (he was to drop the women's in early 2013), a broad and significant portfolio for one so relatively inexperienced in the international game.

Murray's stunning success at the 2012 US Open and the Olympic Games had more than paid back the unprecedented level of investment made in him with the Gilbert appointment. Though that partnership lasted only sixteen months, Murray pointed out several times subsequently how much he had learned from the American's input. But Murray's progress smothered the lack of it elsewhere, even though LTA was stepping up its funding of players further down the scale who were neither good enough to make it, nor that far from retiring.

'I think we should have a bit more of a contract with the players that says if we are going to give you national money, what are you going to give us?' Baker said.

We could make it a bit like a student loan, though I'm not sure I want to discourage people from going into tennis because of the prospect they may have a liability hanging around their necks in ten years when they don't know if they are going to make it or not.

I guess instinctively I'm more comfortable with the idea of saying 'we will back you but in return this is what we would expect. If you do make it onto the tour, you might wear an LTA logo, I don't think it's an unreasonable thing to ask. Heather Watson wears an

AEGON patch, she is a member of Team AEGON and that's how her funding comes about.

Sir Dave Brailsford, the British cycling Performance Director, had argued that it was important for the best to work alongside the best. The sport's gold medal haul at the London Olympics and his subsequent knighthood indicated that he knew what he was talking about. He would argue vehemently about the importance of getting the best together and how good it is for them. 'We are trying to encourage this, to form a bit of a club, so they spar off each other and have the best coaches,' Baker said.

> There is an inevitable dilemma between 'here's the money, go off and plough your own furrow' on the one hand, which some might argue is the best way, or plenty of others who say you should bring them together, have them compete against each other, give them the best off-court support. Certain things suit certain people. I understand there are those who would want the freedom to go off and do what they want to do where they want to do it and say 'give us the money'. I would want some return on that please.

The LTA was able to pay its staff coaches high above the tennis odds, distorting the market, but guaranteeing unquestioned support. No one in their right minds on £70,000-a-year inside the NTC would rock the boat when they knew a job in the private sector would involve a salary less than half what they earned and with twice the risk of the sack if a player suddenly didn't like you. The LTA's performance expenditure in 2012 was £12.3 million and developments in the year included setting up a 'dedicated management team' [more jobs for the boys] to look after the performance programme. £4.2 million was spent on direct support to the men's and women's games through coaching, funding and 'player performance bonus incentive scheme arrangements'.

In his last briefing of the year at the O2 during the ATP Finals, Draper told the media: 'We have had a strong year, our main objective is to grow and sustain the sport. We have a big industry. Over the last eighteen months the British tennis economy has grown from about £1.3 billion to £1.5 billion' – twice the amount the entire gym and health club industry generated in 2012. Where he had got the £1.5 billion figure, no one knew. It was an extraordinary amount but there had been so many expensive flights of fancy since he and his acolytes had taken control of British tennis, there would be no surprise if this turned out to be another one.

At least Baker admitted that the LTA got some things wrong. Draper had not said anything remotely close to 'we cocked up' in six years in charge. Those outside the organisation were astounded by the indulgences inside. Perhaps the appointment of an independent chairman – David Gregson would join the LTA in January 2013 – will lead to a greater level of accountability and responsibility and, after an initial meeting with Gregson, I was left with the impression that things will not stagnate for long.

At another annual meeting of self-satisfied speeches and announcements, we learned that the salary of the 'highest paid director' had risen from £367,000 to £394,000 and his 'variable pay due under short-term incentive schemes' grew from £187,000 to £201,000. When you added pension contributions paid by the company, Draper†'s salary amounted to £640,000. If this was not shocking enough, we learned that the number of employees had risen from an already absurdly high 296 to 311 under the auspices of someone whose initial desire was to trim the staff back.

It was announced in December that Sport England funding was being reduced from £24.5 million to £17.4 million and the LTA

---

† Roger Draper announced in March 2013 that he would be standing down from his role as LTA chief executive in September at the end of seven of the most controversial years in the association's history. Gregson, the new chairman, had met with Draper to tell him of his plans to look more deeply into the governance of the LTA and though he did not raise the question of Draper leaving in that conversation, within days Draper said he would leave. He gave a speech at the NTC at which over 200 staff gathered and gave him a standing ovation. I am told there was hardly a dry eye in the house.

would have to produce a convincing plan for how they would spend the 2014–17 money to enhance participation, otherwise it would be distributed in other ways, perhaps directly to the clubs. One began to wonder exactly what the LTA did right and whether it wasn't worth disbanding the entity entirely.

'Their plan simply wasn't strong enough to justify the four-year investment, it doesn't have a good delivery plan across the country, there is not a good feedback mechanism, it is not really based on customer insight,' the report said. The level of participation among girls in Britain was, I was told, 'horrific'. The statement from Sport England endorsed everything that Angela Billingham had said in the Lords in May and which had sparked the ructions in the first place. She would stand up in the Lords again in December and describe the LTA as 'useless'.

The day the Sport England figures were released, the chief executive had his feet up at the Biltmore hotel in Coral Gables, Florida where he was staying to watch the Orange Bowl junior championship.

And as much as they attempted to espouse the greater inclusivity of their operation – the LTA made much of having held a board meeting in Tower Hamlets in East London as if it somehow suggested they were in touch with the real world – when the Tennis Foundation, its charitable arm which espoused the spreading of the message to all parts of society, held its Christmas celebration, they chose to stage it at St James's Palace. There's inclusivity for you.

♪

It was a wet and wild Wednesday in late November. The group of boys who were trying to practise on the NTC's outdoor clay courts – among them Jack Draper, the ten-year-old son of the chief executive – had been driven inside by horizontal rain. It was the British weather, so often heralded as the reason why we didn't produce tennis players, at its glorious worst.

Maybe one of these would be the LTA's chosen one and if it was young Jack, just imagine the furore. Ahead of them in the queue marked X-Factor were Kyle Edmund, Liam Broady and Oliver Golding, three of the quartet (Luke Bambridge, the fourth, was on tour in the USA) on whom enormous, some would say, incredible hopes were resting. This was the group in the transitional phase, trying to make the step from promise to produce.

Golding had won the US Open juniors in 2011, Broady had reached the boys' finals of both Wimbledon and the US Open in 2011 and 2012, Edmund was the youngest and just beginning to sprout a few bristles. If one or more of these lads 'maximises their talent' maybe the LTA will have its man. They had all arrived belatedly to the NTC, Edmund from Bisham Abbey; Broady, once coached by his father Simon, who loathed the LTA leadership but whose son decided that perennial stand-off was no good for his career; and Golding, the child actor who had initially preferred to do his own thing and had had several different coaches before realising he needed to have a steady foundation.

Individually they were as different as one might expect of teenagers from Beverly, Stockport and Richmond-upon-Thames. Together, they formed a formidable group. All of them were already represented, Edmund by Fraser Wright of IMG who had persuaded him to move from Octagon where he had been managed by Abi Tordoff, who takes care of Laura Robson, at the end of 2012; Broady by Ben Crandell at IMG; and Golding's manager was Cindy Morphy, who had once been a roadie for the Rolling Stones, an eclectic bunch (the managers as well as the Stones).

Edmund is tall, blond, getting bigger and stronger, and no waster of words; Broady, the boisterous one, is shorter than Edmund and whose emotion comes rushing forth; Golding the soft-spoken, off-beat, dark-haired one whose voice the microphone can barely pick up, which is odd for someone who had once had to project himself on stage. They ended the year ranked No. 568, No. 877 and No. 431 respectively. Edmund had won his first ATP Futures event, the initial rung on the professional ladder, in Birmingham, Alabama earlier in the month and received a text of congratulation from Ivan Lendl, no less.

I wondered if Edmund considered himself driven.

> I would say I am. When I'm asked 'do you feel pressure?' – I don't feel it from the outside but from within. I'm setting personal goals and I'm driven to satisfy myself and reach my potential. All I am is a good prospect – that is the reality. I've been a good junior but I'm 568, which doesn't cut it. I am on track but I'm not there and I shouldn't get ahead of myself.

He was given the opportunity to play the Australian Open juniors in January 2013 or more futures events in the USA. Wisely he chose the USA. 'Next year I need to kick on,' he said. 'If I had played juniors, with the travel and missing events, it would have been two months gone by.'

Edmund was appreciative of the surroundings at the NTC. 'I do sometimes look around and wonder how much it costs,' he said. 'We are lucky but it is here and we may as well use it. We get treated well, the food is great, the nutrition, they have all the supplements we need. Sports science is very good. There are a lot of people who buy into what you are doing.' What of the future?

> I do think about it. I was practising with Andy Murray on centre court before his Open semi-final in January, I was trying very hard and was tired out and for Andy it was just a warm-up. I need to improve my fitness levels. This year especially it has been so good to look at Andy, his improvements. I have changed the way I watch tennis, I don't tend to look at the ball-striking but at the movement more and these guys are constantly on the move, it is incredible.

I have known Edmund for a couple of years and Broady almost four. I knew all about Liam's father's struggles and how bitter he was when the LTA stopped their funding for Naomi, his tennis-playing daughter, after her appearance (apparently the worse for wear) on a social media site in 2007 because he considered the behaviour of some in the hierarchy meant that their treatment of her was hypocritical, to say the least. I had had many chats with Simon Broady down the years. He was adamant his son would never play for Britain while Draper was in charge of the sport. Whether this helped Liam as he tried to forge a career was a good deal more problematical.

He admitted to having been in 'a bad place' with his tennis at the start of the year. 'Australia was a real low on and off the court, I was going nuts. I didn't want to be a loser. And then something clicked in my mind and I wanted to go for it.' Broady had been inspired in Manchester by Adrian Tannock, who he described as his mentor, and Ric Moylan, a physical trainer who worked with Scott Quigg, an up-and-coming bantamweight boxer in the stable that turned out Ricky Hatton.

His son's move to the NTC – while it was a dagger to the heart of his father – was essential. 'The arguing that was going on wasn't helping, I had to get away from that but this is a fantastic place to be,' Liam said.

> Obviously it was very sad and I didn't want what was happening with the family but now I wasn't on my own all the time, I'm with the guys, my peers and that is good for us. My Dad did so much for me, no one could have done more, but it wasn't enough.

Golding has been the quintessential outsider, the maverick former child actor who wants to do it his way, with his own people. That worked to a point. He won the US Open juniors but the time came when the gloss wore off.

> You can't live on past success, it doesn't come into my head any more, it was a great chapter and I really enjoyed it and it helped with sponsorships [he remembered to mention Fred Perry, Prince

(rackets) and Ricoh (the imaging and electronics company)] but it doesn't mean anything in the grand scheme of things.

A Wimbledon wild card, guaranteed if he kept up his work rate, would help Golding's budget. The 26.1 per cent improvement in 2012 prize money for those who lost in the first round meant that however disappointed he was with his defeat to Igor Andreev, the Russian, he walked away with £14,500. It was enough for him to be able to afford to place a deposit on his own flat, three train stops from Roehampton.

The way of a budding tennis professional is not all optimum nutrition bars and café lattes at the NTC. Golding had just returned from an ATP Futures in Ashkelon on the border between Israel and Gaza, when the rockets started to rain down. 'The organisers said before the match if the air raid siren goes off you have forty seconds to get to the shelter so just run,' he said. 'That didn't happen but you could hear it going off in the town.' He lost his second round match there 6–2, 6–0 but said his shoulder was hurting from four straight weeks of tournaments and that one of his shoes split in the middle of the second set.

> That level of tournament doesn't get any coverage so they don't know what you have to do. They see Wimbledon and the big events on the TV and there is another whole world going on around it. There are 1,500 people out there with a ranking and the majority are at that level.
>
> More could be done to increase the prize money. $280 for losing a quarter-final and $200 for doubles in Israel is nothing. This is a tough world, and hopefully the money will filter down to Challengers and Futures, because you do see a lot of guys twenty-five, twenty-six and it is impossible for them to make a living from something they love doing.

In Britain, it is not just a case of finding the 'black swan', but thoughts have turned to keeping as many of those who have chosen the profession in work as long as possible. The need for a stronger competitive base is unqualified. It was noted that whereas in the twenty years from 1990 to 2010 the average age of the top players in Russia, France, Germany and the US was increasing and they were playing longer, the trend in Britain was the opposite. The exact same was true of the women.

Comparatively, their earnings were shocking too. Simon Jones, head of 'Performance Support', argued that a League One footballer will be earning £30,000–£45,000 per annum; a twenty-year-old county cricketer £20,000; a stable hand £13,000 and yet tennis players will be lucky to break even, and most lived with a loss.

'Because all the other sports don't have the massive expenses that tennis players have, like travelling to tournaments, accommodation and coaching means this a huge problem for us,' Jones said.

> At the ATP Future and Challenger level very little has moved in recent years in terms of supporting these players. Now, with our AEGON pro series in this country, we have thirty-one weeks of tournaments for men and women and there is the British Tour, which does not offer ranking points but the opportunity to compete and earn. There are forty-one weeks of those and we have increased the prize money in total from £44,000 to £174,000 and doubled the tournaments. There are only two weeks in a year from the age of seventeen to becoming pro when British players can't play for money.

The LTA was about to enter the third year of a bonus scheme, where with victory in a Futures tournament (worth a ridiculously low £830) the LTA would add £600. If a player successfully qualified for a Challenger – the next level up – they would receive £500, with a further £500 if they won a round. 'To have a bit of cash in the pocket gives them a sense of worth and with that our relationship with these players is really improving,' Jones said. 'We give bonuses for doubles as well, we have a specific approach to improving our doubles and this is keeping our players in the game longer, with seven men in the top 100 between the ages of twenty-six and thirty-six.'

Though more money was being offered, it had to be worked for. The entitlement culture that had developed at the LTA – a freebie here, a hand-out there – was being destroyed, or so they said. A culture change had begun: the LTA should not be seen simply as a bank where money could be withdrawn with no questions asked or results required. And yet this was the same organisation that was funding players massively on their talent at fourteen years of age, desperate to find that nugget. For all the decent messages, they were sending out a thousand deplorable ones.

Barry Cowan, a former GB top ten player and now a commentator on Sky TV, had been two years on the LTA Council as a representative of immediate past players and spoke of sitting on committees only to find out that decisions they were supposed to be adjudicating on had already been taken. When the tennis performance committee reflected on five people who could run an International High Performance Centre, the name of Judy Murray – with a proven track record in Scotland – came to the fore, and she was promptly chosen as the LTA's Fed Cup captain, essentially a part-time role.

Cowan would argue that too much money – 'astronomical amounts' as he put it – was being spent on performance players who had no hope of making the top 100. If the LTA felt it was demolishing the entitlement culture, Cowan didn't see it.

This year, only one player should have been able to walk into the NTC and demand a physiotherapist and that is Andy [Murray], otherwise there is a sense of entitlement and [that leads to a] bad environment. Everyone has made everything far too complicated there and it is not that difficult. To become a player means hours on the court, four hours every single day, and I did it as a player for twenty years. There are a lot of people who have got away for too long in the system with all this glossy Microsoft XL statistical mumbo-jumbo. It is all about hours on court.

So much of what the LTA does is bad and they don't know it's bad, and some of the things they do are good and they don't know they are good. But if you are going to do something, just do it properly.

$\mathit{\int}$

Being a tennis coach requires a love of the game beyond the comprehension of most of us. The ones shown so frequently on our TV screens are employed at the whim of players usually half their age. The majority give years of service without fanfare or recognition. I probably speak more to coaches than players during a year. Those I've known for a long time are mates: Bob Brett, Roger Rasheed, Alan Jones and David Felgate. Across the pond, Nick Bollettieri and Wayne Bryan are coaching patricians, bursting with energy and enthusiasm for the game though both are grandparents. The latter American wanted to change tennis and believed he knew the way to do it.

He had brought up two sons who were foremost in the world of doubles. Everyone who knew anything about the sport knew Bob and Mike Bryan, though it would have taken Lieutenant Columbo at his detecting best to tell them apart. I had never seen Wayne without a racket under his arm or a microphone in his hand. He lived for tennis and would have willingly used his racket as an axe against contemporary player development strategies.

An open letter to the United States Tennis Association, delivered with an almighty thud in the spring of 2012, was a lucid piece of testimony against the current trends and caused an enormous degree of angst and controversy. It went viral on the internet. 'Neil, we have to raise hell,' he told me at Indian Wells.

Bryan was significantly at odds with the ITF's new Tennis 10s rule change by which players aged ten and under could not train or play competition with a regular ball on a full-sized court, but instead trained and competed with red, orange or green 'soft' balls on a small court. This would, the ITF believed, 'help players develop the most efficient technique' and 'implement advanced tactics' that in most cases could not be performed using the yellow ball on a full court. Competition for the under tens was tailored to meet these needs, with short sets, tie-breaks instead of a third set and 'no-ad' scoring play. And, of course, having lots of Johnnies and Jennies running around with rackets and balls playing 'little' matches helped swell the participation and competitive numbers that governing bodies required to show that they were doing their jobs properly when they went cap in hand for more state funding.

Bryan was enraged.

As someone who has coached lots of top Southern California Tennis Association under-tens through the years, I can show you all kinds of kids around the country at eight, nine and ten that can flat nail the ball and have very complete games. Mike and Bob play short doubles matches with little kids around the country at their exhibitions and charity events – the points are astonishing and they always use yellow balls. For these kids green balls are a joke.

Let's get some empirical data going. Right now there is not one pro player on the ATP or WTA that grew up playing competitive tennis with green balls in the U10s and the last time I looked there were some pretty damn good players out there. And bingo, the USTA is mandating (and the ITF to be fair) that you must do it this way only. I'll have a bet – you give me 100 kids and let me do my thing from age six to ten and you take 100 kids and keep them on the soft-coloured balls until they are eleven and then track both groups on out until they are all eighteen and see who has got the goods. I know where I would put my money.

More troublingly, Bryan said he had anecdotal evidence of bribes and threats unless parents and coaches adhered to the Tennis 10s guidelines. 'Throwing its weight around is what governing bodies tend to do best – having no real answer to the absurd policies they adopt, re-adopt, re-draft and hope nobody notices the difference is one of the scandals of modern tennis,' he said.

All of this – and Bryan's insistence that the USTA's player development programme should be scrapped – placed Patrick McEnroe in an invidious position. McEnroe, the younger brother of John, a former Davis Cup captain building a significant career as a television commentator, was the $800,000-a-year general manager of US player development, specifically charged with helping to produce more Top 100 players 'with the goal that we have more of them competing into the second week of the majors'.

McEnroe did not believe that Bryan's intervention helped the situation at all. 'The world has changed and tennis has changed with it,' he said.

> Let's face it, in a rapidly-changing global environment, if we're not changing and moving forward, we're essentially going backward. Tennis is simply not the same sport that it was twenty years ago, even ten years ago. Anyone who was paying attention to the second week of this year's Australian Open realises that the bar is being raised as we speak.
>
> In terms of ten-and-under competition, the rule change adopted by the ITF and the USTA has, in fact, opened the door for more kids to get involved in junior competition. Two years ago, fewer than 10,000 kids were involved in tournament play and in the USTA's Junior Team Tennis programme. Now, that number has risen to more than 32,000. We've still got a long way to go, admittedly. We've only begun to scratch the surface of our potential. But more kids are trying tennis, and we feel confident that this rule change will open the door for more kids to get involved – and stay involved – in our sport. And that's a good thing.

McEnroe knew that the maverick will always win the public argument, their voice is louder and the governing bodies spend most of their time on the defensive. Until they have a star to parade, that is how it will be. 'I try not to react too much,' McEnroe told me.

> I am paid to get players in the top 100, and that means hiring the best coaches I believe can help our programme. If you want to tell me about all the money we spend in player development [I asked him what it was, but he would not tell], I know we at the USTA spend a minimum of half what the other big countries spend on development.

Bryan baulked.

> If they were spending $18 million on good causes, I would say well done, I'm the first to clap. What I am here for is to grow the game, this is what I do. I'm not in the pro game, I just want more kids playing tennis and if we have more kids playing tennis, more champions: the broader the base, the higher the pyramid. I would say to the USTA, give us the money and get out of the way, don't waste it.

McEnroe was the man charged now with guiding tennis in a better direction.

> There's a whole division of the USTA for community tennis and their budget is bigger than mine is for developing high level players: it involves giving money to certain local programmes that have a track record of producing players, good junior players, giving them support, giving them dollars. We have a philosophy of how to coach, which is basically to hit a million balls, do what Andy Murray did when he went to Spain and played the way the modern game is played. There's no secret to it. You have to understand if you grow up playing on lightning fast indoor courts and that's all you do, you're not going to become successful because the points are over so fast. The way these guys run, any match they play now is three hours and they possess every shot in the book.
> What I've realised in this job is coaching really matters at a

young age, between twelve/thirteen and seventeen/eighteen. I'm telling you right now we have this one girl, she just turned sixteen, unbelievable, plays like a guy, she is athletic, fast: she never gets tired, but I guarantee if we hadn't got her when we did, she would have no chance of becoming a pro because of how she was getting coached. We have this [fourteen-year-old] kid Stefan Kozlov, his Dad was his coach, Macedonian, and eighteen months ago he came to Boca Raton, saw what we are doing and said you guys take him and that is happening more and more, especially with the girls. Every single good girl there is in the US is training with us now.

The final devastating word on the subject went to Robert Lansdorp, the 74-year-old who had coached Pete Sampras, Lindsay Davenport, Tracy Austin and Maria Sharapova at various times in his career and revelled in his position as the godfather of tennis coaching. Lansdorp had a big beef with the USTA's coaching policy and was not afraid to lay it on the line in an email.

Why does the USTA Junior Development not understand that they will never develop a champion and that THAT is really not their job? The USTA should be a SUPPORTING organisation, NOTHING MORE NOTHING LESS. The most difficult, and most important years of developing are between the ages of six or seven till about fifteen for girls and sixteen for boys. It is a very taxing time developing youngsters. It is about their DISCIPLINE, their FOCUS, their CONSISTENCY, their behaviour and their tennis, their DESIRE TO WIN, loving to COMPETE, their LOVE of WORKING HARD, NOT playing to lose, but the desire to WIN, CONDITIONING themselves, becoming INDEPENDENT THINKERS, and working on the RIGHT TECHNIQUE. The beginning years are hugely important in the development of the child when it comes to the TECHNIQUE. It is crucial. You can ruin a kid in the first couple of years. I have only touched a small part, BUT you can see that the USTA is not interested in doing that. First of all they don't know WHAT to do, but they don't have the time and the desire to do that. That is why they have other coaches and parents do that and then after coaches have worked their butts off, the USTA will come around and basically steal the student, instead of involving the coach or parent in the further development of the junior – instead of asking the coach who has worked with the kid, how they can help. Give the people who developed them your opinion, USTA, but don't take the kid away.

How I wished this note could have been pinned to the gates of Roehampton.

Tennis Twists of Fate

Sweden's Robin Soderling, one of the finest players to strike a tennis ball in the twenty-first century, had missed an entire year on the tour: 'It is the hope and then the hopelessness – they come so fast one after the other,' he said in November 2012. The 2009 French Open finalist did not know if he would play again after being struck down by a particularly virulent virus. We hoped to see him back, but we could not know if or when.

A month before Soderling's plaintive cry, attempting to keep up with the myriad of junior updates in the daily diet of tennis news, a Twitter hash-tag caught my eye, though its consequence did not immediately register. '#prayforsean' may not be catchy but it had a certain power and I followed the link. I did not make a better decision the entire year.

The #prayforsean in question is Sean Karl of Brentwood in Tennessee, a stand-out player for his school Ravenwood High, a three-time state champion and good enough to have been noted by the USTA scouts in his home state, one of the very few I had not visited and always told myself I must one of these days. There is something magical about the Grand Ole Opry and, as my writing colleagues will tell you, I'm a sucker for country and western.

Sean is suffering from Ewing's sarcoma, a rare form of bone cancer that mainly attacks adolescents and children. The prognosis is good, if the cancer is caught early. Sean is eighteen years old. He had been having pains in his back through the early and middle part of the year and, as any teenager would do, dismissed it as one of those things. He is a growing lad and he plays sport, pretty darn well as it turns out, and all those miles he spent behind the wheel, driving himself to tournaments in an effort to make an impact in this tennis world, only added to his discomfort. There was a pain under his ribs he could not properly explain that seemed to move to his hips and then back again. He recalls playing a match in Austin, Texas and not knowing how he had won considering how much his body hurt.

'My family had planned a vacation in Florida so we drove

another eight hours which may not exactly have helped,' he said. 'We were there for four days and all I did was lie on the couch.' The Karls returned home and Sean was planning to go to the chiropractor the next morning but he woke at 2 a.m. in excruciating pain. 'My adrenalin felt as if it was going at 100 miles per hour,' he said. 'I went to the hospital, had the cat-scans and the MRIs and the doctor came out and said they had detected what they believed was a tumour under my ribcage and there was a good chance I had cancer. That came from nowhere. It really hit me.'

Not only did it hit Sean but all of his friends too. The shock was felt not just in his local community but in every tennis community. A 'Pray for Sean Karl' page was launched on Facebook. I joined it instantly and saw a video put together by Taylor Davidson, from Statesville High School in neighbouring North Carolina, which was set to the song 'Jesus take the Wheel' by Carrie Underwood, a truly emotive piece of work. Taylor added her own testimony.

> I am not going to say I know what you are going through, because I don't. YOU can beat this. God is pulling for you. We are pulling for you. Isaiah Chapter 41; verse 10: 'fear not, for I am with you; be not dismayed for I am your God; I will strengthen you, I will help you, I will uphold you with my righteous right hand.' But how can I focus on everyday things while you're fighting for your life? How can any of us?

I choked right up.

The way most of us run around the world – those who hit the balls and those watching those who hit balls – does not often give us pause to consider the world around us. We become blasé. Then we hear a story such as Sean's and the response is remarkable. Following it through to the end of the year – by which time Sean had endured less than half of the thirty sessions required to treat the cancer – was to hear so many tales of hope, prayer and compassion. The professional ranks responded superbly as

Sergiy Stakhovsky (already a campaigner against cancer) led the way and Roger Federer with his coach Paul Annacone, whose brother Steve knows the Karl family, sent a video, which became an instant hit on YouTube.

All of this helped the process no end. Sean Karl wants to be a professional tennis player and views his current trial as a bit of a setback.

> There have been so many different things that have happened, so many positive outpourings, so many people have been in touch, people have been coming around to the house wanting to help with the cooking and doing the laundry for my parents and two brothers, Justin [sixteen] and Steven [fifteen]. It has been just awesome.

As is this young man.

Sergei Bubka had completed his 2012 playing year at No. 186 in the rankings and decided to visit Paris for a couple of days in November to see some old friends. He had taken a rest in a third floor apartment he had never been to before, came to in the morning and wanted to say goodbye when he realised the key had been dislodged and the door was locked. He couldn't raise anyone so decided to look out of a window, leaned rather too far, the sill collapsed and he plummeted twelve metres to what he did not realise at the time was the foot of an elevator shaft in the middle of the apartment block.

Bubka had broken his femur, the entire back of his leg was cut open with the bone sticking out, he had broken an arm, fractured a rib, cut his foot and, amazingly, had not a scratch on his face. He screamed out both in agony and fear, because it was early in the day and he thought that surely someone would get into the elevator, take it down to the ground floor and crush him – as if his body was not savagely twisted enough already. Fortunately, he was heard by a friend. 'I had used so much of my energy crying out for help but I remember being picked up and then I passed out.' He came to over half a day later, of which nine hours had been spent in an operating theatre, where all the various broken pieces of his body were mended.

The doctors told him that they had never encountered someone with such hard bones before and that rendered each of their moves vital and delicate. Fortunately there had been no damage to his spine. Where his bone had split the skin was perilously close to a major artery which, had it been severed, may well have killed him. There had been no nerve damage. He was terribly unlucky but remarkably lucky all at the same time. 'Somebody protected me and saved me,' he said.

It is Bubka's intention to play again and, given his stock, it is not surprising that he is undaunted by a few broken bones. His father Sergey is one of the most renowned athletes in the world, who persevered enough times to have broken the world pole vault record a colossal thirty-five times, and was six times the world champion and an Olympic gold medallist in Seoul in 1988. His outdoor record, set in 1994, stands to this day.

Being blessed with the Bubka genes is one thing, but having such a famous father (and being named for him) is a difficult cross to bear, though one that Sergei junior has faced with fortitude. And this is not the first time he has been seriously hurt, for in 2009 he was in the back seat of a tournament car in Canada when it was involved in an accident not a mile from the hotel where he had been picked up. At the impact, Bubka, who was seated in the back seat, and not wearing a seat belt, went face first in the driver's headrest, leaving him with a three-inch scar right down the middle of his forehead.

Bubka's personality is such that he responded as openly to the force and extent of his injuries as he did when his relationship with Victoria Azarenka, his long-time girlfriend, ended a few weeks before his fall. He even managed to keep a reasonably straight face when he saw Azarenka pictured frequently with Redfoo, the eccentric American singer who was becoming a fixture behind the scenes and in front of the camera on the women's tour. Redfoo [Stefan Kendal Gordy] is the son of Berry Gordy Jnr, the godfather of Motown, and is best known for the band LMFAO. It is an interesting combination, to say the least.

〇

I watched part of the match between Britain's James Ward and Marinko Matosevic of Australia on Court 1 at Eastbourne in June 2012. In my opinion, Ward should have won but he didn't. A couple of times I think he noticed I was watching and, as always, you offer a compatriot a supportive glance or two. What I had no idea about was that, on the same day, his best friend from childhood was being buried.

Jack Groves had, it appeared, committed suicide after several years of suffering from depression. James's father Jim had told his son the news a few days earlier, during Queen's, so that he did not find out from anyone else. Jack's father Bob had watched Ward play Kevin Anderson of South Africa on a chilly day in London. That evening, his son's body was discovered. As we talk about it later in the year, James's words and thoughts come out in a jumble, which is hardly surprising.

Jack yeah, very difficult because [he was] one of my best mates and Bob comes to support me at all the tournaments ... he keeps messaging me now bless him but it is tough ... I think [he suffered from] depression for a long time ... because I saw Bob that day, I played at Queen's and it happened that night and I was none the wiser for a couple of days and my Dad told me so that I didn't find out another way ... for the first couple of weeks ... funeral I was playing at Eastbourne, normally Bob and his wife take a holiday down there ... a shame it really was ... Matosevic ... had break points ... there is a lot of other shit ... you have the same difficulties as anyone else and to have to deal with it ... sometimes you don't want to do it and think 'what's the point?' ... but I know I can be at the level I want to be ... it's being fit and healthy all the time and being able to back up one good week with another good week and not just have the odd good week here and there ... so having a fitness trainer with me all the time will be a massive help. I know there hasn't been a problem with my tennis, it has always been about physically getting stronger. I need to learn more of course. I had problem with my ankles as well which is better now. Loads of injections in my ankle, but you don't tell people those things and let them believe you have weaknesses ... my ankle keeps going ... it is difficult.

Ward's season had been one of disappointing form and debilitating injuries. From starting the year ranked No. 162, qualifying for a grand slam for the first time to having his rackets stolen, to losing both rubbers in the Davis Cup tie against Slovakia in Glasgow, to spotty results on American hard courts, to winning an ATP Futures in Taipei, to taking Mardy Fish to five sets at Wimbledon, to slipping on grass at Newport RI and fracturing his scaphoid, to a loss in the first round of the US Open to Dimitri Tursunov and then having to withdraw from a Challenger in Shanghai because he had torn a tendon in his left wrist attempting to compensate for the weakness in his right. All the time, he had been having trouble with his ankles. When he came back from that trip, his coach James Trotman, who had just become a father for the first time, said he didn't want to travel as much in 2013 and it was best if they parted company.

How does a player at this level survive?

You don't, you are always making a loss, every week of the year. The budget for the year from the LTA [Matrix funding] is £14,000 to spend on hotels and accommodation; by the end of Australia, a lot of that is gone. I have done more travelling than any other British player over the last four years playing at a higher level, Challengers and Tour qualifiers all the time, which means the hotels are nicer, which is more expense, but you need to stay there because there is transport and you're not spending more on taxis. Without the funding I could probably get by but it would be very difficult.

The coach has had a baby and he doesn't want to travel so much, it was very good with 'Trotters' – we had no problems, no other reason to stop. I totally understand but I feel like it is unfinished business but he has to make his decisions. The struggle is the same, tournament prize money, same shit which is embarrassing, so you know what you can earn if you only play those tournaments which is why you have to play the ATP events and the slams. That's the whole idea.

Ward started 2013 ranked No. 250 in the world.

*

I invited Andrew Fitzpatrick to the Lawn Tennis Writers' Association lunch at the All England Club in December and, appropriately, John Beddington was also seated at our table. It was when he read a story about Fitzpatrick in October that Beddington, formerly the head of Tennis Canada and a long-time friend, said he would love to be able to help fund the player home from the worst tennis trip of his life.

The 23-year-old from Solihull, then ranked No. 12 in Britain and No. 456 in the world, was playing a $10,000 ATP Futures in Binh Duong, Vietnam. He had already been robbed of the £1,000 he had saved for three months for a five-tournament expedition to some of the least enticing places in the world but was then the victim of an attempted sexual assault in the single shower in the tournament locker room.

'I was trying to attach the shower head to the wall and suddenly this guy grabbed me from behind,' he said.

My reaction was that he may have had a weapon and I was pretty much trapped with no space to move, and then I realised what he was trying to do, so I punched him. There was only one exit to the locker room so I dashed for that, found the referee and the tournament director called the police. They got the guy but all they really did was give him a telling-off. There was nothing else I could really do. I hadn't been physically hurt.

How much the trauma might have affected Fitzpatrick, he could not be sure. 'I am pretty much by myself here so anything that happens feels so amplified because I don't have anyone to confide in. I just want to survive these next few weeks and then make it home,' he said at the time. Beddington's offer was perfect.

Fitzpatrick books his accommodation via www.couchsurfing. com, which offers sofas to sleep on in local homes. 'I think I've stayed in two hotels this year,' he said. In September [the month in which Andy Murray won a grand slam title] Fitzpatrick put himself up for sale on eBay, for which the leading bid was £870. His rent where he stays with his girlfriend in west London is paid by a friend for whom he plays for Paddington in the National Club League. 'I've always been told I have great potential, I'm working really hard. There are people in Britain who have the resources to help me but, so far, they have chosen not to.'

*

It was as I recovered from a couple of days spent training with Andy Murray in December that I turned on the TV in my hotel room in Florida to be greeted by the harrowing coverage of the Sandy Hook school killings in Connecticut. One could not help but imagine how a few hundred yards down the street Andy – who had survived the massacre at Dunblane in 1996 – would have felt as he watched the same reports.

Andy had only recently felt able to mention the '96 atrocity, hoping that his success in both the Olympic Games and at the US Open would give his town something to smile about having spent so long wreathed in sadness.

One of the children lost in the Sandy Hook shootings was six-year-old Dylan Hockley, whose parents had decided to move to the US with their two children a couple of years earlier. In the midst of the words of comfort and of hope for the future, the Hockley family pastor, Clive Calver, recounted the story of another community, another family that had been caught in such tragedy.

'I told them the story of a little boy from another small town who cowered under a desk as a madman went on a rampage with a gun,' Calver said. 'That little boy and that small town rose from the ashes and rebuilt. That town is Dunblane and that boy is Andy Murray.'

Index